Island No. 10

ISLAND NO. 10

Struggle for the Mississippi Valley

Larry J. Daniel
Lynn N. Bock

The University of Alabama Press

Tuscaloosa

Copyright 1996
The University of Alabama Press
Tuscaloosa, Alabama 34587-0380
All rights reserved
Manufactured in the United States of America

Cover photo: Currier and Ives print *Bombardment
of Island Number 10* (courtesy of the State
Historical Society of Missouri, Columbia)

∞

The paper on which this book is printed meets the minimum
requirements of American National Standard for Information
Science-Permanence of Paper for Printed Library Materials,
ANSI Z39.48-1984.

Library of Congress Cataloging-in-Publication Data
Daniel, Larry J., 1947–
Island No. 10 : struggle for the Mississippi Valley / Larry J.
Daniel, Lynn N. Bock.
p.   cm.
Includes bibliographical references and index.
ISBN 0-8173-0816-4 (alk. paper)
1. New Madrid Region (Mo.)—History, Military.   2. Mississippi
River Valley—History—Civil War, 1861–1865—Campaigns.   3. United
States—History—Civil War, 1861–1865—Campaigns.   I. Bock, Lynn N.
II. Title.
E473.15.D36   1996
973.7′3—dc20   95-31876

British Library Cataloguing-in-Publication Data available

Contents

Illustrations

Figures

Maps

Tables

Preface

NO TRACE OF Island No. 10 now exists. The changing currents of the Mississippi River shifted long ago, leaving it a permanent part of the Missouri shore. It would appear that historians have followed the lead of nature and largely erased the sizable Civil War campaign that was fought in the Madrid Bend area. In their extensive histories of the Civil War, Allan Nevins, Page Smith, and William C. Davis fail even to mention Island No. 10. In their volume *Why the South Lost the Civil War*, Richard E. Beringer and company relegate the campaign to a single sentence. James M. McPherson is only slightly kinder in his *Battle Cry of Freedom;* the subject is treated in a paragraph. The seige of Island No. 10 was every bit as large as and in several respects more significant than the Port Hudson campaign that occurred more than a year later. Yet the latter has been covered by three modern monographs, whereas the former remains ignored.

This historical slighting is perhaps understandable. Island No. 10 was squeezed in between two of the largest battles fought in the West—Fort Donelson and Shiloh. The dismal siege that occurred along the upper Mississippi River appears to the modern reader as unspectacular when compared to the Hornet's Nest at Shiloh. Nor were the participants particularly colorful. Only the most ardent Civil War historian far off the beaten track knows about John McCown and William Mackall (pronounced may-cal, with an emphasis on the first syllable). John Pope is more renowned but is still not a popular study. Even his recent biographers hurriedly glanced over the general's first major campaign (it is covered in seven pages) in an effort to get on to the more glamorous Battle of Second Manassas and the encounter with Robert E. Lee.

Interestingly, during the war the nation took an intense interest in the events that unfolded at Madrid Bend. It was the second time in fifty years that this remote tristate area had captured the country's attention. Between December 16, 1811, and February 1812, a series of violent earthquakes, estimated by historians to have been twenty times stronger than the 1906 San Francisco earthquake, had their epicenters near New Madrid, Missouri. More than thirty thousand square miles were affected, and the Mississippi River actually flowed backward, filling in a depression that would become known as Reelfoot Lake. That lake now formed the right flank of the Confederate defensive system. The press coverage on the siege was so extensive that it almost completely overshadowed early operations on the opposite end of the river at New Orleans.

Even as Port Hudson was not as significant as the loss of Vicksburg, Mississippi, in 1863, so too the capture of Island No. 10 did not compare in scope with the fall of Fort Henry and Fort Donelson and the North's subsequent thrust into the Confederate heartland. The stunning loss at Fort Donelson galvanized the Confederate high command and resulted in a massive counterattack. The Battle of Shiloh ultimately decided control of the upper Mississippi Valley.

Unlike the dramatic drive up the Tennessee, the Mississippi River campaign proved more methodical. The action at Madrid Bend was nonetheless significant. The capture of Island No. 10 consolidated Union control of the upper valley and led to the further decline of Confederate military fortunes in the West. The campaign reaffirmed the strategic value of turning movements and the inability of the Confederates to counter joint operations. Considering the great prestige that the Mississippi River held in the national consciousness, the failure to stop the Union advance further deteriorated Southern morale. General John Pope was propelled into national prominence and received command of the Army of Virginia.

After the fall of Island No. 10, the actions at Fort Pillow and Memphis represented nothing more than anticlimactic holding actions. For all practical purposes, the river lay open all the way to Vicksburg. Indeed, Federal vessels appeared at that town on June 24, 1862, only eleven weeks after the fall of Island No. 10. The Confederacy simply lacked the military and industrial capability to defend the rivers. The Richmond government, however, for political and psychological reasons, had little alternative but to make an all-out effort at defense. It was this dilemma, industrial impotence versus political necessity, that drove the Southern high command to lose one garrison after another. As for the North, it was the navy that time and again tipped the scales in the western theater.

Today a simple marker is all that commemorates the struggle that took place between thirty-three thousand Union and Confederate soldiers and sailors who wrestled for control of the upper Mississippi Valley. Clearly they deserve more. We have attempted to rectify this void by telling the story of a campaign that, from a modern perspective, is perhaps the best-kept secret of the American Civil War.

Larry J. Daniel, Memphis, Tennessee
Lynn N. Bock, New Madrid, Missouri

Acknowledgments

WE ARE DEEPLY indebted to Dr. Richard McMurry of Atlanta, Georgia, and Dr. Leslie Anders of Central Missouri State University at Warrensburg, for reading the manuscript in its entirety and offering valuable criticisms, suggestions, and encouragement. Their candidness has served to strengthen the manuscript, and any weaknesses remaining in it are ours. A debt is also owed to Dr. Jim Wells of Tulane University, New Orleans, who, though working on his own manuscript of the Island No. 10 campaign, unselfishly shared sources and information to assist our efforts. A special thanks to our mutual friend, Dr. Nat Hughes of Chattanooga, Tennessee, who initially got the Daniel-Bock team together.

Several individuals offered research assistance and suggestions and located rare volumes needed to complete this work. These include Marshall Dial and his staff at the New Madrid County Library; Donna Cromer at Kent Library, Southeast Missouri State University; Dr. Linda McCurdy of Chapel Hill, North Carolina; Mark Johnson of Springfield, Illinois; and Jeff Hale of Baton Rouge, Louisiana.

1

The Finest Strategic Position

IN 1861, THE MISSISSIPPI RIVER figured prominently in the national consciousness. In January, Mississippi Governor James Pettus placed a battery of artillery on the bluffs at Vicksburg to command the river. Fearful of the loss of free navigation, politicians and commercial interests throughout the Northwest made a loud outcry. Pettus backed down and the guns were withdrawn, but the struggle for control of the Mississippi had begun. The geographic feature that had unified the western United States would now be viewed in terms of military strategy. The well-publicized "Anaconda plan" of the Federals called for, among other things, the splitting of the newly formed Confederacy along the line of that artery. Confederate leadership in the West became obsessed with its defense, blinding their view to other approaches. In the first two years of the war in the West, it was the control of the rivers, not the railroads, that would prove the key to success.[1]

News of the eight steamers moving up the Mississippi River traveled faster than the boats themselves. On board, Brigadier General Gideon Pillow looked over the flotilla of eight packets and proclaimed them a "beautiful sight" as they churned up the muddy water. The heavily laden boats carried a force of nearly six thousand Confederates that Pillow grandly styled his "Army of Liberation." When the steamers arrived at the hamlet of New Madrid, Missouri, on July 28, 1861, a crowd gathered along the river to cheer the troops as they cleared the gangplanks.[2]

The dynamics behind this push north presented a curious combination of blind ambition, political clout, and perceived danger. The move was strongly influenced by Tennessee Governor Isham G. Harris, who was up for reelection that summer and hoping to fight Tennessee's battles in Missouri, and by Missouri Governor Claiborne Jackson, who had been forced into exile from Jefferson City. Eager to return, Jackson presented Confederate authorities with exaggerated intelligence that Sterling Price and Ben McCulloch were on the Missouri border with twenty-five thousand troops, while Brigadier General William J. Hardee had seven thousand troops in northwest Arkansas. Left without supervision for several weeks as the Confederate government was organizing, Pillow, a vain political general who was as ambitious as he was incompetent, beamed at the prospect of an offensive.[3]

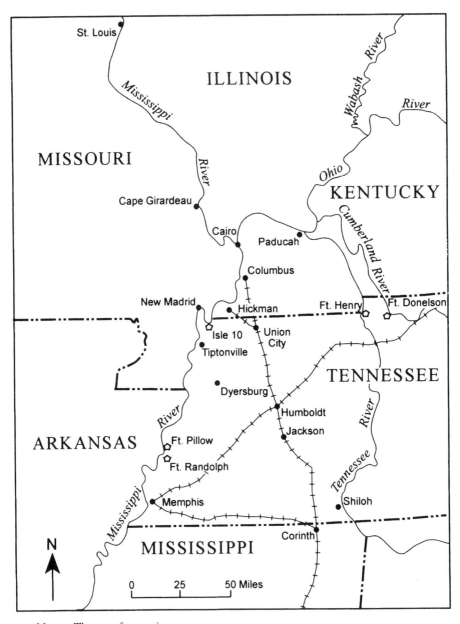

Map 1. Theater of operations

This was the situation as fifty-five-year-old Major General Leonidas Polk arrived in Memphis, Tennessee, on July 13, 1861. In his junior year at West Point, Polk had taken an interest in religion. Upon graduation, he resigned his commission and entered an Episcopal seminary. In 1838, at the age of thirty-two, and only eight years after his ordination, he was appointed missionary bishop of the Southwest. An Academy classmate of President Jefferson Davis, he was assigned command of the newly organized Department No. 2, which included the upper Mississippi Valley. He quickly fell in line with Pillow's invasion plan, one of the last times the two would agree on anything. On the evening of July 23, in front of the Gayoso House, Polk, Pillow, and Jackson all boasted of reclaiming Missouri to a cheering throng.[4]

The plan was for Pillow's forces to link up with those of Price and McCulloch and advance on St. Louis. A main road, the old King's Highway or El Camino Real, led north out of New Madrid and connected with St. Louis 175 miles distant. Pillow, believing that the Federals had largely withdrawn to that city, desired to push ahead to Cape Girardeau, Missouri.

In advance of the move, Brigadier General Jeff Thompson led his command of Missouri state troops and irregulars, some fifteen hundred men, through the Mingo and Nigger Wool Swamps and encamped at Sikeston. The wiry Virginian had emigrated to Missouri after his application to West Point was rejected. At the beginning of the war he served as mayor of St. Joseph. He reveled in the excessive press coverage, both North and South, that his exploits received. His "swamp rats" thrashed about the bootheel of the state, raiding towns and intimidating those of a pro-Union persuasion. In Charleston, Missouri, he even robbed a bank. "Everyone gives me the credit of having 7,000 men, and I have frightened them to death," he boasted to Pillow. He eventually moved up to Commerce, Missouri, where he opened fire on Union steamboats with his artillery but retired when Pillow did not advance.[5]

The entire expedition now stalled. Pillow's force was plagued with sickness and could muster only four thousand troops. He had only 203 wagons and required a minimum of 314 to advance. Polk also discovered that Price and McCulloch had only half as many men as represented by Jackson's inflated figures. Hardee counted twenty-three hundred poorly armed troops. Neither Hardee nor McCulloch, who had independent commands, could come to a consensus with Polk as to objectives. Realizing the futility of an offensive under the circumstances, Polk cancelled the operation.[6]

Pillow, nursing an inflamed boil on his buttocks that further soured his disposition, grew nervous about his position at New Madrid. On August 15, three wooden Federal gunboats dropped down to the town, although no shots were fired and they quickly withdrew. "I have never been in favor of occupying this place [New Madrid] except as a base of operations for movement into the interior," Pillow argued. Polk, too, considered falling back to Fort Pillow and using Union City, Tennessee, as a base for his Missouri operations. The Bishop, however, became increasingly concerned about reports of a Federal buildup at Cairo, Illinois, and Cape Girardeau and about a fleet known to be under construction at St. Louis. He thus sent his topographical engineer, Asa Gray, to inspect the New Madrid tristate area to ascertain its feasibility for defense.[7]

This decision represented a continuation of the strategy initiated earlier by Pillow and Harris. In the spring of 1861, construction began on a string of forts along the Mississippi at the third Chickasaw Bluff (Fort Pickering at Memphis), Point Jackson seven miles above Memphis (Fort Harris), the second Chickasaw Bluff (Fort Wright at Randolph), and the first Chickasaw Bluff (Fort Pillow), the last 115 miles below Island No. 10. Foolishly relying on Kentucky neutrality, Polk was convinced that the Federal offensive would not be made from the north, through Kentucky, but from the west, through Missouri. The Confederate line thus faced south-southeast from Island No. 10, rather than east to the Tennessee and Cumberland rivers. By the end of the summer of 1861, Fort Pillow had emerged as the strongest point, but there was still no concentrated salient.[8]

What Asa Gray found at Island No. 10 was arguably the strongest natural position on the Mississippi in the upper valley. The river at that point made a double bend and appeared on a map like an "S" on its face. The island, so named because it was the tenth island south of the Ohio River, was about one mile long and 450 yards wide. It sat ten feet above low water in nearly the middle of the channel and commanded the river in three directions. The river stretched about three-fourths of a mile on the east and a mile on the west. In past years the main channel had been the Tennessee chute, but in low water it now had snags. Of late the Missouri chute had proved navigable for the largest boats and was the passage of choice, although both channels remained passable in high water. Because of sandbars, the approach to the Missouri chute was not direct. James Price, the only resident of the island, cultivated some of it. He lived in a white cottage surrounded by several slave quarters located in the middle of the island. About 250 acres of corn and a large peach and apple orchard stretched from the island center west toward the bank.[9]

To the north of the island lay Madrid Bend, Kentucky, which was completely severed from the rest of the state. Immediately east of the island was the Tennessee shore, with a nearly impenetrable swamp and Reelfoot Lake, the latter having been formed nearly fifty years earlier by the New Madrid earthquakes. The lake was now forty miles long and in places eleven miles wide. A good road ran from the river, west of the lake, to Tiptonville, Tennessee, six miles distant. All supplies came to the town via steamboat. A road ran east from the town to Troy and Union City, with Barker's Ferry being used at Reelfoot Lake. The strength of the east bank proved to be its weakness. The same

Fig. 1. The Confederate fortifications on Island No. 10 as sketched by the artist of *Harper's* after the surrender (courtesy of *Harper's Weekly*, May 3, 1862)

cypress-entangled waters that kept the Federals out also kept the Confederates in.[10]

The western, or Missouri, shore was marshland cut by bayous and swamp lakes. New Madrid, settled in 1789, was at the apex of the second bend, eleven miles downriver, but north of the island. The town, not protected by swamps, served as the island's left flank and clearly represented the weak link in the defensive system. If it were captured and the river blocked, supplies could only trickle overland from Tiptonville across the neck of the peninsula to the island.[11]

Gray reported that the island had "no superior, in my judgment, above Memphis." He envisioned three batteries—a bastion earthwork on the Tennessee shore, a redan three fourths of a mile from the bastion, and a redoubt on the island, capable of accommodating a thousand men. The furthermost redan would be constructed first with the guns mounted in barbette (peering over the wall). A light garrison, with a battery of horse artillery, would be stationed on the island to prevent a landing. The extended right flank would be protected by a cordon of stations from the river east to Union City, forty-five miles away. New Madrid, although vulnerable, could be quickly reinforced by steamboat. Colonel John McCown, one of Polk's brigade commanders, concurred with Gray's assessment, calling the island the "strongest position for the defense of the Mississippi Valley."[12]

The conclusions of Gray and McCown, coupled with a false report that the Federals were about to descend the river and snatch the island, caused Polk to act quickly. Pillow divided his forces for the defense of New Madrid, Island No. 10, and Union City. The 4th Tennessee, Alexander P. Stewart's artillery battalion, and a company of sappers and miners went to the island. Battery No. 1 on the Tennessee shore, which would become known as the redan, was located after a rapid reconnaissance on August 15, the day after the enemy gunboats had passed down to New Madrid. By August 20, work had commenced on the Tennessee shore, although a shortage of tools hampered the project. With six guns mounted in the redan, Gray, with gross overconfidence, declared that "the enemy cannot now trouble us while erecting the larger works at Island No. 10."[13]

Believing the project to be on course, Pillow arrived on August 28 and was stunned by what he found. In a letter to Polk, he vigorously opposed the redan's location, which had been constructed in an area subject to a three-foot overflow. Positioned so close to the river, the fort's west wall was already eroding. The ground around the redan was muddy bottomland in front of a growth of cottonwoods, and it appeared virtually uninhabitable for troops—"They will die like sheep of the rot," he exploded. At least two batteries would have to be constructed on the island—one at the head to control both channels and the other halfway down the island to cover the main (west) chute. An inspection of the entire vicinity convinced Pillow that "the value of the position [was]

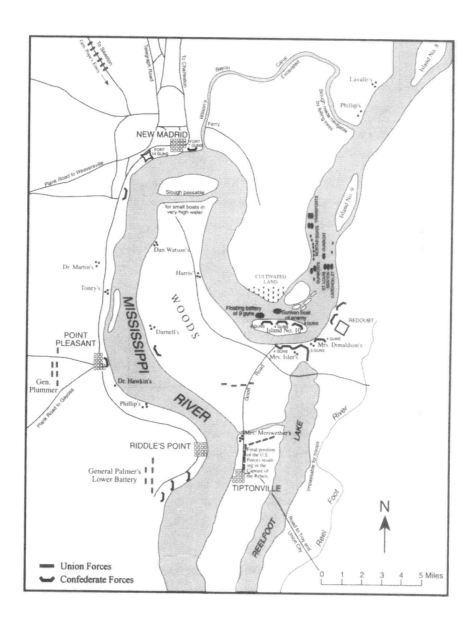

Map 2. Madrid Bend (courtesy of the National Archives)

greatly overrated." He estimated that it would require five thousand troops to hold New Madrid, a like number on the Tennessee shore, and a thousand for the island, making the position "an expensive one." He continued to opt for the bluffs at Fort Pillow as the superior site.[14]

Pillow's gloomy assessment of Island No. 10 was not surprising; he had felt uncomfortable about Madrid Bend from the outset. He may also have had a hidden agenda. Since May, the Tennessee general had been keeping an eye on Columbus, Kentucky, sixty miles upriver from New Madrid. Although his relationship with Polk was by now strained, with only slight urging he was able to convince the Bishop that the occupation of Columbus was a military necessity. Pillow now contended, contrary to his earlier statements, that the river forts in Tennessee could not withstand an attack. Polk believed that he had better move fast before Columbus was captured by the Federals. On September 4, 1861, without informing the War Department, Polk ordered Pillow's troops to violate Kentucky neutrality and occupy the town.[15]

The move to Columbus proved to be a political disaster, although Polk downplayed the consequences. Nonetheless, an entire new front was now undeniably open. General Albert Sidney Johnston, who had superseded Polk in September 1861, and now commanded an expanded Department No. 2, moved most of his forces to southern Kentucky from Columbus (Polk's corps), east through Bowling Green (Hardee's corps), to Cumberland Gap (George Crittenden's command). Johnston, acting more like a corps commander, soon became hypnotized by Federal activity at Bowling Green, as Polk did at Columbus.[16]

The move to Columbus proved not to be as strategically vital as Polk believed it would be. The single advantage was a range of high bluffs consisting of a limestone cliff about seventy-five feet high. It is true that the Federal ironclads were vulnerable to plunging fire, but one Confederate official questioned whether the bluffs posed an advantage. D. M. Frost noted that plunging fire presented the most difficult mode of gunnery for inexperienced cannoneers to master. He argued for placing some of the guns at the base of the bluff, to deliver horizonal fire. The fortifications were eventually tiered to produce high-, medium-, and water-level fire. Although the river defenses were never truly tested, the terrain at Vicksburg, a year and a half later, offered a similar scenario. In that instance, the plunging fire proved ineffective in preventing the gunboats from passing.[17]

Preoccupied with Columbus, Polk neglected Island No. 10. By mid-September 1861, the 4th Tennessee had been reassigned, leaving only the sapper company. The redan, although complete, still had problems. Only four 32-pounders were mounted, two 24-pounder siege guns having been removed to Columbus. The 32s, mounted on iron naval carriages (sliding tracks) made in New Orleans, were positioned in embrasure (a window), which weakened the parapet. Gray recommended that they be placed on siege (wheeled) carriages and mounted in barbette. During high water the area around the redan flooded, but during ordinary stages the enemy could approach from the north via Hickman, Kentucky, or by an amphibious assault. Gray thus saw the need for a twelve-hundred-yard cremaillere line to be constructed from the redan to Black Bayou. There had never been more than eight blacks at work at a time, he complained, and these would soon have to be returned for the fall harvest. He required at least five hundred black workers for fifteen days. Gray had no boat to cross to the island. Two of his most valued assistants had been transferred, and a third lay sick with fever.[18]

On October 16, Gray reported that the lines had been laid off for additional batteries along the Tennessee shore. Work had begun on the lower of these, which would eventually be designated No. 5. Some work had also been done on the cremaillere line, and abatis had been placed. A good deal of timber had been cleared from the island head and the Missouri shore. Only sixty black workers remained, and they had only twenty shovels. Gray was also putting the finishing touches on his map of the area. To complete the survey, however, he had to have the return of his little steamer, *Gordon Grant*, then at Fort Pillow. The steamboat at his disposal was too large and cost an exorbitant one hundred fifty dollars a day.[19]

In late November the 11th Arkansas reported to Gray. These men, armed with old British rifles and squirrel guns, had previously gathered up their arms and sent them to New Orleans for reboring. The weapons were so poorly prepared, however, that most of them burst upon firing. Polk requested six hundred rifles for the 11th, but in the meantime the troops received shovels and assisted in constructing the batteries laid out by Gray. For a week the men encamped on the Tennessee shore. "The lake [Reelfoot] is not as deep as many think," observed Major James Poe. "There are old rotten stumps and a few dead trees. No cows get in it, however, for the bottom of it is soft mud. There are some places where the lake is blue water."[20]

At the end of the month the regiment was ferried across to the island and bivouacked. Farmer Price gave the men free access to his five-acre turnip patch, and a boy crossed over and sold eggs to the troops. Assistant surgeon Junius Bragg nonetheless considered the place dreary enough. "Island Ten is a miserable place to stay at," he wrote his wife. "This is by no means a pleasant locality, but it is the highest and driest spot I have seen since the hills of Fort Pillow." He went on to confide, "The fact of the business is this: we are all liable at any moment to be driven from this place."[21]

Downriver, at New Madrid, progress was more substantive. The only outfit at the town was Jeff Thompson's regiment of Missouri partisans. Pillow promised that New Madrid would receive one of the three floating batteries coming up from New Orleans, but only one arrived and it went to Columbus.

Thompson completed the bastioned fort that bore his name, using the labor
of five hundred slaves. The five-foot-thick parapets consisted of sacks of shelled
corn covered with dirt. The packing of the dirt was accomplished in a rather
unorthodox fashion. Races were conducted with several hundred horsemen ca-
reening along the wall. Thompson remained skeptical of the project. "I have
little faith in little forts," he asserted. He advocated a more extensive line of
works that encompassed the entire line.[22]

In early December 1861, thirty-four-year-old Colonel Edward Gantt arrived
at New Madrid with the 12th Arkansas. An ardent secessionist, he had cam-
paigned throughout the spring of 1861 for a seat in the Confederate provisional
congress. He won the election, but chose instead to command a regiment. The
12th had spent the autumn in Memphis and Columbus, suffering from a bout
of measles and diarrhea and attempting to get their worthless guns rebored.
Neither problem had been resolved by the time the 12th arrived at New Madrid.
Only half the regiment's eight hundred men were fit for duty. Wrote Surgeon
William Jennings, "We still have a great amount of sickness and much fatality,
as Arkansas men cannot stand anything. I have never seen such tender beings
in all my life. Pneumonia and typhoid fever are the primary diseases." He went
on to observe, "New Madrid is quite a low place, and in pleasant weather is a
very pretty village, but in wet weather it must be all mud."[23]

Gantt was troubled by what he found. Nearly completed Fort Thompson,
about a mile from town, was not as large as he had anticipated; it could accom-
modate only two regiments. Barracks would have to be constructed on the river
bank facing the sally port of the fort. The gun platforms had been improperly
placed and would have to be rebuilt. Another fort was needed upriver, just above
town, at the mouth of St. John's Bayou. Jeff Thompson's raiders also presented
difficulties. Their enlistment had expired, and the command was melting away
with each passing day. By the end of 1861, only six hundred remained, and they
refused to do scout duty. "They are a wretched, ragged, dispirited looking set
of men; half armed, undisciplined, careless, and inattentive," Gantt concluded
with contempt. Jennings, too, thought that Thompson's men were the "raggi-
est looking set of men I ever met." The flamboyant Thompson he considered
"quite a case."[24]

Reinforcements slowly arrived. In late November 1861, Gantt received two
companies of heavy artillery—Stewart's and Upton's. In January 1862, the 11th
Arkansas relocated to Fort Thompson. This gave Gantt 1,036 infantrymen and
120 cannoneers, not counting Thompson's cavalry, which now amounted to
only a hundred men. The 46th Tennessee, with only 207 effectives, replaced
the 11th at Island No. 10. A reserve force remained at Fort Pillow—the 40th
Tennessee and the 1st Alabama, Tennessee, Mississippi regiment (a hybrid of
companies from each state). This reserve consisted of 1,064 men, but the latter
outfit was not armed.[25]

Polk remained preoccupied with fortress Columbus. A Federal attack across the river at Belmont, Missouri, on November 7, 1861, although repulsed, convinced him that a major thrust at Columbus was imminent. At the time he had eighteen thousand of his twenty-two thousand troops huddled within the town's defenses. Polk hoped to buttress New Madrid with McCulloch's ten thousand troops, then in winter quarters in Arkansas, but to no avail.[26]

Increasingly aware that some Federal boats might slip past the Columbus batteries, the Confederates began to take a renewed interest in Island No. 10. On January 21, naval officer William C. Whittle recommended to Polk that Fort Pillow be abandoned and the guns and troops sent to the island. He believed that five thousand troops and forty to fifty guns were needed to secure the Madrid Bend area. James Trudeau, a heavy artillery officer, suggested on January 26 that a four-gun redoubt be constructed at Hickman and that regular naval patrols be made between that place and Columbus. As for Madrid Bend, he concluded: "The strategic importance of Island No. 10 is so great that it now becomes indispensable to occupy it strongly and permanently."[27]

For good or bad Polk had decided on Columbus as his primary river fortification. The far more difficult question related to whether the ironclads could be stopped at any point. These dreaded vessels were a technological innovation that would alter the course of the war in the West. Essentially four modes of defense were available to the Confederates, and all were utilized at Columbus.

Polk relied heavily on his shore batteries. He boasted 140 guns at Columbus, but the number was deceptive. Some of these faced east to protect the city against land attack. Many of the cannon were old smoothbore 32- and 24-pounders that could not penetrate the armor of the ironclads. The only weapons effective against this armor were rifled 32- and 42-pounders and smoothbore 8- and 10-inch columbiads. The Confederates also had a huge 128-pounder rifle cast at the Tredegar Iron Works in Richmond and dubbed "Lady Polk." It exploded shortly after the Battle of Belmont, nearly killing the husband of its namesake—General Polk.[28]

Some of Polk's officers raised serious questions as to whether artillery alone would be sufficient to repulse the flotilla. J. T. Trezevant, an ordnance officer, informed the general in November 1861, "If the enemy should send down their ironclad steamers it is questionable if you have any guns at Columbus to stop them, especially if they pass at night. . . . In the excitement of the moment, your gunners would not hit them once in a hundred shots." Colonel Marsh Walker, commander of the 40th Tennessee and a West Pointer, was of a like mind. He predicted that the Federal naval captains would "shut their eyes and go by in any dark and stormy night when they chose."[29]

A second method of countering the Union fleet was to obstruct the channel. Colonel Edward Fontaine suggested to Polk that pilings be placed in the

Mississippi with tree trunks lodged against them. He surmised that the gunboats might be slowed enough to give the batteries more time to do their work. Although never attempted at Columbus, it was tried at Fort Pillow. Engineer Montgomery Lynch theorized that the pilings would reduce the channel to six hundred yards. The project, condemned by many from the outset, proved unsuccessful because flood waters obstructed the progress.[30]

Sinking barges and boats in the channel presented another possibility. This method was attempted in the much smaller Cumberland River, against the advice of Colonel Adolphus Heiman. "This will be a fruitless operation in a river which rises from low water at least 57 feet, and which I myself have often known to rise ten feet in 24 hours," he wrote. The project was nonetheless attempted at Ingram Shoals, where, in November 1861, five barges with twelve hundred tons of stone were sunk. Engineers gave assurances that this would be sufficient for any rise less than twelve feet above flood stage. Only a few days later, however, a Federal gunboat passed over the obstruction at flood stage without difficulty.[31]

Yet one more way remained to block the river. In July 1861, Pillow stretched a large chain across the Mississippi at Fort Pillow, and, although it was soon swept away by the current, Polk liked the idea. At Columbus a mile-long chain was laid over rafts placed strategically in the river. Each link weighed nineteen pounds, and the entire chain was secured to the bluff by an enormous six-ton anchor. The current eventually broke it, but if a similar experiment in New Orleans in April 1862 was any indication, it would not have worked anyway. In that instance the Federal vessels easily cleared the chain barrier.[32]

The third defensive possibility involved the use of mines, or "torpedoes." Trezevant believed this method to be the only real hope of stopping the ironclads. He recommended that five hundred to a thousand be placed in the Mississippi River channel. On December 4, 1861, Matthew Maury wrote Polk from Richmond that six torpedoes were ready for shipment and that another twenty-five were under construction. The next day inventor A. L. Saunders in Memphis informed the general that nineteen of his "improved submarine batteries" were being shipped to Columbus and that work was proceeding to complete the entire order of fifty. These primitive devices often failed to ignite, and, more often than not, the swift current and debris swept them away. The torpedoes, in fact, created more of a threat in thought than in reality because the Northern press created a near hysteria concerning them.[33]

The final hope of stopping the ironclads was in the development of a counter fleet. Work began on three lightly armored steamboats, but they would hardly be sufficient to challenge the Federal flotilla. The only way to stop an ironclad was with an ironclad, and for that Polk turned to Captain John T. Shirley of Memphis. The captain oversaw the construction of two ironclads, the hulls of which were laid at Fort Pickering at Memphis in October 1861. The engines were built at a foundry on Adams Street, and the timber was cut locally. The armor consisted of railroad bar iron bolted to the sides, hull, and ends. Shirley decided to concentrate his efforts on the CSS *Arkansas* first, but the work went slowly. By late March 1862, the keel had been laid and the ribs and framework put in place. A naval officer was disturbed with the work that had been completed. "She is a humbug, and badly constructed," Henry Stevens informed his wife.

A large crowd gathered in Memphis on March 29 when the hull of the *Arkansas* was launched. A band struck up to "Dixie" amid the cheers of the spectators. When New Orleans fell in late April, the vessel was towed downriver. At that time, the woodwork had been completed, except for the captain's cabin, and the hull mostly armored. The casemate still had no sheathing, however, and the engine and two boilers were aboard but inoperative.[34]

The Confederacy was simply outclassed in the industrial capacity required to construct ironclads. Construction began on two such vessels in New Orleans, which had several local foundries, including the large Leeds & Company. The Tredegar plant also assisted in engine and armor production. Even so, neither ironclad had been completed when the city fell to Union forces in late April 1862. Even if the *Arkansas* had been completed, it alone could not have contested the combined power of the Federal flotilla. The Confederates in the West had to complete not only one ironclad, which proved to be impossible due to the time constraints, but also two or three for the upper Mississippi Valley.[35]

Although Polk did not get his ironclad, his pleas did not go unanswered. In late November 1861, six converted river steamers from New Orleans, a rag-tag flotilla, were ordered to the general. Commanding the fleet was sixty-two-year-old Commodore George Hollins, who had fought the British in the War of 1812 and later scrapped with Algerian pirates. In an American reprisal action, he commanded a ship that shelled a Nicaraguan town. At the beginning of the war he commanded the USS *Susquehanna*, stationed at Naples, Italy.[36]

The fleet that initially arrived at Columbus consisted of six vessels, two others coming in January and February 1862. The flagship *McRae*, armed with eight guns, was formerly a Mexican screw seized as a pirate in 1860. The *General Polk*, built in 1852, was a sidewheeler carrying five guns and cased with railroad iron on the forward deck. A converted tugboat built in 1845, the *Ivy*, carried one gun forward and aft. The *Livingston*, a sternwheeler built in 1861, had been used as a ferryboat. Mounting six guns, the boat's only protection was heavy timber positioned around the boiler. So slow was the boat that the crew jokingly complained that they could not sleep when at full speed downriver because driftwood bumped the stern as it passed. The *Jackson*, a sidewheeler built in Cincinnati in 1849, had two guns.[37]

The most powerful addition to the flotilla was the floating battery CSS *New Orleans*, fashioned from the immense Pelican Drydock of Algiers, opposite the Crescent City. Measuring 60 feet by 180 feet, it had a slanting cover of timbers on the starboard side with sheet iron. A pumping system made it possible to lower the structure until only the iron plating was out of the water. Lacking motive power, it had to be towed upriver and then anchored in position. Six 8-inch columbiads were mounted at the time, making it a formidable vessel.[38]

The most curious-looking member of the squadron was a cigar-shaped, iron-plated boat named CSS *Manassas*. It had been converted from a river towboat and mounted a single 32-pounder in a bow trapdoor. The vessel got snagged around Memphis and had to be returned to New Orleans for repairs. Word of its approach had already been reported in the Northern press, which greatly magnified the boat's potential.[39]

The Southern populace placed an inflated hope in this flimsy fleet, yet there were those who knew better. Wrote a crew member of the *McRae:* "Day after day, without sufficient power and great draught, we struggled against the mighty current of the Mississippi, occasionally bumping into a mud bank and lying helpless there until pulled off. At the cities of Vicksburg and Memphis we received ovations. The dear people were very enthusiastic and knowing nothing about naval warfare, they felt sure we could whip the fleets of the universe."[40]

Frankly, no one knew whether these methods could in fact stop the ironclads. The alternative was simply to concede the rivers and contest the Union advance as it moved inland, an option that was politically unacceptable. Having done all that he could, Polk nervously awaited the Federal advance.

2

Too Much Haste Will Ruin Everything

HISTORY WOULD CREDIT James B. Eads with the construction of an iron-clad flotilla that would time and again tip the scales in the western theater in favor of the Federals. It is an interesting notoriety because he had never built a boat before undertaking the contract. His involvement was gained to a large extent through political ties. The flotilla, the result of a national effort, combined the expertise of both the military and the civilian industrial complex.

An aging General-in-Chief Winfield Scott gave birth early in the war to the idea of a brown-water ironclad fleet. The flotilla, designed to implement his Anaconda plan, called for offensive operations down the Mississippi River. John Lenthall, the chief of the navy's construction bureau, designed the boats, but the plans were significantly modified by naval architect Samuel A. Pook. Various firms bid for the contract in August 1861, including well-established Hill & Payne of New Albany, Indiana, and Hambleton & Cowan of Cincinnati. Eads's competitors shouted foul play when he landed the contract. Although submitting the low bid of $89,000 per boat, he had never before built a boat and had no facilities to do so. One irate bidder even termed him an "unscrupulous speculator."[1]

Eads, an energetic forty-one-year-old St. Louis businessman, was born in Lawrenceburg, Indiana, and had grown up along the river. He formed a river salvaging partnership, became rich, and retired in the 1850s because of poor health. It was his political ties that would ultimately land him the inside track on the ironclad fleet contract. He had the backing of President Abraham Lincoln's attorney general, Edward Bates of St. Louis. Charles Blair, an influential member of the Republican party in Missouri, and the brother of Montgomery Blair, Lincoln's postmaster general, petitioned to have the boats built in St. Louis, giving Eads an additional edge. Such a move, it was argued, would help stabilize Missouri for the Union.[2]

Although Eads lacked the facilities, he did have the administrative genius and energizing force needed to pull together the diverse aspects of this huge project. He divided the work between the Marine Railway & Drydock Company of Carondelet, Missouri, seven miles below St. Louis, and the Hambleton, Collier & Company docks at Mound City, Illinois, near Cairo. Some five hundred hands were employed in Missouri and three hundred in Illinois. At Mound

City the keels of USS *Cairo,* USS *Cincinnati,* and USS *Mound City* were laid, as the Carondelet yards construction began on USS *Louisville,* USS *St. Louis,* USS *Carondelet,* and USS *Pittsburg* (the city was not spelled with an "h" at that time). The fleet became known as the "City Series."[3]

By the time Captain Andrew Foote, the new western naval commander, arrived in St. Louis, construction had begun on nine ironclads. These included Eads's seven and two others, USS *Essex* and USS *Benton,* the latter converted from a steamboat purchased by the Western department commander, Major General John C. Fremont. The *Benton* would play a major role in the Island No. 10 campaign as the flagship of the Mississippi River squadron. After the war Eads proudly wrote of the conversion of the vessel. He failed to mention that the double-hulled boat was originally *Submarine No. 7,* one of his own underpowered salvage boats that he had sold to the government at an inflated price. He even attempted bribery in the process. After awarding the conversion contract to Eads, Fremont then named the vessel in honor of his father-in-law— Thomas Hart Benton. Despite these shenanigans, the mammoth *Benton,* much larger than Eads's ironclads, proved to be the strongest craft afloat in the West. Carpenters tore the decks down to the bottom and sides and rebuilt the entire vessel, which mounted sixteen guns.[4]

Another project initiated by Fremont in August 1861 was the construction of thirty-eight mortar rafts. These unpowered rafts measured 25 by 60 feet and were surrounded by slanting bulwarks six to seven feet high. Each raft, with a crew of fifteen, carried a single 13-inch mortar capable of lobbing a shell three and a half miles. Some doubted that the rafts could withstand the recoil, claiming that they would fall apart after 250 rounds. The public remained quite fascinated by the mortars, which it was touted could fire with impunity out of the range of rifled cannon. By January 1862, extensive work remained. This was in part because Fremont's successor, Major General Henry W. Halleck, showed no particular interest in the project.[5]

As construction continued on the ironclads and mortar rafts, Captain Foote turned his attention to manning them. In November 1861, the Navy Department dispatched five hundred sailors, Jack Tars from the blue-water navy who were at Fort Ellsworth at Alexandria, Virginia, near Washington, D.C. A deficiency of a thousand men remained for the fleet (each ironclad had a complement of 251 men), not to mention eight hundred men for the mortars. The void was partially filled by the army. By December 1861 Halleck had collected 1,200 volunteers at St. Louis—a hodgepodge of river men, farmers, and shopkeepers. In February 1862, an additional six hundred volunteers arrived from the Army of the Potomac, one naval officer describing them as "Maine lumbermen, New Bedford whalers, New York liners, and Philadelphia sea-lawyers."[6]

Guns and ammunition had to be secured from arsenals back east. Each of Eads's ironclads required four 42-pounder rifles, six 32-pounders, and three

Fig. 2. The *Baron De Kalb, Cincinnati,* and *Mound City* (courtesy of Paul H. Silverstone, 1981; U.S. Naval Historical Foundation)

8-inch Dahlgrens, except for the *St. Louis,* which had an additional 32-pounder and one less Dahlgren. The *Benton's* armament included seven 42-pounder rifles, a like number of 32-pounders, and two 9-inch Dahlgrens. On November 20, 1861, the steamer *Maria Denning* arrived at Cairo with 82 cannon, 120,000 solid shot, 100 shells, and 400 grapeshot for the fleet. A huge unauthorized order for 11,200 mortar shells astounded even Foote, who cut the number in half.[7]

Foote found himself working under the time constraints of nature, as well as those of the War Department. Observing the dropping river gauge, a St. Louis correspondent expressed apprehension that "the gun-boats not quite finished, will not be able to get out of the Mississippi River, unless they are sent away in a few days." By early December the Carondelet vessels had arrived at Cairo, although the *Pittsburg* and the *Benton* grounded in the process. By the end of the month Eads informed Foote that the Mound City boats would be ready to move, although the *Cairo* was delayed. A frustrated Foote informed Secretary of the Navy Gustavus Fox: "I only wish that you could have spent one day here [Cairo], for the last six weeks, as no imagination can fancy what it is to collect materials and fit out Western Gun Boats with Eastern men without Navy yard—in the West, where no stores are to be had."[8]

By January 1862, the flotilla was at long last ready. Underpowered and vulnerable to plunging fire, they were nonetheless formidable and more than a match for anything the Confederates could put against them. The boats had never been tested against earthen fortifications, however, and whether they were up to that task remained to be seen.[9]

Looking much older than his forty-seven years, Major General Henry W. Halleck possessed a stern schoolmasterly appearance and had a habit of conversing with a bug-eyed stare. His prewar career had been spent mostly in staff and engineering assignments. Although well suited for the managerial aspects of the huge Department of Missouri, which stretched west from the Cumberland River, he was essentially a theorist. In comparison with his predecessor, Fremont, however, he was a welcome replacement.[10]

Halleck arrived in St. Louis in November 1861 and established his headquarters at the Planter's House Hotel. Fremont had left a legacy of chaos and defeat, his subordinates having lost at Wilson's Creek and Lexington. Many of the troops in the department lacked blankets and arms. "Reports come to me daily of troops in a suffering, disorganized and mutinous condition," Halleck wrote on November 28. An offensive prospect was put on hold as he consolidated and reorganized his department.[11]

If Halleck was preoccupied with intradepartmental affairs, Brigadier General Ulysses S. Grant pushed for a fight. Just before "Old Brains" arrived, the Illinois general had been eyeing New Madrid, and he planned to move against the town on November 8, 1861. None of the particulars are known; the incident is mentioned only once in the navy records. The movement was cancelled "owing to the inability of the gunboats to cooperate." Halleck held a more conservative view of the town. He understood New Madrid's importance and believed that its occupation would relieve the garrison at Cairo. New Madrid could be taken by Brigadier General Samuel Curtis's army from the direction of Springfield, Missouri, but Halleck doubted that it could be permanently held, being vulnerable to Confederate attack from Arkansas and west Tennessee.[12]

From the beginning of the war, a movement down the Mississippi from Cairo to New Orleans had been a pet project of Lincoln, Scott, Fremont, and George B. McClellan. The press, the Northern public, and clearly the Confederates believed such a move was in the making. President Lincoln even mistook the Battle of Belmont for the vanguard of Halleck's offensive down the river. The strategic emphasis now shifted. When Winfield Scott resigned, his Anaconda plan no longer dominated military thinking. Halleck and Brigadier General Don Carlos Buell, commanding the Department of Ohio, were being urged to cooperate, and this necessarily focused attention on the Cumberland River, the dividing line between the departments. Although cooperation between the two men remained virtually nonexistent, Halleck nonetheless did not have an immediate interest in the Mississippi. In January 1862, he wrote that he considered "the idea of moving down the Mississippi" to be "impracticable, or at least premature." Increasingly, he was being drawn to the Confederate center—the twin rivers.[13]

In February 1862, the St. Louis commander permitted Grant and Foote to move up the Tennessee River to Fort Henry. The fort proved a soft target and was neutralized after a two-hour fight. This action seemed to affirm the invulnerability of ironclads and the inability of earthen forts to defeat them. In truth, the gunboats had been shot up, and three of the four ironclads had to return to Cairo for repairs. Hoping to repeat success, however, Grant got permission to move on Fort Donelson.[14]

Even though the Cumberland River fort had less firepower than Fort Henry's, its location and engineering strength made it formidable. Foote's boats attacked on February 14, but after an hour's bombardment, at ranges down to 400 yards, not a single Confederate gun had been disabled. By contrast, Foote's fleet had been badly bruised, with two ironclads being forced to withdraw and the flag officer himself being painfully wounded in his foot. The Southerners were encouraged. Lieutenant Colonel William T. Withers wrote the secretary of war on February 28: "The fight at Fort Donelson has developed the fact that the boasted invulnerability of the enemy's gunboats is a myth."[15]

While the inept Confederate leadership concentrated on the river, Brigadier General Grant closed in on the land. It was this dual aspect of joint operations that made it so deadly. Even if the gunboats could be stopped, a garrison had to be exposed to protect the shore batteries. Only by defeating the gunboats *and* keeping the Federal army at bay some miles from the fort was there any hope for Southern success. If Grant could not have been stopped on the march between Fort Henry and Fort Donelson, as Thomas Connelly suggests in his book, then the Confederates should have abandoned the fort and saved the troops.[16]

With the capture of Fort Donelson, Grant had scored one of the greatest victories of the war. Johnston had lost one-third of his army. Even with interior lines and unified command, the Confederates proved unable to develop an effective counter to joint operations. All across Johnston's line, his troops now reeled back in disorder. Nashville fell, and Columbus, "the boasted 'Gibraltar of the West,' " as Halleck referred to it, would soon follow. Even in defeat, modern gunboats had gained the strategic advantage. Halleck concluded that the Confederates were now "completely turned on both sides of the Mississippi."[17]

3

Defense to the Last Extremity

IN EARLY February 1862, forty-four-year-old Louisiana General P. G. T. Beauregard, the hero of Fort Sumter and Manassas, came to the West. Unfortunately, he arrived just as Johnston's position in central Kentucky disintegrated. Following the fall of Fort Henry and Fort Donelson, Johnston's center and left wings were isolated by the Tennessee River. Beauregard was given command of the troops between the Tennessee and the Mississippi, while Johnston pulled the Bowling Green column back to Murfreesboro, Tennessee. Initially Beauregard proposed an extravagant plan whereby his forces and those in Arkansas, now under Major General Earl Van Dorn, would unite at Columbus or New Madrid for a joint movement against Cairo, the southernmost base of Union operations, or even against St. Louis. He and Johnston eventually agreed, however, that the wings of the army should merge at the strategic rail junction of Corinth, Mississippi. It was essential to make a preemptive strike against Grant's army advancing up the Tennessee River before it merged with Buell's army coming from Nashville.[1]

Beauregard's planned trip to Columbus was aborted because of illness. He stopped at Jackson, Tennessee, and summoned Polk to his side. The bishop arrived on February 19 and discovered, much to his dismay, that the main item on the agenda was the evacuation of Columbus. Beauregard's views had already been expressed to Johnston. He believed that Grant could easily march westward from Fort Henry to Union City or Clinton, Kentucky, and invest Columbus from the rear. He recommended that the town be evacuated, a move Johnston had already approved, contingent on War Department acceptance.[2]

Already bristling at being superseded in command, Polk loudly protested. For six months he had labored to strengthen Columbus, and he was not prepared to give it up. "I felt in leaving it as if I were leaving home," he wrote his daughter. He bargained with Beauregard, offering to hold the town with just five thousand troops, but the Louisiana general held firm. What happened next became a matter of postwar contention. According to Beauregard, the two finally concurred that the town could not withstand a determined attack. William Polk, the bishop's biographer-son, insisted that his father went along to maintain harmony, but in fact never agreed with the decision. Yet on March 12, Polk conceded to Davis that Island No. 10 was acceptable as a defensive position and could be "held by a much smaller force." William Polk concluded, however, that nothing was later done at Island No. 10 that could not have been accomplished at Columbus and that, for good or bad, the town should have been held.[3]

The truth was that Polk had become too comfortable. A static defense also served as a convenient shield against decision making. In seeing Columbus as "home" rather than the trap it really was, he lost sight of the big picture, even as Johnston had done with the Bowling Green defenses. To survive, Polk's corps had to remain mobile. If the bishop could have had his way, it is conceivable that Columbus might have become an early day Vicksburg, Mississippi. Losing the equivalent of a corps at Fort Donelson and another at Columbus so early in the war might well have broken the back of the rebellion in the West.

Underlying the Beauregard-Polk split was the basic dilemma facing the western Confederate command. Polk subscribed to an all-out point defense, something that Beauregard adamantly resisted. The Louisiana general wanted no more Fort Donelsons. Realizing that fortifications would be required to stop the Federal fleet, he adopted what might be termed a "modified point defense." Forts designed for small garrisons would be constructed, leaving the bulk of the troops to maneuver in the field. Small garrisons, however, were always subject to being gobbled up unless relieved by the maneuvering field army. Whether Beauregard could disengage from his opposing force to offer such relief was uncertain. On February 23, he wrote Polk: "The great point is . . . to be able to support in time the garrison of Island No. 10 if attacked."[4]

Beauregard thus set about to modify the construction of Fort Pillow. Even as the Columbus works had been overbuilt, so too was Fort Pillow being prepared for a garrison of fifteen to twenty thousand. What Beauregard had more in mind was three thousand. He believed such a force would be sufficient "until reinforcements, in an emergency, could have come to their relief."[5]

The Madrid Bend area was made to order for Beauregard's strategy, even though New Madrid was admittedly vulnerable. Its natural strength made it almost inaccessible from the east. Captain David B. Harris, Beauregard's chief engineer, was sent with instructions specifically outlining construction plans. Madrid Bend, nevertheless, remained far removed from the new defense line that Beauregard would establish. Island No. 10 formed roughly the apex of a right triangle that extended down the Mississippi River to Memphis, east to Corinth, and then diagonally back to Island No. 10 through Humboldt, Tennessee.[6]

Was the main battle for the Mississippi River to be fought at Madrid Bend, or was that position simply to buy time for the primary defense at Fort Pillow? In postwar years Beauregard insisted that he had intended the latter. At no time, however, did he express such a thought to either Polk or Johnston. On February 21, he wrote Adjutant General Samuel Cooper that in the meeting with

Fig. 3: Beauregard later insisted that the main battle for the Mississippi Valley was to be fought at Fort Pillow (shown above) (courtesy of *Battles and Leaders*)

Johnston it had been decided to hold both Island No. 10 and Fort Pillow "for defense to the last extremity," the implication being that both were of equal value. On February 26, he wrote Polk: "New Madrid is all important. In my opinion [it] must be watched and held at all costs. All troops at Fort Pillow but mere guard should be transferred with utmost celerity." On still other occasions he expressed the idea that Fort Pillow was merely a backup for Island No. 10. Whether his later contention was mere postwar hindsight or that there might have been a certain schizophrenia within the general on the subject cannot now be determined.[7]

The plan was set in motion. Polk's seventeen-thousand-man corps at Columbus would be divided, one division being transported forty miles downriver to Madrid Bend, there to join the fifteen hundred troops already in garrison. The one thousand infantry at Fort Pillow were also directed to the area. The balance of the corps was concentrated at Humboldt. An infantry-cavalry outpost would be maintained at Union City to protect the Mobile & Ohio railhead and the right flank of Madrid Bend. Some one thousand cavalry remained on outpost at Paris, Tennessee, keeping an eye on Grant's army, estimated at fifty thousand. Johnston's Confederate army continued to be pressured by Buell's estimated forty thousand. In addition, a threat to the Mississippi Valley existed from a Federal army forming in that arena.[8]

The issue of the western rivers—their vulnerability, method of defense, or even whether they should be defended—was set in the context of Davis administration policy. Early in the war President Davis, motivated by political and social concerns, adopted a policy of territorial defense. A concerted, though fruitless, effort was made to hold all areas. This policy not only prevented concentration of troops, but also created a defacto two-front war for Johnston— the Mississippi Valley and the Tennessee Valley. Which of the two held greater importance was problematic; the issue was still being debated a year later in the Vicksburg campaign by Davis and Joseph E. Johnston. The point is that Sidney Johnston, until the fall of Fort Donelson, made no attempt to concentrate his widely scattered forces, despite the fact that he enjoyed unified command.[9]

In the Mississippi Valley, the issue of river defense—its practicality or even its necessity—never reached the level of a regional debate. The populace merely assumed that the Mississippi would be the battleground. The Mississippi Valley (from which President Davis came) had a powerful constituency—Governor Isham Harris, Sam Tate (president of the Memphis & Charleston Railroad), the Memphis Military Board, wealthy plantation owners, and local congressmen, who formed a powerful lobbying bloc in Richmond, all demanded that the administration attempt an all-out defense. Harris did not even wait for Davis's imput but, as has been noted, began his own river construction sites without consulting Confederate authorities. Thomas Connelly suggests that the western Confederate military establishment would have concurred anyway, since half of Johnston's division and brigade commanders held business or residential ties to the Mississippi Valley.[10]

News concerning Columbus and its fate was slow in reaching the capital. Richmond insider Robert Kean noted on February 20, "Columbus is cut off, and will of course be, probably has been, evacuated." By March 6, however, attorney general Thomas Bragg noted that no definite news had been received concerning the town. War Department clerk John Jones was certain that Beauregard would "not be caught in such a trap as that [Columbus]." At the same time he jotted in his diary, "But he is erecting a battery at Island No. 10 that will give the Yankees trouble. I hope it may stay the catalogue of disasters."[11]

It is clear that the government mindset still held static defenses in high regard. Writing from his home outside the capital, renowned secessionist zealot Edmund Ruffin remained baffled at the administration's inability to grasp the issue. "We no longer hold any portion of Ky, except an island (No. 10) in the Mississippi. . . . I should think that we had had enough of risking armies in fortifications in reach of the enemy's naval forces. An island is the place most exposed to their attack, and the least capable of being reinforced, or the garrison escaping in case of defeat."[12]

Political tensions also affected strategic concerns. The main advocates of deemphasizing river defense were Beauregard (in 1862) and Joseph E. Johnston (in 1863)—both archenemies of the administration. A Davis prejudice toward these individuals might well have blinded him, and probably did, to their alternative strategy.[13]

By late February 1862, Beauregard and Polk had become increasingly concerned about the security of New Madrid. Although he had never personally visited the position, Beauregard could not resist making certain suggestions as to its defense. He stated that the gorges of the fortifications should be palisaded only so that Confederate gunboats could fire into them if captured. He envisioned a triangular defense, with three forts of about equal size (five hundred men to each), two to be on the river and a third a little in advance of the others, forming an apex. Meanwhile, Polk ordered five of Hollins's gunboats to Madrid Bend—four to protect the flanks of the forts at New Madrid and the other to remain at the island.[14]

Reinforcements were also sent to New Madrid. Thirty-three-year-old Colonel L. M. "Marsh" Walker, a West Pointer and a nephew of President James K. Polk, led the 40th Tennessee. Thirty-three-year-old Colonel Alpheus Baker of Eufaula, Alabama, commanded the 1st Alabama, Tennessee, Mississippi. At 1 P.M. on February 26, the 40th received orders to move upriver, along with the 1st if it were armed. Regrettably, Baker's guns were only a notch above worthless. The rifles, prepared in a Memphis shop, had mainsprings that often broke. Only days earlier, a shipment of eighty such rifles had been received, twenty-four of which malfunctioned when test-fired. Some men in the outfit had only old squirrel guns and shotguns, and others remained unarmed. Indeed, there were only twenty-five decent arms in the entire regiment. Rather than be left behind, however, Baker loaded his men aboard the steamer *Vicksburg*. An additional 180 Memphis rifles arrived just before departure and were issued to the men; inferior as they were, the weapons were an improvement on nothing at all.[15]

Brigadier General A. P. Stewart commanded the New Madrid defenses. His West Point diploma had won him a brigadier's commission in November 1861, but in truth he had virtually no military experience, having spent the previous nineteen years as a mathematics professor. He had turned down the chancellorship of Cumberland University in Lebanon, Tennessee, where he taught, to remain "close to the students." Although he considered secession legal, he believed it unwise and voted against it. His heavy artillery had performed adequately during the Battle of Belmont, but whether "Old Straight," as he was called, would prove to be a fighter remained an open-ended question.[16]

Colonel Walker hurried work on the town's defenses. Gantt's brigade already occupied Fort Thompson with fourteen heavy guns. Construction also began on Fort Bankhead, a smaller and less substantial work at the mouth of St. John's Bayou. The technical supervision was largely under the direction of Captain T. B. Hogue of the engineers. Dirt and bags of shelled corn made a parapet ten feet thick. The garrison included Baker's and Walker's regiments and Captain Smith P. Bankhead's Tennessee battery, a Memphis outfit, that had come down from Columbus. At the dead end of the Sikeston Road, the Confederates rigged a battery of Quaker guns—logs placed on carts and positioned to look like cannon. From the outset, Jeff Thompson had opposed the New Madrid works, believing that they could be easily invested. He asserted that the stand should be made at Jones's Ford at the swamp. Baker's men, meanwhile, remained dispirited about their inferior arms. The regiment lined up along the river bank to take target practice at trash and floating logs, but many of the guns did not discharge, and several burst. Three hundred additional Memphis rifles arrived, but like the rest, they were almost useless.[17]

On March 14, in response to a letter from Harris, Beauregard agreed that his idea of an advanced lunette could be eliminated, "as the gunboats appear[ed] to be able to cover the front effectively, and keep off the enemy." He also directed that Harris could dispense with abatis on the Missouri shore. Postponing the construction of additional redoubts at Madrid Bend was also approved, but General Beauregard remained concerned that a number of substantial traverses be built.[18]

Morale remained generally poor. Gantt's Arkansas troops were still recovering from an outbreak of measles. Knowledge of Confederate setbacks in other areas also resulted in gloom. "I have been afflicted with the blues ever since I heard of our disasters in Kentucky and the evacuation of Bowling Green by Johnston," remarked surgeon Jennings. "Nor is that all. New Madrid is going the same way, for when it falls Columbus is doomed."[19]

Construction began to lag at Madrid Bend. Piecing together a project of such proportions in such a remote swampy bottomland was proving laborious. There was only enough lumber for the gun platforms, leaving none for the storehouses. The redan was inundated, and a shortage of tools remained. By working day and night, however, work crews began mounting guns. On February 16, Gray informed Gantt that the steamer *Commodore Whittler* had gone to Fort Pillow for thirteen additional guns and that the *Ohio Belle* had been sent to pick up slave laborers. "I think the lumber can be sawed and ready for the boats to take up in a few days, if they will go immediately at it," he concluded.[20]

In the meantime, the *New Orleans Picayune* of February 20, 1862, assured its readers that the rumored evacuation of Columbus was false. Its correspondent had received it "on the authority of Gen. Beauregard" that the town was to be "held at every hazard." Despite this assurance, four days later the vanguard of the Columbus garrison arrived at Island No. 10. Aboard the transport *Marie* was Colonel J. B. G. Kennedy and twenty-five men of his 5th Louisiana Battalion, two hundred blacks, and supplies of commissary stores and lumber. The colonel found engineers Harris and Gray, and Captain D. Wintter's company of sappers hard at work, as well as the 46th Tennessee, of which only 155 of 400 men were fit for duty. The situation appeared discouraging. A week and a half later an entire division of the Columbus garrison would be withdrawn, and all the heavy guns that had been holding back the Federal fleet would go with it. Yet there were only two works on the Tennessee shore: the redan with three 32-pounders and Battery No. 5, a mile and a half distant, with a single 32-pounder. Nine unmounted guns lay scattered about, and no work had commenced on the island batteries. Beauregard remained concerned about the slow progress and warned Polk about prematurely disengaging at Columbus. A dearth of slaves had slowed construction. Colonel Ed Pickett, commanding the post at Union City, was ordered to send five hundred slaves to Island No. 10, but he gathered up only eight.[21]

On the morning of February 26, the new commander of Madrid Bend arrived. Forty-seven-year-old Brigadier General John P. McCown was a graduate of West Point with twenty-one years service in the Regular Army. A veteran of both the Mexican and Seminole wars, he had served in the 5th United States Artillery. His qualifications and political connections in Tennessee had landed him the job of commander of the artillery corps of the Tennessee Provisional Army at the beginning of the war. On paper he looked good for what promised to be a campaign with little field maneuvering. On the debit side, he was essentially an unknown (his role in the Battle of Belmont had been largely passive), and he had never had an independent command. Lieutenant Colonel John F. Henry of the 4th Tennessee met the general in October 1861 and was unimpressed, describing him as "an old delapidated fellow with very little energy."[22]

McCown arrived on February 26, and went directly to New Madrid. Hollins was already on the scene with his gunboats. Should the enemy's ironclads pass the island batteries, McCown predicted that the town could hold only six hours. The next day he conducted a thorough inspection of the upriver defenses, admitting that he was not prepared for what he found. "I find that little or nothing has been done by Captain Gray," he informed Polk on February 27. Kennedy had more recently made progress, and fifteen guns were now mounted—five in the redan, seven in Battery No. 5, and three in between. "Upon examination I believe that the upper battery [redan] is not equal to what is expected of it," he observed. As for the island, "nothing was done until yesterday [February 26]." McCown concluded: "Every hour I can get is of great importance. I fear I will have to defend this place with the bayonet unless I can get time."[23]

Chief of Artillery James Trudeau arrived on March 1. A member of a prominent Louisiana family (his grandfather was former Governor Zenon Trudeau), forty-five-year-old Trudeau had studied in a Swiss military school and later became a physician, practicing in Philadelphia and New York. He was acquainted with the celebrated ornithological artist James Audubon and frequently supplied him with rare bird specimens.[24]

Trudeau immediately realized that the "post we were about to occupy was in no measure fortified." The ten Tennessee heavy artillery companies, some 536 cannoneers, also arrived on March 1. The companies of William Y. C. Humes, James A. Fisher, and Thomas Johnston were assigned to the island. The last was a mobile siege battery with four 8-inch siege howitzers, each with thirty rounds, three 24-pounders, and a 12-pounder. The balance of the companies encamped on the mainland behind Battery No. 5. Captain Andrew Jackson, Jr., the adopted stepson of the former president, directed his men and two companies of the 11th Louisiana in the preparation of platforms for Battery No. 4. The large Battery No. 5, which had been started the previous fall, was placed in the hands of W. C. Jones's, Paul T. Dismuke's, and J. B. Carruthers's companies, along with the sapper company. Robert Sterling's men worked the redan, and Edward W. Rucker's and Frederick W. Hoadley's men labored on Batteries 2 and 3.[25]

During the first three days in March, the Columbus garrison began to disembark. Twenty steamers carried McCown's undersized division ("it is more

Fig. 4. Major General John P. McCown (courtesy of the Massachusetts Commandery Military Order of the Loyal Legion and the U.S. Army Military History Institute)

properly a brigade," observed Beauregard) and Brigadier General Alexander P. Stewart's independent brigade, some thirty-seven hundred infantry. Bankhead's Tennessee Battery rolled off the gankplank with six guns. Unfortunately, the flatboat transporting Captain Richard "Black Dick" Stewart's Pointe Coupee Louisiana Artillery sprang a leak, causing the loss of one field gun and all the

ammunition. A couple of cavalry companies, with three hundred troopers, re-
ported for scouting purposes. Coupled with Gantt's brigade, downriver at New
Madrid, Beauregard had committed seventy-five hundred troops by early
March.[26]

Men and equipment came in so hurriedly that chaos resulted. A frustrated
Trudeau wrote: "Everything had been piled on the steamboats in such a way,
at the time of the evacuation of Columbus, that upon landing nothing could
be found. The chassis of a gun would be at one point, the gun and carriage at
another; the pintle-blocks and pintle pins had all been stowed away in a flatboat, and we had already made ourselves such as we required when they were
discovered. Such confusion I have never witnessed." Even McCown conceded:
"The guns, ammunition, etc. have been brought down without any person
knowing what was on each boat."[27]

By March 5, all five mainland batteries had been completed. The redan had
several problems yet to be resolved. The armament consisted of three 8-inch
columbiads and three smoothbore 32s. The former had been procured from the
floating battery. With such a pool of talent available to McCown, it is difficult
to understand why such an obvious mistake was made in the placement of guns.
Because the redan was the initial contact battery, and range was far more a
factor here than at any other point, the 32s should have been replaced with
rifled guns of the same caliber. This arrangement would have given the extra
range required and the penetrating power needed against ironclads. Smoothbores would have been more functional at one of the lower forts protecting the
Tennessee chute. The redan smoothbores would be useless in a long-range bombardment. Even for close-in work, the smoothbores could still not penetrate
the armored bows of the boats.[28]

Other problems remained. The flooded redan would be "next to useless"
in a fight, McCown admitted. The base of the earthen wall was twenty-four
feet thick, which was probably adequate to absorb solid shot. The erosion remained so serious, however, that the three 32s had to be placed in barbette,
which made them vulnerable.[29]

Gray also encountered difficulties with the wooden gun carriage platforms
for the columbiads in the redan. The timber could not stand up to the repeated
recoil unless it was topped by an iron traverse plate, which could be obtained
in the immediate area only from the floating battery at Columbus. Gray urgently requested the plates "as our artillerymen in drilling use up our platforms
very fast." The iron carriages themselves remained three to nine inches below
the high-water mark, making them vulnerable during flooding. Commodore
William C. Whittle traveled to Fort Pillow to hurry the steamer *Vicksburg* with
additional guns for the island.[30]

The remaining shore batteries were of varying strength. Batteries 2 and 3,
some 2,000 and 2,175 yards, respectively, from the redan, were essentially sand-

bag earthworks thrown up above the overflow. To position the emplacements any further back from the bank would have reduced the fire control of the channel. Number 2 had a parapet ten feet high and twenty feet thick, and it mounted three 32-pounder rifles and a single 32-pounder. This battery commanded the redan in the event of its capture. Battery No. 3 had three 32-pounder rifles. Battery No. 4, at this time, had only one gun, but others would be mounted. To the rear and left of No. 4 was a three-hundred-square-foot fort with eight-foot-high walls surrounded by a seven-foot-deep ditch. Battery No. 5, the most elevated and substantial of the shore batteries, was four hundred yards from No. 4. It had two bastion fronts meeting at an obtuse angle. The wall was eight feet high, twenty feet thick, and a hundred feet long, lined at the top with sandbags. It contained seven guns, including three 8-inch columbiads, a rifled 32, and three smoothbore 32s. Behind the batteries and extending to the tree line were numerous tent streets. A few permanent structures existed, including a white cottage used as headquarters.

On the head of the island, timber had been cleared back five hundred to six hundred feet. Square-shaped Battery No. 1, the Belmont Battery, was fifty feet from the river. The wall, 250 feet long, eight feet high, and fifteen feet thick, consisted of earth and sandbags. The guns, placed in four compartments divided by three gabions, each had a magazine beneath. In a mistake similar to the armament placement in the redan, four of the Belmont guns were smoothbore 32s. The battery did contain, however, the most powerful weapon in McCown's arsenal—a monster eight-ton rifle capable of hurling a 128-pound projectile. Dubbed "Lady Polk, Jr.," it was named after its twin sister at Columbus, which exploded shortly after the Battle of Belmont. Commanding the Belmont Battery was Captain William Y. C. Humes, a young Memphis lawyer and a graduate of the Virginia Military Institute, whose company consisted mostly of Irish laborers from the "Pinch District" of Memphis.

Some progress had also been made on the remaining island batteries. Crescent-shaped Battery No. 2 was seventy-five feet long and divided by a single gabion. Its armament of three smoothbore 32s and a rifled 24 made it suitable for close-in work only. Battery No. 3, 375 yards from the Belmont, covered the main channel and served essentially as a back-up battery. It was an angular formation with walls ten feet high, two hundred feet long, and gabions positioned between each gun emplacement. Work remained to be done, and no guns had been mounted. Batteries 4 and 5 were a quarter of a mile below the Belmont Battery and positioned in Price's peach orchard. Each of these batteries, which were not extensive, had a pair of Hamilton's eight-inch siege howitzers. The real protection for the main channel remained the floating battery, which had been moved from the Tennessee shore on March 2. It had on board one rifled 32 and eight 8-inch columbiads, making it, in terms of metal weight, the most powerful of the batteries.[31]

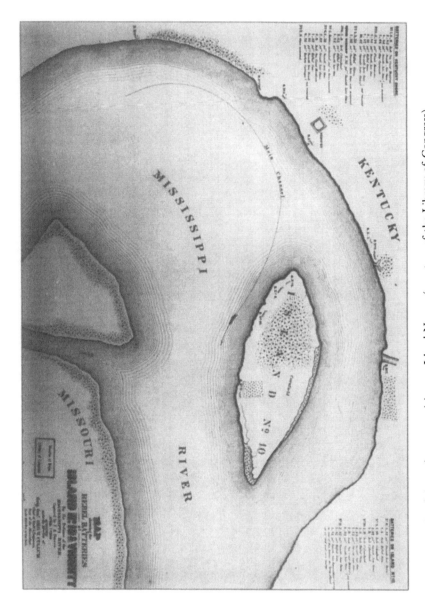

Map 3. Confederate battery positions at Island No. 10 (courtesy of the Library of Congress)

McCown thus had in readiness thirty-seven guns on March 5, but still he fretted: "All I fear is that the Federal gunboats may close their ports and run past," he confided to Polk. Engineer Harris shared his concern. He questioned whether "they, the batteries, will be able or not to prevent them from passing . . . the future alone can disclose."[32]

According to Harris's March 9 report, progress had been made, although serious problems remained. The five Tennessee shore batteries had twenty-four guns: five 8-inch columbiads, nine 32-pounder rifles, and two 32-pounder smoothbores. The water in the redan had risen above the gun platforms, and he feared that the battery would be of little use until the river fell. The entire Tennessee bank was "caving in very fast," and it looked as though new batteries might have to be constructed in the rear of existing ones. Harris warned, "We will be fortunate if we do not lose any of the guns, if what we hear [is true] in regard to the landslides that sometimes occur on the Mississippi." Fortunately, the river bank, although by no means commanding, was ten to fifteen feet higher than the opposite shore.

The island head, heavily timbered except for a cleared area, had ten guns mounted in Batteries 1 and 2: one 128-pounder rifle (Lady Polk, Jr.), one 8-inch columbiad, and seven 32-pounders. The Missouri shore remained heavily wooded, but Harris did not consider its clearing a priority. A strip of cleared land one half to three fourths of a mile wide directly opposite the island offered a good view of the approaching enemy. The work force on the island and Tennessee shore consisted of 200 blacks, 128 Irish, and Wintter's company of sappers and miners with about 40 men. Recognizing Beauregard's extensive engineering expertise in the Regular Army, Harris concluded: "I very much regret the general has not been able [because of illness] to make a personal inspection of this position and give Captain Gray and myself the benefit of his suggestions." The Louisiana general did attempt to have Jeremy Gilmer, Johnston's chief engineer, sent to New Madrid—"the safety of the place may depend upon it," he wrote. Johnston denied the request.[33]

Even Trudeau was amazed at the progress made between March 1 and March 12. "I can say with pride that 1,000 men performed in that time more and better work than was ever done at Columbus in three months," he boasted. By March 13, twenty-two guns had been mounted on the mainland and nineteen on the island. The floating battery supplemented these forty-one pieces.[34] (See Chart, Table 1, Confederate Armament on March 13, 1862.)

Although the number appeared impressive on paper, serious logistical problems remained. In a long-range bombardment, the mainland and island batteries No. 1, the redan and the Belmont, would receive the brunt of the action. The first was now at the upper end of a mile-and-a-half sheet of water three feet deep that separated it from the lower batteries. The redan remained

Table 1. Confederate armament on March 13, 1862

Battery	Commanding	Armament	Total
		Mainland	
1	Edward W. Rucker	3 8-inch columbiads 3 32-pounders	6
2	Robert Sterling	1 32-pounder 3 32-pounder rifles	4
3	Frederick W. Hoadley	3 32-pounder rifles	3
4	Andrew Jackson, Jr.	1 8-inch columbiad 3 32-pounder rifles	4
5	W. C. Jones J. B. Carruthers Paul T. Dismukes	3 8-inch columbiads 1 32-pounder rifle 3 32-pounders	7
			24
		Island	
1	W. Y. C. Humes	1 8-inch columbiad 1 128-pounder rifle 4 32-pounders	6
2	W. Y. C. Humes	3 32-pounders 1 24-pounder rifle	4
3	James A. Fisher	1 8-inch columbiad 2 32-pounders 2 24-pounder rifles	5
4	Thomas Johnston	2 8-inch siege howitzers	2
5	Thomas Johnston	2 8-inch siege howitzers	2
			19
Floating Battery	Samuel W. Averett	1 32-pounder rifle 8 8-inch columbiads	9
Total Guns			52

so badly inundated that the magazines had seeped water, and shells had to be lined along the parapet. Gray insisted that he had never intended to use the redan at high water, but rather for the gunners to fall back to the lower batteries that commanded it. "General McCown, however, thinks the locality so fine for a cross-fire, that he has ordered a detachment to use the guns as long as they can. They can retire along the cremaillere line if the enemy's fire gets too severe for them," he informed Polk. Mainland Battery No. 2 still had no magazine. A shortage of rifled ammunition also remained, the guns averaging only thirty rounds a piece.[35]

A welcome relief had been received the previous day, March 14, with the arrival of the 1st Alabama, a regiment that had been thoroughly drilled on the heavy guns at Pensacola, Florida. Nearly a year earlier some of the men had posed in checked shirts and nondescript uniforms at their gun emplacements for a local photographer. Their youthful commander, twenty-six-year-old Colonel I. G. W. Steadman, was a graduate of the South Carolina Military Academy and of the University of Louisville Medical School. On March 5, 1862, the regiment was loaded aboard flat cars for Tensas Landing, where a steamer took them to Mobile, Alabama. From there the men boarded railcars for the trip north to Corinth and west to Memphis, where they arrived on March 12. A leaky old steamer was used for the final leg to Island No. 10. "We had a very disagreeable trip up the River sleeping out on the deck," a member wrote his wife. On their arrival, McCown notified Polk: "The First Alabama Regiment is here, with mumps and measles."[36]

The 1st Alabama had barely arrived when Steadman was ordered to report to Trudeau. His men were to be divided to assist the Tennessee heavy artillerymen: two companies for the island batteries, one for the floating battery, and a detail of sixty-five men each for the five mainland batteries. "This gave four detachments for each—an invaluable resource in a prolonged action," Trudeau noted.[37]

On the strategic front, in early March 1862, Beauregard shifted his defensive line. His new crescent-shaped deployment ran south-southwest from Island No. 10, through Humboldt, Tennessee, to Corinth. He counted 37,000 effectives, one fourth of whom were committed to river defense. In addition to the guns coming to McCown from Columbus, the Louisiana general ordered ten cannon from the now abandoned defenses at Pensacola. General Braxton Bragg's corps from the Gulf Coast had been directed to join the concentration at Corinth. Three of his regiments, along with a sapper and miner company from New Orleans, were sent to Fort Pillow to rebuild the depleted garrison at that place.[38]

4

We Have Received Marching Orders

HALLECK FAILED IN his bid to obtain top command of all Federal armies in the West. Secretary of War Edwin Stanton sternly replied that the president "expects you and General Buell to cooperate fully and zealously with each other, and would be glad to know whether there has been any failure to cooperate in any particular." It was precisely in the particulars that Halleck and Buell parted company. Halleck advocated a massive joint venture up the Tennessee River, but Buell did not want to use the river. He favored an overland march from Nashville (within his department), cleaning out pockets of resistance as he advanced. The Tennessee River, he believed, should be used as a shield against Beauregard, while his and Halleck's forces remained concentrated at Florence, Alabama. The parochial bickering that characterized the winter of 1861–62 thus continued.[1]

Forts Henry and Donelson had now been neutralized. Beginning on February 10, 1862, General Samuel R. Curtis's eleven-thousand-man army chased Sterling Price's eight thousand Missourians into northwestern Arkansas. The time was right for Halleck to make his turning movement on Columbus by way of New Madrid, a move entirely within his own jurisdiction. There was a particular urgency about New Madrid. Realizing that the Columbus garrison was untenable, Polk would probably attempt to withdraw his troops and escape downriver. Rumors were already afoot to that effect. The capture of New Madrid would thus cut off the southern escape route. The man Halleck tapped to lead the expedition was the energetic Major General John Pope. Summoned to Western Department headquarters in St. Louis from central Missouri, Pope arrived at the Planter's House to confer with Halleck on February 18, 1862.[2]

John Pope's career was on the rise. The thirty-nine-year-old West Point graduate had taken advantage of every opportunity the war had presented him thus far. He was an Illinois Republican with family ties to Mary Todd Lincoln; the president had even practiced law in the federal court of Pope's father, Judge Nathaniel Pope. This connection had landed him an invitation to accompany the newly elected president on the perilous journey to Washington for the inauguration. Besides political connections, Pope had a solid military background. He had served on General Zachary Taylor's staff during the Mexican War, where

Fig. 5. Major General John Pope (courtesy of the Massachusetts Commandery Military Order of the Loyal Legion and the U.S. Army Military History Institute)

he was brevetted twice for bravery. Although displaying an aptitude in the engineers, he had never led any sizable command in combat. Given to self-aggrandizement, he was scorned by many of his peers. "I don't care for John Pope one pinch of owl dung," wrote one western general. Despite the criticism, Pope received his brigadier's commission early in the war and was assigned to command the District of North Missouri.[3]

Just two months before the meeting at the Planter's House, the relationship between Pope and Halleck had become strained due to what Halleck termed Pope's "decided spirit of fault-finding." The situation was salvaged by a small Federal victory in Missouri, initiated, though not personally led, by Pope. A jubilant Halleck promised him a "suitable command." Pope's subsequent appointment thus appeared a reward, yet it was a logical move. The Rebels had been driven out of Missouri, and his idle troops would be the core of the new army to move on the Mississippi River.[4]

Commerce, Missouri, served as the staging area for the planned offensive. Twenty-five miles north of Cairo, the town was located on the Mississippi River on the southern extremity of the Missouri high banks. From this point to Helena, Arkansas, the west bank of the Mississippi was low and flat, and the interior was seasonally inundated by floods and always swampy. Commerce had the advantage of having a relatively high and dry road leading west to Benton, Missouri, where it intersected with the main road to New Madrid. The previous autumn Grant had used the town as a landing area as part of his overall demonstration against Columbus. To expedite operations on his two fronts, Halleck placed his chief of staff, Brigadier General G. W. Cullom, at Cairo, and his friend, Brigadier General William T. Sherman, at Paducah. Wasting no time, Pope went down to Cairo, where he stopped at the arsenal to place a requisition for siege guns. He also made defensive plans in the event of an attack from Columbus, a fear that proved groundless. Moving back upriver to Commerce, he arrived on the evening of February 21.[5]

Pope initially brought just his staff and two companies of infantry—about 140 troops. "The wharf at Commerce is narrow, and the road leading into town muddy and bad, and it was with some difficulty that they managed to get their wagons up from the boat," wrote an accompanying St. Louis journalist. The transports *War Eagle, Atlantic,* and *New Golden State* would soon follow from Cairo with the 47th and 59th Indiana and 46th Illinois. A virtually new army began to form, very few of the regiments having served together. "Regiments were sent me rapidly from St. Louis, from Cincinnati, and from Cairo, most of them entirely raw, having had their arms first placed in their hands when they embarked on the steamer to join me," commented Pope.[6]

A Cincinnati reporter accompanying the 27th Ohio chronicled the events of that regiment. The unit had been apart on detached duty for the past five months, half of the men on the Hannibal & St. Joseph Railroad and the other half in southern Missouri. They reunited at Benton Barracks near St. Louis in mid-February. On February 21, the regiment "passed through the streets of St. Louis amid the cheers of its citizens for the 'Buckeyes.' " The men boarded a transport at 6 P.M. and began the downriver journey. February 22, George Washington's birthday, was celebrated by singing and speechmaking. On Sunday morning, February 23, worship services were conducted aboard the vessel as it approached Commerce. The regiment camped on the river bank that evening, but the next day it moved to a wooded area three miles from town.[7]

The river between St. Louis and Cairo bustled with activity. "We have received marching orders," Michael Freyburger of the 7th Illinois Cavalry wrote his wife. "We leave here tomorrow for Commerce 15 miles below here. I suppose we will march on New Madrid." On February 17, Martin Smith of the 5th Iowa wrote of his experiences to a friend. "Left the levee at St. Louis this morning 10 o'clock. On board is the 5th Iowa, a battalion of the 2d Iowa Cavalry and Capt. Powell[']s Battery of rifled cannon with about 500 horses, camp equipage etc. We left St. Louis amid the cheers of a large concourse of people on shore with brass bands playing on board." By February 24, ten regiments and a battery, some sixty-five hundred troops, had arrived at Commerce. "The whole place here is one camp of soldiers. We are certainly going to war now. I think the object is New Madrid but we may go farther down, particularly if we get possession of New Madrid," noted an Illinois soldier. Brigadier General John Palmer frankly admitted that he did not know the destination. "I only know that we go either West or South on the West side of the Mississippi. Whether [we] go to Arkansas or Kentucky crossing the river below Columbus I don't know."[8]

Pope brigaded his troops as quickly as they arrived. The First Division, with five thousand troops, was commanded by forty-year-old Brigadier General Schuyler Hamilton, a West Point classmate of Pope's and a veteran of the Mexican War, during which a cavalry lance had passed entirely through his lung. He could also lay claim to distinguished family connections—as grandson of Alexander Hamilton and Halleck's son-in-law. Brigadier General John M. Palmer, leading the Second Division with fifty-five hundred troops, was a political general. He had been instrumental in the formation of the Republican Party in Illinois and, in 1859, ran, for Congress, but was defeated. His 14th Illinois had seen little action while in Missouri, but Palmer had strong ties to President Lincoln and Illinois Senators Lyman S. Trumball and Orville H. Browning. It was through their petitions that he received his brigadier's commission.[9]

Pope also had two thousand cavalry, placed under the capable leadership of another friend, Colonel Gordon Granger of the 2d Michigan Cavalry. Granger was also a West Pointer, a veteran of the Mexican War, and an avid hunter. He had already distinguished himself in the Battle of Wilson's Creek, but he had an unmistakable brusqueness about him. Just before the campaign commenced, one of his regiments rode in review past Pope, the commanding general. "Pope, look here!" Granger blurted out. The general teasingly replied: "What of it?" Granger could not restrain himself. "What of it? You damned fool! You never saw a better looking regiment nor a better drilled regiment in your life!" Words were exchanged, but the dispute ended on a friendly note.[10]

Also attached to the expedition was the large engineer regiment of the West (25th Missouri), under the command of Colonel Joshua W. Bissell. The outfit had twelve full companies, comprised chiefly of mechanics and carefully selected workmen. Most of the officers and about six hundred of the men would be engaged in the upcoming campaign.[11]

A generally good rapport existed among the general staff. Pope, Granger, Colonel Joe Plummer, assistant adjutant general Speed Butler, and Aide-de-Camp Louis Marshall were all Regular Army, and they readily formed a pleasant social set. They congregated about the campfire at night and discussed various matters. Pope was "very agreeable and a very witty man and often turned the laugh on his staff and others." The notable exception to this close-knit military fraternity was the politician John Palmer. His bitterness was evident. He denounced those in the clique as "profoundly ignorant of everything outside of their own profession. One would be greatly surprised at the flabbiness of character exhibited by such men as Pope and others who lead armies," he confided to his wife. He went on to admit that he would prefer to resign and be done with them, "but that would only be to increase their chance of the perfect Military Aristocracy."[12]

Halleck diverted all new regiments from Grant to Pope and scaled down his upriver garrisons in an effort to free other outfits. On February 27, he drastically pledged to Pope whatever it took—"The object must be accomplished if it requires 50,000 men." Time was increasingly of the essence. A recent copy of the *Memphis Appeal* indicated that the Rebels might soon evacuate Columbus.[13]

On February 24, Colonel James R. Slack's brigade from Palmer's division advanced eight miles to Benton. Martin Smith found the town "very pleasantly located on an eminence and completely surrounded by a dense forest. It is indeed a rural spot. . . . I have learned that the inhabitants are strongly tinctured with secessionism." Captain Aden Cavins of the 59th Indiana noted that the troops took up quarters "in the deserted homes of the rebels, some of which are fine, but all the furniture has been ruined or destroyed, and the white walls are bespotted with the lowest vulgarity." Some of the Federals ransacked the courthouse and scattered the lawbooks. The next day Palmer arrived with the remainder of his division. Being a lawyer, he had the lawbooks gathered up and returned.[14]

Pope planned to move his army forward on February 28. Hamilton's division was to advance as far as the Hunter farm, to be followed the next day by

Palmer's division. Hamilton's troops would occupy Sikeston, a small hamlet with a tavern run by a Rebel sympathizer, on March 1, while Palmer would move to within five or six miles of the village. One battery was to accompany each division, with the extra battery traveling in the middle of the column. The wagon trains would bring up the rear of their respective divisions, each escorted by three infantry companies. Captain O. L. Jackson, commanding Hamilton's guard, was in charge of 140 six-mule wagons. "Some of the rear teams are overloaded and we have had great trouble with them," he admitted.[15]

From the outset, seasonal conditions and geographical features were significant in shaping the campaign. The Mississippi River was experiencing the worst flooding since 1858. Both banks of the river overflowed from Cairo to Island No. 10. Fort Holt at Cairo was partially under water. The entire country for thirty miles west of the river was under from one to ten feet of water. "The strong and muddy current of the river had . . . carried away every movable thing. Houses, trees, fences, and wrecks of all kinds were being swept rapidly down-stream," wrote a naval officer. Past Benton, Missouri, the road to New Madrid dipped from the Scott County hills into swampy bottoms, known as the Great Mingo Swamp. The swamp, from five to twenty-five miles wide, stretched from the Arkansas-Missouri border north to an area parallel with Cape Girardeau and had long served as Jeff Thompson's hiding ground. The road at this point was a corduroy that had been built upon an old embankment, forming a kind of broken causeway. It had not been repaired in years, and in some places it proved nearly impassable.[16]

The first day's march, February 28, was an unpleasant one, according to a Cincinnati journalist who accompanied Hamilton's division. "The troops were compelled to cross deep swamps, most of which had to be waded; the larger ones we crossed by means of impromtu bridges," the latter being constructed by Bissell's engineers. At one point the division had to halt for more than two hours to allow the battery to catch up. Colonel W. P. Kellogg's 7th Illinois Cavalry, spearheading the march, soon encountered Jeff Thompson's handiwork. "There is a swamp about one mile wide that is cross-laid with timber all the way across, with an occasional bridge. Here we found trees felled into the road and the bridges burned or destroyed and by the signs, we knew it had been done a very few hours ago," a trooper recounted. It was now dusk, and the column halted. The troops bivouacked on the ground, without benefit of tents or blankets. The engineers completed the work early the next day, and the march was resumed about 11 A.M.[17]

On Saturday afternoon General Thompson appeared again south of Sikeston with about eighty-five horsemen and his battery of six 1-pounders. The cannon were experimental breechloaders manufactured by Street, Hungerford & Company of Memphis. Each piece was mounted on four wheels and drawn by teams of two horses, giving the appearance of a regular field battery.

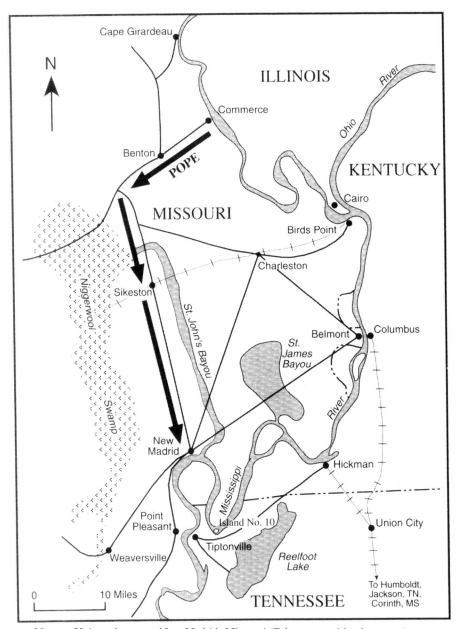

Map 4. Union advance to New Madrid, Missouri (February 28–March 3, 1862)

Believing the Sikeston force to be a small contingent that might be easily intimidated by his guns, Thompson unlimbered his battery astride the road and marked the spot with his large staff flag. The general's nephew, Willie Thompson, rode out and met a Federal vedette, about eighty yards separating them. "Whose men are you?" the picket demanded. "Jeff Thompson's," came the response. "What are you doing here?" shouted the Yankee. "Hunting a fight," yelled Willie. "By God, you'll get it!" came the response.[18]

Thompson quickly discovered he had "waked up the wrong party." James D. Morgan's contingent was soon reinforced by the advance of Hamilton's division. The chase was on. Wrote a member of Kellogg's 7th Illinois Cavalry: "Then the fun commenced. We chased him for fifteen miles over a splendid, straight, wide, level road which he strewed with blankets, guns, hats, and at last his artillery." At times the blue troopers trailed at three hundred yards, at other times a hundred yards, and occasionally they closed to within pistol range. Thompson lost all his cannon in the fray; one man was killed, two wounded, and six captured, including Captain Hogue of the engineers. The one fatality was a seventeen-year-old boy, although it is uncertain whether it was Willie Thompson, as the Federals later claimed. The Missouri Swamp Fox had been soundly thrashed, and the Northern press touted the capture of some of "Jeff Thompson's gang." Morgan reported with disgust: "Jeff Thompson escaped, as usual."[19]

During the early hours of March 2, it began to drizzle, and this continued as Pope's troops began their march at 7 A.M. By 11:00 it was pouring. "I do not think it ever rained so much harder. I was soaked to the skin. Such flashes of lightning and peals of thunder, I scarcely ever heard," remarked Colonel Slack. The march slowed to a crawl as the troops trudged through swampy backwater. A member of the 46th Indiana estimated that his regiment made only five miles in five hours. A correspondent noted that the men "waded in mud, ate in mud, slept in it, were surrounded by it." The army camped nine miles from New Madrid that evening, as half-inch-thick ice formed on the wagons and field guns.[20]

As the army inched forward, Pope attempted to size up his opposition from sketchy intelligence reports. Thompson's captured men were doing a lot of talking, but whether their stories were reliable was another matter. They claimed that New Madrid was held by four brigades (ten thousand infantry), nine hundred cavalry, and four batteries. Columbus, according to them, was being rapidly evacuated. Other reports indicated that New Madrid had been reinforced from Randolph. Halleck continued to press for quick action, advising Pope that if he could just reach the river a little above New Madrid, he could cut off the Rebel reinforcements from Columbus.[21]

The upcoming campaign would be won as much by logistics as speed. A wagon train of two hundred teams had to be kept constantly employed transporting supplies from the Sikeston railroad. Bissell's engineers were employed virtually full-time in repairing the New Madrid road so that supplies could be moved. They collected almost every fence rail for eighteen miles to corduroy the road. Meanwhile, Brigadier General Eleazor A. Paine's division advanced from Bird's Point, repairing the railroad and telegraph line along the way. By March 11, the track had been completed, and trains began to run regularly between Bird's Point and Sikeston.[22]

5

I Consider New Madrid of Great Importance

POLK KNEW OF the Federal buildup at Commerce and by February 26 had correctly guessed Pope's objective. He directed McCown to "work your regiments day and night until the armament is complete." By the evening of February 27, scouts had confirmed the Union destination. Reports placed a Yankee brigade at Benton. An additional twelve thousand Federals were at Commerce, with five thousand more en route. By the time Pope reached New Madrid, his strength had reportedly swelled to twenty thousand. McCown hysterically placed the number at between twenty and thirty thousand, which even surpassed bloated newspaper estimates.[1]

Colonel Baker went into New Madrid early on Saturday morning, March 1, searching for a suitable headquarters. Along the way he viewed more than one hundred graves, the deaths caused by sickness in Gantt's brigade. The partially destroyed town was to host the exiled Missouri legislature on Monday. Shortly after Baker entered town, three shots rang out in quick succession from Fort Thompson. Marsh Walker galloped up and announced that the enemy was nearby and ordered Baker to move his regiment forward as quickly as possible. The men shed their knapsacks and double-quicked up the Sikeston Road. Baker shouted, "Hurrah for Mississippi, Alabama, Tennessee," and the troops responded with a rousing yell.

Inwardly, Colonel Baker was far from confident. His regiment, armed with such inferior weapons, could not begin to hold its own in an extended engagement. One company did not even possess weapons. "What should I do, Colonel? You know our situation," inquired a lieutenant. Baker instructed the men to tag along with the regiment and simply do the best they could. As the troops passed along the road, they encountered fleeing citizens coming in from the countryside. "Where are the Yankees?" the soldiers yelled, but they got no response. Women aboard a docked steamboat enthusiastically waved their handkerchiefs as the regiment departed. Reaching Fort Bankhead, Baker encountered some of Jeff Thompson's scouts, who claimed that the Federals were barely three miles distant. As the hours ticked away, however, nothing came of the incident, and the regiment returned to town.[2]

A cold wind and overcast skies characterized Sunday, March 2. A downpour during the early morning hours had washed out some of the streets in town. At breakfast the Confederates heard the faint booming of cannon upriver, which turned out to be the shelling of evacuated Columbus. The men soon went to work on the entrenchments.[3]

That morning Colonel Thomas Jordan, Beauregard's aide, happened to be in New Madrid on a fact-finding mission. Riding out of town with Stewart and several other officers, he encountered some scouts riding hard, who claimed they were being followed by twelve hundred enemy cavalry. Half believing the story, the party rode out a little further. They suddenly encountered a significant number of Yankee troopers not two hundred yards distant. Hurriedly, the officers wheeled about and made their escape.[4]

Shortly after lunch several of Thompson's pickets, some hatless and without muskets, galloped wildly into town, reporting that the enemy were closing rapidly. Panic erupted in the village with slaves yelling, children crying, and women darting in every direction. "It was so amusing to me that I could not help laughing outright, for I was well aware that it was nothing but the enemies [*sic*] cavalry, and that they would never come in reach of our long-range guns," surgeon Jennings informed his brother. The long roll sounded, and Walker's 40th, along with Bankhead's battery, marched a mile out the Sikeston Road. Baker's 1st formed ranks across the road immediately in front of town.[5]

As Jennings suspected, it proved to be nothing more than a reconnaissance patrol, consisting of the 43d Ohio and the 7th Illinois Cavalry. Walker deployed for an ambush. While Bankhead's guns unlimbered astride the road, supported by the right wing of the 40th, the regiment's left wing hid behind a fence that bordered the road. "We had not been there but a few minutes before the advance guard of the enimy [*sic*] came up. . . . They were cavilery [*sic*] about five hundred in number," noted Lieutenant Smith C. Twitty of the 40th. The unsuspecting Illinois troopers might well have fallen into a trap but for the impetuousness of Bankhead's cannoneers, who opened fire at a range of one thousand yards. One shell burst directly under the nose of a horse, dismounting, but not seriously injuring, its rider. The Federal horsemen quickly filed off the road into a cornfield. After waiting an hour and a half, Walker's men returned to camp.[6]

Colonel Baker conferred with Stewart that afternoon. Stewart remarked in an excited tone, "I wonder what the bloody rascals intended? I don't believe they will come up tonight." A few officers believed that the enemy would not make an attack until their fleet simultaneously assaulted Island No. 10. Baker dispatched Company B of his regiment as pickets that evening. Forced to stay in a wet bottom all night in the bitter cold and without fires, the men returned at daybreak, saying that they could stand it no longer.[7]

Despite the frigid cold, there was a flurry of activity among the Confederates on Monday, March 3. Colonel W. E. "Buck" Travis's 5th Tennessee was

Fig. 6. New Madrid, Missouri, shortly after the fall of Island No. 10 (courtesy of *Battles and Leaders*)

ferried down from Island No. 10 to Fort Bankhead. A steamboat that had come up the night before brought a welcome sight—about eighty Sharps and Mississippi rifles, which were quickly farmed out to Baker's men. The Missouri legislature convened only long enough to reschedule the session for Thursday at Gayoso, about twenty-five miles downriver. Indeed, many of the legislators and Governor Jackson himself had still not left Memphis. A nervous Jeff Thompson approached McCown about removing his two hundred men. "I told him frankly that my men were too valuable to be caught in a trap, and that he was in one," he recalled. McCown conceded that Thompson's troopers would be of more value operating in Pope's rear and released them. That afternoon they boarded a boat and departed downriver from Point Pleasant.[8]

About 1:00 PM Hamilton's division approached to within two and a half miles of town and deployed skirmishers. Observing the terrain, Pope noted that the country "is perfectly level for miles around this place." Several open cornfields separated the armies. The Rebel pickets were driven in, and the town soon invested. At 1:30 Pope probed the defenses. The 27th Ohio advanced on both sides of the Sikeston Road. About a mile to the rear, Colonel John Groesbeck's 39th Ohio followed on the right, and Colonel J. L. Kilby's 43d Ohio proceeded on the left. The 11th Ohio Battery unlimbered in the road, and the balance of the division followed in the rear, with the 7th Illinois Cavalry and part of the 2d Michigan Cavalry protecting the flanks. Hollins's gunboats, the cannon of which peered over the banks of the flooded Mississippi, suddenly opened fire. A shot rang out from the CSS *Ivy,* passing over the Federal line and kicking up the dirt. The cannonading became general and was taken up by the guns of Fort Thompson.[9]

Shells exploded across the large cornfield through which the Yankees advanced. "I had the first one [shell] thrown at us, but it was too heavy to take or send home," Colonel James R. Slack wrote his wife. Captain Oscar Jackson noted in his diary that "some [shots] came very near us. It was our first experience under fire but the boys took it coolly!" One shell, weighing nearly eighty pounds, landed within a few feet of a St. Louis journalist, but failed to explode. Despite the crashing sounds, the Federals counted few casualties. Although under fire for more than three hours, they suffered only one killed and three wounded, including a trooper accidentally shot by a comrade. "Artillery fire is terribly noisy and makes a great stink and that is about all," concluded Brigadier General Palmer to his wife. He dismissed it as a "humbug of a cannonade."[10]

Pope believed that he could carry the works but could not hold the town long, due to the support fire of the Southern gunboats. "The river is so high the hulls of the gunboats are plainly visible, and their guns look over the bank, with a sweep at least a mile and a half," the general reported. Having no immediate expectation for the arrival of Foote's flotilla, he concluded that little could be done until the siege guns arrived from Cairo. Pope withdrew his troops to the rear and established camp.[11]

About 7:00 that evening a Memphis reporter noted that the Federals were "concealed in a piece of woods and a cornfield, but [could] be distinctly seen from the pilothouse of the gunboats." Some thirty or forty rounds had been fired from *Ivy* and Fort Thompson. The enemy force, known to be Hamilton's division, estimated at six to ten thousand troops, was apparently waiting for the balance of Pope's army. The only Southern casualty for the day was a member of Baker's regiment who accidentally shot himself in the head with one of the worthless Memphis rifles.[12]

McCown continued to reinforce New Madrid on Tuesday, March 4. The *John Simonds* transported the 4th Tennessee downriver at daylight. Two recently arrived cavalry companies remained on the Tennessee shore, however, for the level Missouri plain, with its perpendicular river banks, offered no shelter for horses.[13]

Because a general attack was now possible at any time, several houses in the line of fire could no longer be spared and had to be burned. Hollins assigned the task to young midshipman James Morgan of the CSS *McRae*. Ironically, it was Morgan's great-grandfather who had founded the town. In vain did the sailor explain the history of the community and plead that it not be destroyed. "The old commodore simply remarked that it would be a singular coincidence and that it was all the more appropriate that I should destroy my ancestor's town," recalled Morgan.[14] A party went ashore and torched a dozen houses.

Unfortunately, unauthorized looting of all abandoned houses in town also occurred. Soldiers ran uncontrolled throughout the streets and stole curtains, ladies' hats, and household souvenirs. Piles of pork, sugar, and even medicine from a local drugstore were strewn about. An expensive piano was pulled from a residence, defaced with a knife, the strings jerked out, keys scattered, and the legs hacked to pieces. The courthouse and sheriff's office were gutted. One soldier noticed a tangled pile of papers and ledger books, one of which was written in French and read: "District of New Madrid, Louisiana Territory, December 1798." "We tell the people we come to protect them, and yet we treat them *worse* than the enemy could do," wrote Jennings. "This has been done almost wholly by the Tennessee and Louisiana troops, with the aid of those devils in human shape that man the gunboats."[15]

The Federal force before New Madrid remained inactive throughout the day, being "kept off by the damn gunboats," according to one Northerner. Some looting of chickens and pigs occurred in the vicinity until Pope dispatched a cavalry squadron to put an end to it. The ground received a dusting of snow during the day. Some soldiers observed that "the top of their [New Madrid's] courthouse was covered with men looking at our army."[16]

At 11:00 that evening a patrol under Colonel W. H. Worthington probed the northern suburbs of town. The command included the 43d Ohio, five companies of the 5th Iowa, two companies of the 59th Indiana, and two guns each of a Missouri and Michigan battery. Advancing along the Sikeston Road, the Federals encountered pickets of the 4th Tennessee, who quickly withdrew. The field guns unlimbered on either side of the road, and a brisk fire opened. Three of the Rebel gunboats, one at Fort Thompson, one opposite town, and one above town, replied. According to the colonel, the boats "soon obtained our exact range, but few of their shells exploded." After holding their position for an hour, his men retired. The withdrawal came none too soon for Company E, 4th Tennessee, which unknown to the Federals had been hiding in a house only fifty yards from their position. The Northerners sustained three casualties in the midnight action, one of whom was left behind and buried by the enemy. Etched on his tombstone were these words: "W. Beaser. Welcome here. Here is the spot where [lies one] who was not satisfied with leaving other people alone. . . . This Yankee said he belonged to the 5th Iowa Regiment."[17]

Halleck banked on quick results from Pope so that his troops could reinforce the Army of the Tennessee. On March 4, he notified Sherman at Columbus that if New Madrid fell before Pope's reinforcements arrived, they should be immediately redirected up the Tennessee River to Major General C. F. Smith, who had temporarily replaced Grant. It soon became apparent that Pope could not, or would not, move as rapidly as expected.[18]

With his operation stalled, Pope pointed the finger at Foote, who had been promoted to flag officer and commanded the Mississippi River squadron. He believed that a cooperating naval demonstration at Island No. 10 was essential to draw off the Rebel gunboats at New Madrid. When naval cooperation was not forthcoming, Pope reciprocated with stubbornness of his own. He did send a brigade under Colonel J. B. Plummer south to Point Pleasant in an attempt to disrupt river communications. To block the river effectively, however, he boldly told Halleck, would require thirty thousand troops. Besides the main force at New Madrid, he envisioned a dozen movable columns, each with five hundred men and two field guns, operating in a sniping fashion along a twenty-five-mile stretch of the river. The Confederate gunboats would thus be forced to descend the river to protect their supply line.[19]

From Halleck's perspective, the suggestion must have appeared ludicrous. Pope had, or soon would have, eighteen thousand troops to oppose a force that, even by his own inflated estimate, did not exceed five thousand. As though odds of three and a half to one were inadequate, he now clamored for six-to-one odds. His request came at a time when Halleck desperately needed to reinforce Smith on the Tennessee River. Halleck had set himself up for such a request, however, by earlier overzealously promising fifty thousand troops to accomplish the mission.

The St. Louis commander now notified Pope that he had given up the entire operation and decided to send his forces to Smith. There are two possible interpretations. Stephen Ambrose in his biography of Halleck suggests that the plan was merely a bluff to nudge Pope to action. "Thoroughly frightened" at the prospect of losing his independent command and chance for glory, Pope immediately replied that he had successfully outflanked New Madrid. Kenneth Williams presents a more plausible explanation in his Lincoln biography, claiming that Halleck was frustrated by Foote's lack of cooperation. On March 7, he had even wired this to the department chief of staff, Brigadier General George W. Cullom, at Cairo: "As Commodore Foote declines to cooperate, General Pope's army will be immediately withdrawn." Whichever interpretation is correct, it is clear that Halleck dropped the subject on hearing of Plummer's success.[20]

Colonel Plummer's expedition had actually produced mixed results. His command of about three thousand troops consisted of the 11th Missouri, 26th and 47th Illinois, Bridge's Wisconsin battery, six companies of the 2d and 3d Michigan Cavalry, and an engineer company. Beginning at noon on March 5, the brigade marched a circuitous fourteen-mile trek to Point Pleasant, avoiding a five-mile stretch of river road. He was ordered to establish a lodgement along the river bank and construct rifle pits for a thousand men. The troops camped three or four miles from the town that evening, and, although a light snow covered the ground, no fires were allowed.[21]

Early on March 6, Plummer occupied Point Pleasant. Two Confederate transports were docked for refueling—the *Mary Keene,* at Point Pleasant, and the *Kentucky,* lower down on the opposite bank. Though surprised, both managed to escape, a shell exploding over the *Mary Keene.* Hundreds of bullets riddled the cabin and skylights, scores of which were picked up in the hallway of the boat. Learning that the Federals had gained the rear of New Madrid, Hollins immediately proceeded downriver on Captain John Dunnington's CSS *Pontchartrain.* Dunnington's crew fired a few rounds, forcing the Federals into the interior. Seeing a white flag on shore, Dunnington cautiously steered his vessel to within forty yards. A devastating volley of musketry opened, killing one aboard and wounding two others. The fatality was a fourteen-year-old boy serving as a powder boy. John Reeder, about the same age, hurriedly ran forward and shouted: "Captain, I will be your powder boy now."[22]

That evening Plummer had his infantry and engineers dig gun emplacements and trenches for 280 men. On March 7, 8, and 9, Hollins's gunboats vainly attempted to repel the Federals. Every time the boats navigated near the Missouri shore to close the range, they were harassed by small-arms fire. Midshipman Morgan recalled: "The levees were breastworks ready made, and day after day our gunboats had to go down and clear them out. We would be drifting down the apparently peaceful river, when suddenly a row of tall cottonwood saplings would make us a graceful bow and fall into the stream as a dozen or more field pieces poured a galling broadside into us." To guard against small-arms fire, the boats were forced into a stationary position opposite Point Pleasant, where the river was a mile and a half wide. There they could shoot with impunity but likewise with little success. Colonel Baker expressed his disgust. He and others had been led to believe that the gunboats could prevent the banks from being occupied, but as he noted, "that was yet another delusion."[23]

McCown may well have missed one of his few opportunities in the campaign for an offensive action. Since the Federals offered no pressure upriver at the island, he could have marched some of his infantry—for instance, Colonel R. P. Neely's and Brigadier General Stewart's brigades, supported by the Pointe Coupee Artillery and a company of cavalry, about twenty-six hundred troops—down to Tiptonville, where they could easily have been ferried across the river.[24] A joint land—naval operation might well have jarred the Federals loose from Point Pleasant. In the event of a reversal, the Confederates could have withdrawn to the protection of the gunboats or escaped along the west bank. That McCown failed to take any action may not have been as significant as the fact that nothing indicates he even considered such a bold tactic. The Federal move on Point Pleasant was utterly predictable, yet not even a picket had been posted to give warning or a gunboat permanently positioned at the dock. McCown's thoughts were upriver, watching the Federal navy, rather than downriver, on the Union army.

The Southerners belatedly established counter-battery fire. At noon on March 9, two rifle guns from the Point Coupee Artillery were positioned directly opposite Point Pleasant, south of the Daniels's house. The first shot, fired from a Parrott rifle, sent the Federals scattering. Some fifteen to twenty rounds were discharged, temporarily keeping the Yankees away from their works. On March 10, the Confederates brought down two 24-pounder siege guns. After several hundred rounds, however, the only Federal casualty was a dead artillery horse. "Many of their shells have been well directed, and shells have burst over our guns and rifle pits without success," summarized Plummer.[25]

The peppering shots of the Federals likewise proved little more than annoying. Southern transports continued to slip by at night escorted by the gunboats. On the night of March 7, the *Kentucky* extinguished its lights and safely passed with only one shot being fired at it. The next day the steamer *Mears* was safely escorted upriver past the Union guns. Two nights later the *Victoria* passed without damage. Gray sounded a note of caution. He knew that as soon as the river began to drop, the boats would have to run very close to the Missouri shore to remain in the channel and commented that "we shall be troubled very much."[26]

The significance of the Point Pleasant move was not so much its impact on Confederate communications as its effect on Halleck. The knowledge of Plummer's lodgement convinced him to salvage the campaign. It is probable, however, that Pope's army would have been kept in place anyway. Only days later, on March 11, 1862, Halleck received his long-desired promotion to the command of the newly created Department of the Mississippi, giving him unified command in the West. He could now accomplish what he had intended all along: namely, to keep Pope in place and reinforce the Army of the Tennessee with Buell's army in Nashville.

Beauregard was having problems of his own. Increasingly, he was developing a crisis of confidence in McCown, who appeared to be panicking. In early March Polk had come to Beauregard's headquarters in Jackson. Even though McCown was corresponding with the Bishop as his immediate superior, Louisiana General Beauregard was also privy to the contents of the telegrams. On March 4, McCown wired Polk: "I am virtually besieged. . . . My position is critical in the extreme." The next day he again sent a message claiming that he was confronted by thirty thousand Federals and that Union forces under General Franz Sigel were marching on Point Pleasant with an additional ten thousand troops. That same night he telegraphed: "It is useless to deny that my position is critical in the extreme."[27]

Beauregard was troubled by the tone and content of these dispatches. First, he believed the number of Federals to be fifteen to twenty thousand, not the thirty thousand claimed by McCown. Second, he had reliable information that Sigel was not moving on Point Pleasant, but was in western Missouri confronting Van Dorn. The hysterical overtones of the correspondence struck Beauregard as unbecoming a professional soldier. He thus concluded that he could "not place much reliance in a subordinate commander who was thus timorous under responsibility, and who apparently gave way to nervous apprehension as to the strength of his adversary." The same day that Beauregard received McCown's March 6 telegram he notified the War Department that "for the sake of our cause and country," Brigadier General William W. Mackall, Johnston's adjutant general, should be promoted and dispatched to his headquarters without delay. If the Louisiana general had not already definitely decided to replace McCown (he later claimed that he had not), he clearly was leaning in that direction.[28]

On March 7, McCown informed Polk: "I consider New Madrid of great importance." He gave assurance that the town would not be relinquished without a fight. At 10:00 the next evening, however, he dispatched another gloomy summary that seemed to indicate his fate was sealed. He then estimated Pope's army at thirty thousand troops and sixty guns. "How long I can hold New Madrid against such odds is a question. I believe the enemy will soon be fifty thousand strong."[29]

This latest litany of despair decided the issue for Beauregard. Although

McCown's personal bravery was never in question, his steadiness as a commander was very much in doubt. Beauregard concluded that McCown's "fear of responsibility was most apparent." Under the circumstances, he replied that "the country expects us to do our duty with a fearless heart." His remark was as much a veiled warning as it was encouragement. Clearly, although the actual change of command had not yet come, Beauregard had made his decision.[30]

It is true that McCown's reports sounded more like those of an hysterical civilian than a West Pointer and long-time Regular Army officer. At the same time, McCown was telling Beauregard something that he did not want to hear. Emotionally and physically, the Louisiana general was approaching a breakdown. His overriding concern was in concentrating all available forces at Corinth for a merger with Johnston. Under the circumstances, he had little patience with the New Madrid sideshow. McCown's dilemma also underscored the weakness of Beauregard's "rescue" theory, that is, that a small garrison could be relieved in the event of an emergency.

McCown pleaded either that he be reinforced or that Pope be attacked from the rear. On March 5, he suggested that forty thousand troops be thrown against the Point Pleasant force. Even if such a move had been feasible, it assumed that the Federals would remain obligingly passive while a large Confederate force crossed the Mississippi and moved into Missouri. If an ironclad managed to slip past the Island No. 10 defenses in the meantime, the reinforcements would be stuck on the west bank. Again on March 7, McCown recommended that his New Madrid command be heavily reinforced so that an offensive operation might be attempted. "I see no other course to pursue. If I had 20,000 more men, such a move would be my course," he wrote.[31]

Beauregard had no intention of doing either. Realizing that he could not be strong everywhere, he had to decide where to be weak. On March 4, he had thirty-seven thousand troops under his command, one fourth of whom were committed to river defense. This river force included McCown's seven thousand (Beauregard's figure—but actually closer to eight thousand) and twenty-five hundred new troops that had recently arrived at Fort Pillow. He could, and perhaps should, have stripped the latter of its infantry, perhaps fifteen hundred troops, to reinforce McCown. This addition would not have been decisive, however, considering the numbers that McCown faced. On March 13, it seemed as though Beauregard had a momentary change of heart when he directed Colonel Robert M. Russell's brigade of three regiments to Tiptonville via Memphis. No sooner had the order been cut, though, than a report was received of a forward movement by the Federals up the Tennessee River. Russell's orders were immediately countermanded. As late as March 14, Beauregard was still hoping that he could defeat the Federal Army of the Tennessee in time to relieve McCown. This represented a tenacious, if not naive, clinging to his original concept of river defense.[32]

What McCown received was not more troops but considerable advice and a promise of more slave labor. On March 7, six hundred shovels were sent to Island No. 10 on the *Hartford City,* and others were promised by way of Union City. Polk assured McCown that a thousand slaves would be impressed for his use. Regarding the battery at Point Pleasant, Polk could only counsel that he hoped Hollins's gunboats could clear the shore "as successfully as their boats cleared the same shore of ours above Columbus." Concerning reinforcements, the Bishop stated that with the flotilla and heavy guns already at McCown's disposal, "we [meaning Polk and Beauregard] believe you may keep at bay 50,000 men."[33]

The obvious signal being sent to McCown was to dig in and be prepared to go it alone. Even the technical advice was simplistic. The advanced salient at New Madrid that had been earlier proposed by Beauregard was in an area already covered by the fire of the gunboats. The work had to be done at night to avoid enemy fire, and, even so, McCown did not have the troops to occupy it. McCown understood these shortcomings and, although he promised to "erect it as soon as I can," work never began. Beauregard later criticized him for this inaction. Rather than offering minute management, the Louisiana general should have attempted to formulate an alternative strategy. Not having the latter, he concentrated on the former.[34]

The only hope for McCown at this point was for Sidney Johnston to relieve him with Van Dorn's sixteen-thousand-strong army in Arkansas. On March 7, 1862, however, just as operations at New Madrid were heating up, the diminutive Van Dorn suffered a staggering defeat at Pea Ridge at the hands of a numerically inferior Union army force commanded by Samuel R. Curtis. It took the Confederates two weeks to regroup their scattered forces. Van Dorn was not in a position to move against Pope, although he suggested he was on March 17. By then, time had run out on the garrison. The projected move was cancelled, and Van Dorn's army moved east of the Mississippi River to link up with Johnston and Beauregard at Corinth.[35]

McCown assured Polk on March 5, and again on March 9, that morale was high. The letters and diaries told a different story. The level terrain gave a panoramic view of the Federal campfires at night, which extended for three miles. A Union prisoner captured on March 7 revealed that Pope had three cavalry and twenty-five infantry regiments and a dozen batteries. It was commonly believed in the Southern ranks that the Federals had forty thousand troops. "The Yankee force is so vastly superior to ours that they will certainly attack us in a few days," believed D. A. Turren of the 11th Arkansas. William A. Mack, also of the 11th, concluded that it was a "question of whether we should evacuate in time to avoid a trip to Chicago, or remain and fight to the death." By March 10, Colonel Baker admitted that the troops had become despondent. Sickness reduced the regiments to 250 to 320 men each. As early as February

26, Surgeon Jennings considered the prospect of holding New Madrid "extremely doubtful" and wrote that he soon expected "to take a trip to St. Louis."[36]

Surgeon Bragg of the 11th Arkansas was disquieted by the seemingly impotent Confederate leadership. "McCown and Stewart . . . are officers who do not know what they are doing," he confided on March 10, believing that the chances were "good to visit St. Louis." The comparison to Fort Donelson was more than subtle when he wrote: "Both [Stewart and McCown] have their headquarters on Steam Boats, so they can play the Pillow and [John] Floyd game on the army, if we are defeated." His reference was to those generals' unceremonious departure from Fort Donelson before their surrender had been consummated.[37]

On March 4, 1862, thirty-four-year-old Brigadier General David S. Stanley arrived at New Madrid. A broken leg suffered in a horse-riding accident the previous fall had prevented his earlier arrival. Stanley, a West Pointer and Regular Army veteran, quickly fell in line with the Pope clique. A reshuffling of regiments occurred so that Stanley then commanded the First Division, Hamilton the Second, and Palmer the Third. Palmer, more disgruntled than ever, expressed his disgust. "My situation here is rather disagreeable. . . . Pope has given all the choice divisions to these army chums of his," he wrote his wife. He also conceded a measure of frustration: "I have too been deprived of all Illinois troops so that after the war I will have no [political] benefit whatever goodwill or popularity I may earn. My troops are all from Indiana and their goodwill will do me little good."[38]

Pope's organization, labeled the Army of the Mississippi, was at best inefficient and at worst grandiose. Each of his divisions had two brigades of two regiments, except for the Second Brigade of the Second Division, which had three. These so-called divisions were little more than brigades, which together formed the equivalent of a fair-sized division. Two additional "divisions" arrived later, meaning that Pope actually commanded a corps, not an army. Many of the officers were acting under field commissions that had not been approved by the Senate or various state legislatures. This prompted Gilbert to comment: "Mr. Pope is only a Brig. Gen., yet for months he has been *acting* Maj Gen, a great many captains in this army are *Acting* Col & a great many Col *acting* Brig. Gen & so on it goes & we often wonder whether our *acting* will be considered by prosperity as farce or tragedy." Pope did take a progressive step with his cavalry and artillery, however, forming them into separate entities, thus bucking the early trend of keeping these branches as appendages of the infantry.[39]

Meanwhile the siege continued. Snow still blanketed the ground at New Madrid on Thursday, March 6. At noon a party of four Confederate officers foolishly chased some Yankee scouts back to their picket line. In the process they encountered a large body of Union cavalry and quickly found themselves the ones being pursued. Captain Helms of Arkansas, a gray-haired veteran of the Mexican War, dismounted and attempted to get off a shot with his Maynard rifle, which he had borrowed from Brigadier General Stewart. A bullet struck him in the neck, but he managed to hang on to the mane of his horse long enough to get away, blood flowing profusely from his mouth. A lieutenant in the Confederate party was also wounded.[40]

Brisk skirmishing continued throughout the day. At one point Stanley's division pushed to within seven hundred yards of Fort Thompson before being driven back by artillery fire. Although exposed for three and a half hours, the Federals sustained only three wounded. A patrol under Gordon Granger, consisting of the 46th Indiana and two companies of the 5th Iowa, pressed the Confederate left, but after two hours fell back under heavy fire. Granger boasted that his men "behaved like veterans, and quite surprised me by their coolness and indifference to the danger which surrounded them."[41]

The next day, March 7, Stanley's division was ordered to demonstrate against the lower part of town. While the Confederates were thus occupied with this feint, Colonel W. H. Worthington's brigade would assault and occupy the enemy's trenches at Fort Bankhead. Stanley advanced Kirby Smith's brigade and three pieces of artillery. No sooner had the guns been positioned, however, than "the enemy opened on [them] with shot, shells and every conceivable missle," according to Captain Jackson.[42]

James Morgan of the *McRae* related what happened next. "I was standing by the commodore on the poop deck watching the firing when we saw a light battery enter the other end of the main street. Our nine-inch gun was trained on them, and when it was fired the shell struck the head of the column and burst in about the middle of the company. To see horses, men, and guns cavorting in the air was a most appalling sight." Flushed with success, the officer in charge of the gun immediately ordered it reloaded and fired again. This time the weapon exploded; the huge muzzle splashed into the water, and half the large breech crashed onto the dock beside the carriage. The other half of the breech flew into the air and grazed the side of the boat as it descended. The gun was replaced by a cannon from the floating battery.[43]

Stanley's division failed to deceive the Confederates. The Southerners simultaneously "commenced throwing shells into the woods occupied by my troops, evidently expecting the main attack to come from that quarter," noted Worthington. Indeed, most of the gunboats now zeroed in on the hapless colonel. The plan having obviously backfired, Stanley considered a move on Fort Bankhead as utterly impossible and aborted the attack. Palmer wrote his wife: "I was ordered to place a regiment in some woods to protect artillery. . . . A shell burst in front of them about thirty feet and half of them fell flat. I told them 'they never knelt down half as quick at an Indiana campmeeting.' They got to laughing and in a few minutes they were as unconcerned as if nothing was going on." Federal casualties for the day totaled six wounded.[44]

Men on both sides commonly believed that the only factor preventing the capture of the town was the gunboats. Alfred Gilbert noted: "We are hourly looking for the Federal gunboats from above and then I suppose we will get in and take the place. The Rebels are only some 4,000 strong and we have 12 or 14,000 here. We could take the place now but could not hold it long against the fire of their boats." Palmer concurred: "We could soon occupy this town in an hour if the gunboats were not present to shell us as we go in." Surgeon Jennings believed the gunboats were equivalent to a thousand men each. A crewman aboard CSS *McRae* agreed: "But for our [naval] presence there, I believe . . . the Enemy could have carried that place in twenty-four hours."[45]

With Cairo no longer threatened, Cullom channeled an additional six thousand or so troops to New Madrid, even though he admitted to Halleck that Pope did "not ask for reinforcements." The troops arrived via the repaired railroad between March 10 and March 13. Included were Brigadier General Eleazor A. Paine's division of four regiments, Colonel Nicholas Perczel's brigade of two regiments, and some unattached outfits. At least one regiment, the 26th Missouri, had to march the entire way. Thirty-year-old Colonel George B. Boomer informed his wife: "I have had hard times of late, as we marched thirty-eight miles in two days to get here [New Madrid], without tents or baggage, or scarcely anything to eat."[46]

The 8th Wisconsin, the famed "Eagle Regiment," also arrived. Before leaving Eau Claire, the outfit was given an eagle, "Old Abe" by name, which had been a family pet. The men received the mascot with some skepticism. Before the war was over, however, the bird would become a legendary national symbol. At New Madrid, an Illinois soldier remarked that close to the 8th's regimental flag was a man carrying a shield, "and above the shield there was a bunch of arrows and perched upon these arrows was a live eagle. It seemed as well as anything you ever saw. It attracted the attention of thousands as the Regiment passed through the grounds."[47]

Pope now permanently disengaged from Commerce and shifted his supply base to Bird's Point. The 18th Missouri and four companies of the 22d Missouri garrisoned the latter. The 22d Illinois and two companies of the 1st Illinois Cavalry, all from Paine's division, formed a garrison for Charleston, Bertrand, and Sikeston. Pope also did some additional restructuring, promoting Plummer to brigadier general and giving him the newly formed Fifth Division—a reward for his earlier performance at Point Pleasant.[48]

Because he had little else to do until his siege guns arrived, Pope now began to drill his troops, virtually within the view of the Rebels. "The country is perfectly plain; we can see from our tent door the smoke stacks of their gunboats, and the music of their bands mingles with our own yet 'tis confounded dull,' " commented a trooper. A lieutenant in the 10th Illinois recalled that the commanding general "rode down our front at break-neck speed on his dapper-gray charger. This performance was intended to be very impressive, but something in the appearance of the horse and the rider made it both ridiculous and comical." The drilling did coalesce the men, especially the Illinois and Iowa boys who, according to a soldier, "seem[ed] to have more family feeling between them."[49]

Even in the midst of the routine, the daily skirmishing continued. A Confederate wrote on March 6 that a brief encounter had occurred that day in which two Southerners had been wounded. The next day a passenger from Island No. 10 arrived in Memphis aboard the *Kentucky*, reporting that McCown had lost seventeen men killed and wounded. On March 12, a Captain West, McCown's provost, foolishly rode beyond the picket line and was accidentally wounded by his own men as he returned. The abdominal wound proved mortal. "He was a useful man but crazed by whiskey," wrote Colonel Baker. That evening two Rebel deserters appeared in the Federal camps, telling of dissatisfaction among the Southern troops.[50]

For a week and a half the Federal army thus sat, occupying the time with minor skirmishes and limited engagements. The clock was ticking for Pope, however, and the pressure to deliver was intense. The dilemma of New Madrid had to soon be resolved.

6

The Cowardly Rebels Run Away

POPE'S SIEGE GUNS, three 24-pounders and an 8-inch howitzer, were on the way, being sent overland to Mound City and thence by boat to Commerce. Once there, they were loaded on railroad cars and hauled to Sikeston. Drawn over the ordinary roads with four huge four-wheeled sling carts, the guns arrived at New Madrid on the afternoon of March 12.[1]

The general lost no time. At dusk Colonel James Morgan's brigade of Paine's division advanced to within eight hundred yards of Fort Thompson. The site had been previously selected by Major W. L. Lathrop of the artillery and Colonel Bissell of the engineers. Throughout the evening one regiment worked feverishly on the gun emplacements and trenches, while the other stood guard. The men piled fence rails lengthwise, lapping the ends over and covering them with dirt. The work went on within 150 yards of the enemy picket line. In the darkness a Captain Carr of the 10th Illinois ventured too close to the enemy vedettes. As he struck a match to light his pipe, he was shot. "Oh, God," he yelled when struck. A Rebel sentinel shouted back: "Hah! Hah! Did that hurt you any?" As the captain staggered back, he was hit again. He made it back to his lines but died within hours.[2]

The Federal activity began to draw attention. At midnight Gantt was informed of some enemy movement in front of Fort Thompson. Determining that the Yankees were moving up heavy artillery, he ordered the picket strengthened, although one-fifth of his men were already on the line. As the Federals nudged forward, the Southerners retired three hundred yards. Stewart was informed of these developments, but short of bringing on a general engagement, little could be done. Gantt shifted several of his mobile siege guns to the east parapet. The 11th and 12th Arkansas were also directed to be in readiness, a portion of the troops to enter the fort and the balance to occupy the rifle pits below.[3]

By 3 A.M. the Federals had completed two redoubts with flanking rifle trenches for two regiments. Captain Joseph A. Mower, with two companies of the 1st United States Infantry, manned the siege guns. J. D. Morgan's 10th Illinois and R. F. Smith's 16th Illinois were assigned to the trenches, supported by Bissell's engineers. Seven companies of the 2d and 3d Michigan Cavalry, armed with Colt revolving rifles, anchored the far right, beyond the breastworks. Colonel Gilbert Cumming's 51st Illinois was positioned on the extreme left flank along the wooded slough that stretched from the river. Slack's brigade moved into a cornfield to the left of Cumming's regiment. Stanley's Ohio division, backed by a dozen field guns, moved in the rear of the main line of battle astride the road. More than ten thousand men were deployed to support the siege batteries, with Hamilton's division and Palmer's brigade in reserve.[4]

At dawn on March 13, a deafening roar jolted the Confederates, followed by a thunderous cheer throughout the Union army. "We took them completely by surprise. The gunboats had no steam up and it was some time before they got into position," wrote Gilbert. Because ammunition was limited, Mower's gunners concentrated on the gunboats. The CSS *Mohawk*, which had left Madrid Bend at midnight with McCown aboard, received a hit. T. B. Ball, McCown's medical director, happened to be in the pilothouse with the general. A 24-pound ball severed his legs below the knees, the grisly wound proving mortal. In Fort Bankhead two heavy guns became dismantled with two men wounded. A 32-pounder in Fort Thompson was likewise struck, killing two gunners and wounding one, as the Federal regulars continued to fire with amazing accuracy.[5]

Morning fog and the smoke of the guns made visibility poor. "The smoke clearing off revealed to us the enemy's batteries, with four regiments of infantry more than half a mile from them, partly secreted from view by the timber in front of us," noted Gantt. He directed three heavy guns and two field pieces on the northern bastion to concentrate on the infantry, while three 24-pounders on the northwest bastion trained on the enemy's artillery.[6]

After regaining their composure, the Confederates began scoring some hits of their own. At 9 A.M. one of the Federal cannonballs that had landed inside Fort Bankhead, killing two mules, was reloaded and returned with devastating effect. One of Mower's 24-pounders was struck squarely on the muzzle, disabling the piece, killing one cannoneer, and wounding six others. Gantt directed all the guns in Thompson to focus on the field battery to the left. The first shot came from the eastern bastion, followed twenty-five seconds later by another, and so on down the line in quick succession. The enemy battery was soon silenced, two guns being dismounted. Slack's brigade, in advance of the siege guns, came under a heavy fire and withdrew. Jackson noted: "When we made a good shot, our boys would cheer and when the rebels did, they would yell like devils." Throughout the action, the 10th and 16th Illinois regiments, protecting the siege guns, kept their regimental flags flying, making a tempting target for Southern gunners. Stanley ordered the flags lowered, but the men refused. "No, General, the flag flies wherever we are." Stanley relented: "Very well. If you take the risk, I won't say a word."[7]

At 10 A.M. Palmer's division moved up in support of Paine's troops, positioned in some woods about eight hundred yards from Fort Bankhead. About

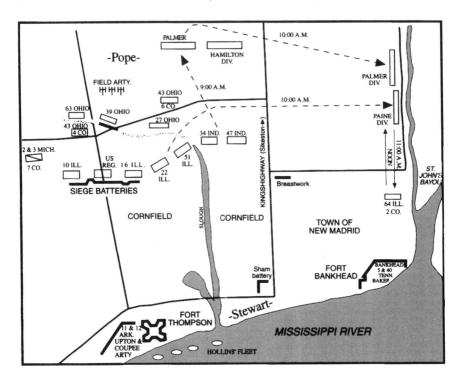

Map 5. Union assault of March 13, 1862

an hour later Paine received orders to attack the fort. The fire of three gunboats concentrated on the division, forcing a withdrawal after half an hour. Although never mentioned in Pope's report, Palmer refused to cooperate in the attack, claiming that two thousand men would be lost. Pope relented, and the assault was cancelled.[8]

At noon the firing tapered off, but surged again in the afternoon. "The hair breadth scrapes were very numerous," commented Gilbert. "[One] man lying on the ground with his knapsack strapped to his back had a 32 pound ball shot pop right on his back and bounce off without doing more than knock out his breath out of his body for a time." A ricocheting artillery shot passed through the line of the 47th Indiana, bowling off the legs of four men. The shots from a gunboat and the guns of Fort Thompson subjected the 63d Ohio to a blistering crossfire. The regiment quickly moved to a slight rise that offered some slight protection. "Again the solid shot would skim along the top of the ground and bury themselves in the earth but a short distance before or behind us, throwing the dirt sometimes to the height of seventy or eighty feet." One heavy artillery shot struck the breastwork of the 16th Illinois and literally covered a squad of men with dirt and sand. After digging out, they jumped up on the embankment and, hats in hand, gave the Rebels a salute and cheer.[9]

Colonel Morgan, pacing with his arms behind him, became irritated with his men as they continually jumped for cover, dodging incoming shells. "Stop that dodgin'," he shouted. No sooner had he spoken than a shell narrowly missed his head, causing him to dive for cover. The men broke into laughter, and the old colonel reluctantly joined in.[10]

In mid-afternoon Stewart and McCown met aboard the *Mohawk* at Fort Bankhead. McCown raised the possibility of an evacuation. Stewart thought that it might be possible to withdraw the heavy guns at night. Returning to his New Madrid headquarters, the commanding general vowed to meet with Stewart again in a few hours.[11]

Early that evening a conference was held aboard the *McRae*. Casualties throughout the day had been light—two killed and five wounded—but McCown still considered evacuating. Hollins was ready to pull his boats out, fearing that they would be sitting ducks for the Yankee siege guns. Damage had already been sustained on some vessels, the CSS *Polk* having been hit four times. The fact that the Federals had an 8-inch siege howitzer (confirmed by the recovery of a shell fragment) had a disquieting effect. Neither could the Federal numerical superiority be easily dismissed. Stewart claimed that his three thousand troops (Gantt placed the number at thirty-five hundred) faced an estimated twenty-five thousand men with fifty guns. Reports from civilians and two of Jeff Thompson's scouts who managed to get through the lines claimed that Franz Sigel was within two miles of New Madrid with forty regiments. An evacuation was ordered.[12]

McCown clearly hoped to pull off the same type of smooth withdrawal that had won Polk such acclaim at Columbus. It was not to be. Almost from the outset a fiasco developed. As the transports moved upriver to bring off the troops, the CSS *McRae* and CSS *Pontchartrain* headed in the opposite direction. The transport *Louisville* went to Fort Thompson, protected and assisted by the gunboats CSS *Polk* and CSS *Livingston*. The transports *Desoto, Winchester,* and *Ohio Belle* proceeded to Fort Bankhead. The last two never appeared, however, because their captains refused to obey orders. The lone *Desoto* was thus left with the task of transporting fifteen hundred men and their equipment.[13]

Gantt, at Fort Thompson, placed thirteen of his infantry companies on the picket line. With the remaining seven companies, plus the artillerymen and sailors, he began the task of loading supplies. The men acted "sullen and indisposed to work." A 24-pounder siege gun sank in the mud and had to be abandoned. The remaining guns were spiked. The infantry hurriedly scrambled aboard as the officer commanding the *Polk* shouted that he "intended to save his boats" and let the troops "shift for themselves if the enemy fired." Coupled

with these blunders was sheer bad luck. At 11 P.M. an unusually violent thunder-
storm erupted, making it difficult to see except for the flashes of lightning. By
3 A.M. the boats passed downriver to Tiptonville. The *Livingston* towed a hospital wharf boat with one hundred patients aboard. Thirteen soldiers were left
behind, mostly pickets of the 11th Arkansas who abandoned their posts during
the storm to seek shelter.[14]

The situation at Fort Bankhead rapidly deteriorated. A panic erupted as the
men ran pell-mell onto the transport. Lieutenant William Polk, son of the major general and an officer in Bankhead's battery, wrote his sister: "It was more
like a rout than an evacuation. Everybody seemed to be panic struck but a few."
The bow of the *Desoto* literally dipped in the water under the tremendous
weight. Bankhead's field guns were saved, but the caissons and limbers had to
be dumped into the river.[15]

The activity did not go unnoticed by the Northerners. "I could plainly
discern by aid of the lightning flashes through the darkness, their transports
plying up and down the river," recalled Ephraim Wilson of the 10th Illinois.
At 2:30 A.M. a shrill whistle blast from a transport could be distinctly heard.
William H. Davis of the 22d Illinois informed his mother: "We heard their
boats running at night but we did not know what they were doing. Some
thought they were getting reinforcements, others that they were leaving." In
his report, Stanley noted: "During the stormy night I heard the enemy's boats
constantly moving but could not devise whether it was an evacuation or preparing to attack my left flank."[16]

During the early morning hours of March 14, Hamilton's division, wading
through pools of knee-deep water, relieved Stanley's men, while Slack's brigade
replaced Morgan's. Though a heavy morning fog shrouded the surroundings,
preparations proceeded for a dawn attack. As the fog lifted, two Confederate
deserters, approaching under a flag of truce, related that the forts had been
evacuated. Advancing with two companies of the 1st United States Infantry,
Captain Mower scaled the parapets of Fort Thompson and found only two
Rebels—both asleep. The Stars and Stripes was raised as wild cheering spread
throughout the Federal ranks.[17]

The town was quickly occupied. A trooper of the 7th Illinois Cavalry observed: "I rode through what was left of the town, for the Rebels burned many
houses to give their guns a better chance at the approaches, and cut down nearly
all of the shade trees. . . . The boys are now fishing out of the river whole boxes
of quartermaster's goods—clothing, blankets, etc. that the secesh rolled in as
they ran." The withdrawal had obviously been hasty. Dead men were left un-
buried, food sat on tables, and candles still burned in tents. "The cowardly
rebels run away in the night," remarked a disappointed William Davis. Captured material included twenty-five siege guns, five hundred tents, hundreds of
boxes of ammunition, and an immense amount of baggage. The reporter of

the *Cincinnati Gazette* commented: "Near the camp is a wagon-yard and a corral containing probably two hundred mules and horses. Very few wagons, however, were found."[18]

The fifteen-day campaign had been won with amazingly few casualties. Pope claimed that between February 28 and March 14 he sustained losses of eight killed, twenty-one wounded, and three missing, but this total is likely too low. Anecdotal material establishes the loss of two killed and fourteen wounded between March 3 and 7. Palmer informed his wife that his division alone lost ten killed and twenty wounded in the March 13 attack. The Cincinnati paper listed by name eight killed and twelve wounded in that assault, and it is known that one had been killed the previous night. The *Republican* claimed that the 10th Illinois had eight killed and fifteen to twenty wounded on March 13. Pope's earlier statement of about fifty killed and wounded throughout the campaign proved more nearly correct. Confederate losses were about the same, including those captured.[19]

The evacuation of New Madrid was costly for the Confederates. Bragg, at Corinth, wrote gloomily: "[We] shall be seriously damaged by the result at New Madrid." Although the captured siege guns, easily unspiked, presented no threat to Island No. 10, the Federals now had a base of operations against that position. Supplies would have to be hauled overland from Tiptonville. Hollins's fleet, with the exception of the floating battery, was forced back to that town. McCown was aware of the ramifications. Earlier he had written: "New Madrid must be in our possession. To hold this [Island No. 10] without New Madrid would require a much larger force than I have." Again on March 8 he wrote: "The river would be closed if New Madrid is abandoned." On the strategic front, the loss of the town caused Beauregard to cancel a proposed offensive.[20]

The damage, nonetheless, was not fatal. From the beginning the town had been the weak link in the tristate defense. The key to Madrid Bend was not the town, but Island No. 10. Polk had written on March 11: "If he [McCown] should have to give up that point [New Madrid], it would not involve by any means a surrender of the river. He could hold the island and the bend, and keep the enemy off from the Tennessee side by his gunboats." The primary function of Hollins's flotilla was not to stop the ironclads, which his boats were clearly unable to do, but to prevent the Federals from crossing the river by rafts or transports. Hollins's gunboats would have been forced backed to Tiptonville anyway, as the river began its annual drop. Thus, a correspondent of the *Appeal*, though obviously putting the best face on a bad situation, was not incorrect when he wrote: "The movement [capture] gives no particular advantage to the enemy as the position is not one of any strategic importance in defending Island No. 10."[21]

Considering the numbers that McCown faced, the town could not have been held indefinitely. Even if all his infantry had been thrown into the fight, reinforced with Russell's brigade and the infantry at Fort Pillow, McCown still would have had only ten thousand troops to oppose Pope's eighteen thousand. The men who fought at New Madrid, from both the North and the South, believed that it was only a matter of time before the town fell.[22]

McCown's defense, nonetheless, had been unspectacular. He had failed to anticipate the capture of Point Pleasant, which was the most obvious move the Federals could make. Once the village was captured, McCown never considered an offensive against Plummer's unsupported force. Without a doubt, however, it was his botched and, many believed, premature evacuation that subjected McCown to the harshest recriminations. "I cursed the General [McCown] to provide such a mockery of transportation when I knew 7 or 8 large boats were lying within 6 miles [Tiptonville]," stated Colonel Baker. In speaking of the evacuation, the editor of the *Memphis Appeal,* though not singling out any officer, concluded: "We must begin to purge our army of blunderers, and make merit the basis of military promotions." The *New Orleans Delta* soberly reported that it was now widely rumored in Memphis that the island would be evacuated and the forces withdrawn to Fort Pillow.[23]

McCown was on the defensive from the outset. On March 14, he informed Polk that the evacuation "was not satisfactory to me for want of discipline of the troops" and that officers "acted under authority other than mine." On March 17, he explained: "I abandoned New Madrid because it involved a constant loss of life to hold it. It was of no use, with Point Pleasant in their hands, except to make a landing for offensive action. I could not do that with my force." McCown later had to fight back rumors about his own drunkenness during the episode.[24]

An angry Beauregard ordered an investigation to determine culpability. The investigating officer, Major George W. Brent, concluded that the entire evacuation had been badly bungled. He also believed that the position could have been held longer. "This was the poorest defense made of any fortified post during the whole course of the war," expressed Alfred Roman, Beauregard's biographer. The evacuation amounted to a "stampede" and was done "in a manner far from creditable to the general commanding." Roman stated further that the "hasty and unnecessary evacuation" of the town "destroyed the little confidence General Beauregard had felt in the commander of that subdistrict."[25]

If McCown was mired in denunciation, Pope's star was on the rise. He had captured New Madrid without the help of the navy, something that many, including Pope himself, doubted could be accomplished. "Though small, the operation had been skillful; and Pope had shown he could meet emergencies and act decisively," concludes Lincoln biographer Kenneth P. Williams. Pope also excelled as a logistician. Within a day of Plummer's arrival at Point Pleasant, Pope confidently wrote him that tents and ten thousand pounds of coffee were on the way. Gilbert believed that Pope's victory was "one of the most thorough and complete victories [they] had with very little loss of life." He affirmed that "the generalship displayed by Gen. Pope is entitled to all the praise." Gilbert was miffed when he read the Cincinnati, St. Louis, and Louisville papers, which, in his opinion, gave Halleck too much credit: "Had Gen'l Pope been at Fort Donaldson [sic] and in chief command I have no doubt that stronghold would have been taken at much less loss."[26]

Halleck was jubilant, not only for the capture but also for the culmination of a campaign that he alone had initiated. On the day of the capture he telegraphed Pope: "I congratulate you and your command on the success which has crowned your toils and exposures. You have given the final blow to the rebellion in Missouri and proved yourself worthy members of the brave Army of the West."[27]

7

Why Can't Foote Move?

FIFTY-SIX YEAR old Andrew Foote, "Old Flag" to his men, had a well de-
served reputation as a fighter—both on the high seas and as a crusader
against what his deep Calvinist beliefs perceived as immorality—specifically
whiskey and slavery. He had fought the Chinese at Canton and chased slavers
in the South Pacific. As a Presbyterian elder, he conducted Bible classes each
week, whether at sea or in dock. On the Sunday following the fall of Fort
Henry, he preached a sermon in a church at Cairo. His lifelong ambition was
to see the whiskey ration in the navy abolished, a dream that would be realized
before the end of 1862. Years later a naval comrade recalled that the flag officer
was "not a man of striking personal appearance, but there was a sailor-like
hardiness and frankness about him that made his company desirable."[1]

In many ways the action at Fort Donelson had been a turning point for
Foote. The battering taken by the fleet had shaken his confidence, and he was
now cautious to the point of being reluctant. "I will not go [attack] near
[fortifications] again," he wrote his wife. "You must have no fears about us
now, as we will keep off a good distance from Rebel forts in future engagements." Again he noted: "I won't run into fire again, as a burnt child dreads
it." He bitterly blamed Halleck for the naval repulse at Donelson, both because
he had urged the attack before the flotilla was ready and because he had not
given mortar support.[2]

Halleck desired that the Island No. 10 batteries be neutralized. On March
2, Sherman had advised Halleck that the position might be captured "if we
move quickly." Foote, however, was not anxious for another hasty action. After
securing Columbus, his boats returned to Cairo for repair and refitting. "I am
fully impressed with the importance of proceeding to New Madrid," he wired
Secretary of the Navy Welles, but he said he would refuse to budge "unless . . .
ordered to do so by the Secretary of the Navy." The Fort Donelson action had
left damaged hulls, disabled machinery, and riddled pilothouses. So bad were
the last that the pilots refused to go back inside them. Halleck, who already
had his hands full because of a recent rift with Grant, was miffed by Foote's
sluggishness. He wired that the flag officer must not wait for repairs, as an attack
on Island No. 10 was imperative. New Madrid must fall soon, Halleck insisted,
because Pope's forces were "needed for movement up the Tennessee." He curtly

Fig. 7. Flag Officer Andrew H. Foote (courtesy of the National Archives)

concluded: "I have much better information than you on the condition of affairs and where possible, my instructions should be obeyed." The St. Louis commander projected the attack for Monday, March 10, but Cullom telegraphed Halleck that Foote still refused to budge.[3]

Foote, under extreme pressure, finally agreed to a move, but gloomily predicted "the most disastrous consequences to the flotilla." To a relative he complained that Halleck was again making the same rash decision that he had made following Fort Henry. But the department commander then suddenly reversed himself. On March 7 Halleck wired Cullom: "I do not wish Commodore Foote to attack Island No. 10 with his gunboats. On the contrary, I directed that they should not be exposed to the enemy's batteries. All they were to be used for was to protect the mortar boats from sharpshooters and field batteries. I believe that a few hours' bombardment with the mortar boats would have caused the enemy to evacuate. . . . I repeat, I do not want the gunboats to fight till they are ready." His theory about the decisiveness of a mortar attack later proved untrue. More to the point was his sudden shift in tone. Whether Halleck had been shaken by Foote's gloomy comments and backed down, or whether his original intentions had been misrepresented by Cullom, through whom his messages were passed, cannot now be determined.[4]

Foote's concerns were not without foundation; Island No. 10 presented far greater difficulties than the twin rivers. Because the Cumberland River flowed north, the assault on Fort Donelson was made upstream. A disabled boat would thus float away from the enemy's guns. On the Mississippi the situation was reversed. Because this river flowed south, a disabled boat would drift helplessly into the enemy's guns. The Rebels might even capture an ironclad. There was also the problem of the inadequately powered engines. The swift current made it difficult to manage the unwieldy ironclads. Once the boats proceeded downriver, Foote feared that they would be unable to return. The USS *Benton's* engines proved especially troublesome. It could barely stem the five-knot current of the Ohio River, while the Mississippi was presently flowing at seven knots. On March 2, the USS *Mound City,* while going up the Cumberland, had scraped bottom and received damage on her starboard side. The USS *Conestoga,* a wooden gunboat that would accompany the fleet, had broken a piston head, which could only be repaired in Cincinnati.[5]

While these technical difficulties were real, Foote also had lost the will to fight. The condition of the boats offered an excuse for inaction, but in truth he was broken both physically and emotionally. Still suffering from the foot wound he had received at Fort Donelson, Foote hobbled about on crutches. His devotion to duty caused him to push himself to the point of exhaustion. Rarely did he go to bed before midnight. "It [job pressure] has added ten years to my age and is quite enough to break any man," he wrote to a friend on March 9. Three days later he described himself as "almost crazy" from the burdens placed on him. His deep religious convictions resulted in a certain war weariness. "Oh! how I long for this war to terminate! I have had enough of it," he confided. He was also professionally discontented, having been displeased with his assignment from the outset. He saw himself as a blue-water officer and referred to the West as a "wilderness." "I would this moment give all I am worth could I have been on the Atlantic, a captain of a good frigate, instead of out here," he related to a friend.[6]

Foote grossly exaggerated the consequences of a naval defeat at Island No. 10, believing his gunboats to be the only factor blocking a joint Southern operation on St. Louis, Cincinnati, and the entire Northwest. Even Foote's brother joined in the national chorus for quick action and wrote the flag officer that the country expected "dash and close fighting, something sharp and decisive." An exasperated Foote quickly responded: "Don't you know that my gunboats are the only protection you have upon your rivers . . . that without my flotilla everything in your rivers, your cities and towns would be at the mercy of the enemy? My first duty then is to care for my boats, if I am to protect you." Too old, too lethargic, too fearful of making a mistake, Foote was, in short, the wrong man for the job. Halleck was caught in a delicate balancing act. Because he and Buell could not agree on strategy, Grant's army, temporarily commanded by Smith, was now advancing unsupported up the Tennessee River, deep into enemy territory. Pope had to either score decisively on the Mississippi or disengage his army for service elsewhere.[7]

His patience exhausted, Halleck was in a rage by March 10. "Why can't Commodore Foote move tomorrow? It is all-important. By delay he spoils all my plans," he barked at Cullom. On March 12, only two days later, however, Halleck wired Foote not to attack until further orders, since Pope had to get his heavy guns in position to cut off the Rebel retreat from New Madrid. For his part, the flag officer insisted to Welles that he had no "jealousy against the Army" and that he remained on "best of terms with Generals Grant, Smith, [and John] McClernand," pointedly omitting Halleck and Pope.[8]

On March 13 Foote, not intimidated by Halleck's pressure, still offered excuses. The ironclads could not hold in place when anchored by the stern in the present current. Since the sterns were not armored and had only two guns, the vessels were bow heavy. "We must therefore tip up to the shore the best we can," he wrote. The paddlewheels, placed amidship, caught driftwood that clogged the rotation. He also raised such a row about the lack of supporting infantry that Halleck was forced to send some troops from Cairo along with the expedition.[9]

There is evidence that the Federals did not have an entirely accurate picture of what awaited them at Island No. 10. Intelligence reports indicated a small river battery at Hickman and additional fortifications in the Madrid Bend vicinity. In late February 1862, the St. Louis *Republican* failed to mention Island No. 10 and claimed that Forts Pillow and Randolph were so weak they could not hold out an hour against the fleet. In early March the same paper stated that the Confederates had withdrawn from Randolph. Military reports placed fifteen thousand Confederates at Island No. 10, with a dozen heavy guns. The more powerful position was considered to be Fort Pillow, with a garrison of seven thousand troops and fifty-five guns. The Southern fleet was dismissed as being "old New Orleans tugboats, which could be easily sunk by a single broadside [from an ironclad]." Interestingly, a laborer who had worked at Island No. 10 escaped and arrived at Cairo on March 11 telling a very different story of what to expect. He stated that the position had twenty thousand Confederates, sixty guns, five gunboats, and a floating battery. The information was apparently not taken seriously because a naval officer later admitted: "We were greatly surprised when we arrived above Island No. Ten and saw on the bluffs a chain of forts extending for four miles along the crescent-formed shore, with the white tents of the enemy in the rear."[10]

At 7 A.M. on March 14 the squadron, accompanied by a bevy of eastern correspondents, at long last departed Cairo. There were five gunboats—Commodore Benjamin M. Dove's USS *Louisville,* Commodore R. N. Stembel's USS *Cincinnati,* Commodore Henry Walke's USS *Carondelet,* the flagship USS *Benton,* commanded by Lieutenant S. L. Phelps, and Lieutenant George M. Blodgett's wooden USS *Conestoga.* The steamboats *A. F. Wilson* and *Ike Hammitt,* lashed together, towed four mortars, while *Pike* and *Wisconsin No. 2* towed a like number. *Alps* followed with the coal barge. Two ordnance boats, *Judge Torrence* and *Great Western,* carried the shells and powder for the mortars. The transports *Silver Wave* and *Rob Roy* had on board about fifteen hundred troops: six companies of the 15th Wisconsin, the 27th and 42d Illinois, Battery I, 2d Illinois Light Artillery, and one company of the 2d Illinois Cavalry. Six tugboats capped off the expedition. By 9 A.M. the fleet docked at Columbus, where it was joined by Lieutenant Egbert Thompson's USS *Pittsburg,* Lieutenant Leonard Paulding's USS *St. Louis,* Commodore A. H. Kilty's USS *Mound City,* and the steamboat *Lake Erie,* which towed two additional mortars.

At 2 P.M. the squadron again steamed downriver. "The broad Mississippi was soon dotted with steamers, both large and small and in less than half an hour Columbus had disappeared," observed a reporter. The fleet proceeded part of the time under steam and occasionally floated with the current, watching for snipers and masked batteries. The squadron anchored at Hickman around 5:00. From the decks of the boats, several horsemen could be seen on the hill above town, while others galloped along the streets in haste. The reception proved less than cordial, although a few ladies waved handkerchiefs from their windows. While at Hickman, the USS *Cincinnati's* boilers began leaking, and it returned to Cairo for repairs.[11]

The riders seen galloping off happened to be three Confederate officers and Merit Harris, the Hickman telegraph operator. The next day Harris, then at Union city, clicked off a taunting message to the Federals at Hickman: "Did you think the water is always this high? Wouldn't you like to have caught the old [train] engine yesterday? Ha! Ha! If your men can't do any better than that they had better stick to their old business of making wooden clocks. . . . Not one of your boats passed up or down but I reported it."[12]

The sailors awakened to a dismal morning on Saturday, March 15: rainy, cold, high winds, patches of fog. At 5:30 A.M. the fleet weighed anchor and proceeded downriver. At 7:00, just behind Island No. 8, the USS *Benton,* two miles in advance, sighted the Confederate scout steamer CSS *Grampus,* known as "Dare Devil Jack" to the Rebels and commanded by Captain Marsh Miller. The boat "suddenly appeared across her track and 'close abroad.' She stopped her engines and struck her colors, and we all thought she was ours at last," related Walke. After giving four long warning blasts from its whistle, however, the boat escaped under a full head of steam. The USS *Benton* fired four shots, all plopping in the water short of the target. "She [*Grampus*] ran and holloed [whistled] worse than [a] scared dog with a tin pan after him," a sailor humorously wrote, "and soon dodged behind a bend, and being much faster than our boats, escaped unhurt."[13]

At 8 A.M. the flotilla approached Phillips's Point. Round the bend and through the dead timbers and patches of cottonwood trees, the head of Island No. 10 could be plainly seen, the surface "white with tents." A number of Rebel transports hugged the Tennessee shore. With the use of a long glass, the names *Ohio Belle, John Simonds, Mears, Red Rover* (still bearing her old inscription "U.S. Mail Packet"), and *Grampus* could be detected, along with one other unmarked vessel and the floating battery. Two refugees informed the correspondents that the last bore the sign: "Bound to take Cairo."[14]

An hour later, the fleet rounded the bend, Phelps's USS *Benton* several hundred yards in advance. For several hours Foote cautiously reconnoitered the island and shoreline. "We could see the Rebel flag flying over their battery [the redan], and everyone was all excitement to 'pitch in,' " commented a sailor aboard the flagship. "But the Commodore was more considerate than us hot-head greenhorns and kept us back. . . . " The *Chicago Tribune* correspondent described the scene for his readers: "Looking through a glass, the upper battery [redan] seemed to be a simple earthwork 8 or 10 feet in height. . . . The Stars and Bars was flying from the lower corner of the works, and the artillerists could be plainly seen walking along the parapets. . . . In the rear and right [downriver] fortifications are a number of buildings, over which flies a yellow flag, indicating a hospital." The *Times* reporter claimed that he counted forty-six guns, including those of the floating battery.[15]

From Captain Edward W. Rucker's view in the redan, the ironclads "seemed to be examining for a position to commence an attack." Israel Gibbons, a member of the 5th Louisiana Battalion and a soldier-correspondent of the *New Orleans Crescent,* viewed the approaching fleet from the island. He wrote: "The enemy's boats loitered the greater part of the day, smoking and steaming back and forth plentifully. There appeared to be five or six gunboats, with a number of transports and little tugs, or mortar beds—it is hard to tell which."[16]

Foote made his move in the early afternoon. At 1 P.M. the Federal transport *Lake Erie No. 2* dropped down to the Missouri shore with mortar boats 11 and 12, where they were moored to the bank. Dropping a twenty-pound powder bag into the stubby muzzle, the crew then used a derrick to hoist the shot. At 2:40 a lanyard was jerked and No. 12 belched forth the first shot, flames leaping from the muzzle, followed shortly by a round from No. 11. Since the mortars fired diagonally across Phillips's Point, the crews could not see their targets. The fire control was directed by signals from the fleet. At 3:00 the USS *Benton* joined in the action with its bow guns. The first shell fell short, bursting prematurely, but a second struck within a hundred yards of the Confederate tender *Red Rover*, causing the Rebel transports to move a mile and a quarter downriver, where only their stacks could be seen. The firing now became general, directed at both the island and the redan.[17]

Soldier-correspondent Gibbons of the *New Orleans Crescent* was on the receiving end of the bombardment on the island. "The first shot fell in the water just across from us near the Missouri shore," he observed. "The second shot came much nearer, and was well in line with one of our silent batteries." The USS *Benton* trained its guns on the redan, but the range was so great it soon went back to the larger target—the island. "One round shot and one shell passed over our quarters falling in our rear, in the interior of the island, without damage to anybody," remarked the Louisiana journalist. The Rebel gunners at the Belmont Battery impatiently waited to return fire, but it proved useless at such ranges.[18]

The redan was also slow in responding. A full half hour elapsed before a single shot rang out, which a Northern reporter described as "a cloud of white smoke, which suddenly turned to blue and was followed by a report [discharge]." In a few seconds the shot "came glancing along the river; but it was far to the right, and fell short at least three-fourths of a mile." The second and third shots likewise went wild, but the fourth was more accurate, though still short a half mile.[19]

Shells now filled the air. One of USS *Benton's* shells struck the redan parapet and "filled the air with flying dirt. We could see the men running away." Although the flagship did not venture much further, two more batteries could be detected downriver among the tents and barracks, with a yellow hospital flag between them. Foote broke off the engagement before sunset. An intense but bloodless opening act, the USS *Benton* expended forty-two shots and thirty-four mortar shots. A correspondent aboard the flagship noted that the vessel was so deep in the water that the firing of its guns produced only slight jarring. Nonetheless, those spectators who stood above the wheelhouse, the highest point aboard, complained that night of headaches.[20]

About 5:00 that afternoon, Rucker spotted some tugs and transports making a reconnaissance near a slough just above the sandbar near the Missouri shore. A few shots chased them away. At 2 A.M. the Confederates sank the transport *Winchester* in the wash channel to prevent passage.[21]

Captain E. H. Cummings and two assistants of the signal corps arrived the next day at the redan and established a flag post. An engineer officer whom Beauregard had brought with him from Virginia, Cummings had been trained in wig-wag signals by Captain E. P. Alexander. Upon arriving in West Tennessee, he was forced to advertise for spyglasses, as none could be purchased in the department.[22]

Chilly, disagreeable, and with every indication of rain, the nasty weather continued on Sunday morning, March 16. At 7 A.M. Foote's flagship signaled for the fleet to follow its movements. The Federal gunboats USS *Benton,* USS *Cincinnati,* and USS *St. Louis* formed a line of battle and eased into the main channel, with USS *Mound City* and USS *Carondelet* holding back near the Missouri shore. These two vessels were in advance of eight additional mortars that had been towed into position and moored to the bank. The *Philadelphia Inquirer* correspondent noted: "At 8:30 we had dropped low enough down to see the enemy's tents and one of two batteries. The encampment extended a distance of fully two miles along the Kentucky [Tennessee] shore." At 9:00 the Rebel steamer *Ohio Belle* peeked around the bend, apparently to reconnoiter, but was quickly chased off by a few shots from the flagship.[23]

Confusion set in about 9 A.M. Trudeau received word that Rucker had given a distress signal from the redan and shown a white flag. Mortified, the chief of artillery ordered a skiff and immediately proceeded upriver. As he approached the small fort, much to his dismay, a Federal transport neared under a flag of truce. A New York reporter recorded the exchange that took place between the Federal officer, a Lieutenant Bishop, and Trudeau, whose Cajun accent misled the correspondent into thinking that Trudeau was a foreigner.

> BISHOP: "Do we understand your signal right, that you wish to communicate with us?
> TRUDEAU: "No, sir, it was a mistake."
> BISHOP: "Then why did you display a white flag?"
> TRUDEAU: "I acknowledge that it is our fault; I myself was deceived by it. I have only just arrived here and learned that it was merely a signal to our fortifications below. I regret the mistake."
> BISHOP: "Good morning, sir."
> TRUDEAU: "Good morning."

Fig. 8. The Federal attack on Island No. 10, March 16, 1862 (courtesy of *Frank Leslie's Illustrated*, April 5, 1862)

The color of the flag was changed, but the Federals had seen the redan. Practically under water, it had ammunition placed along the parapet wall. Thirty minutes later, the Confederates viewed what appeared to be a Federal transport under a flag of truce. The CSS *Grampus* was sent out under a white flag to investigate. When the Federals did not respond, it quickly returned.[24]

Foote continued his long-range shelling. At 10:00 the USS *Benton* fired a few rounds from its stern guns, but received no response. An hour later the mortars opened with a deafening roar, the first shell exploding directly over the island. Israel Gibbons noted that four of the 13-inch shells exploded directly over the island headquarters, with a number of men barely escaping injury. The troops of the 5th Louisiana Battalion and the 46th Tennessee moved to cover at the rear of the island. Wrote the Philadelphia journalist: "With the aid of a glass we could plainly see where our mortar shells had torn and cut the limbs and trees, and barked the timber back of the enemy's position."[25]

"Throughout the afternoon, the ten mortars continued their work, lobbing 200 shells at the island and the redan, while USS *Benton*, with two and sometimes three of the big mortars, would 'let go' at once, with a tremendous thundering roar, the loudest we have ever heard," described a reporter. One correspondent was awed when the mortar shells made a direct hit; they would "toss up a column of dirt a distance of from 50 to 100 feet." On the Confederate side, Gibbons wrote that many of the men flirted with death, laughing at and ridiculing those who ran from the shell explosions. Shortly after 2 P.M., the redan fired a few shells, but all fell short.[26]

At 5:00 the transport *Silver Wave* dropped down to the mortars. Several companies of the 27th Illinois debarked, as well as Battery I, 2d Illinois Light Artillery (the Joliet Light Artillery). The contingent supported a fatigue party building a bridge over a slough. The activity did not go unnoticed, catching the attention of the cannon crew for the Lady Polk, Jr. at the Belmont Battery. Though silent up to this point, the cannoneers could not pass up such a tempting target, even though the range was in excess of three miles. The huge gun fired a shot, the shell landing only twenty yards astern of the transport. The Federals quickly reboarded, and the transport returned upriver.[27]

At 6:00 that evening a 6-pounder in the Illinois battery unlimbered and opened fire to feel out the Confederates. This awakened the floating battery, which returned nine shots in quick succession. A shell fragment struck one of the Yankee gunners in the leg just below the knee; his wound proved mortal. The Federal battery quickly withdrew. Parting shots came from the navy that night. At 6:30 the USS *Benton* sent several rounds toward the redan, but got no response. Later that night the USS *Mound City* fired twenty rounds at what was termed the "middle battery." The mortars continued a harassing fire at thirty-minute intervals until dawn. After two days of long-range bombardment, however, the situation remained stalemated. About four hundred rounds had been expended by the navy on Saturday, without inflicting a single casualty.[28]

Throughout the night of March 16, the Confederates worked frantically to repair the redan parapet. McCown also used the respite to shift his infantry. Three Federals captured in a skiff that night claimed that the main attack would come the next day. McCown placed the 55th Tennessee within a mile and a half of the redan to act as a support in the event of an amphibious assault. The 4th Tennessee was placed at Trudeau's headquarters, behind mainland Battery No. 3. Colonel Steadman prepared two detachments of fifteen men each from his 1st Alabama to be kept at Trudeau's headquarters as a relief for Rucker's gunners. The balance of the regiment remained in reserve. The 5th Louisiana Battalion and the 46th Tennessee were relieved from island duty and replaced by Walker's 40th Tennessee, armed with Enfield rifles.[29]

The weather finally took a friendly turn on Monday morning, March 17, being sunny and offering the clearest view in days. Summoning the naval captains aboard the flagship for a conference, Foote announced that a direct assault would be made against the redan. The attack would be made bows-on at a range of two thousand yards due to the rapid current. Because of USS *Benton's* inadequate engines, it would be lashed in between USS *Cincinnati* on the left and USS *St. Louis* on the right, making a powerful floating battery.[30]

The crews hurriedly prepared for action. The three vessels spent much of the morning testing their engines in concert. Meanwhile, USS *Mound City* and USS *Carondelet* went into action. "At 9:45 A.M. the drum beat for quarters, and all was excitement to see the 'ball open,' and at 11 A.M. the *Mound City* opened fire on the battery with her three bow guns—two rifle[d] sixty-four's [42s] and one 8-inch shell gun," noted a sailor. The parting salvo of the *Carondelet* struck a tree overhanging the redan, making a tremendous splash in the water, having the appearance of an explosion. *Mound City* signaled: "Well done, old *Carondelet*." The eight mortars along the Missouri shore also got into the act, targeting both the island and the redan. The first shell burst prematurely, showering fragments into the water.[31]

A St. Louis reporter recorded some of the banter between the crew members aboard the *Carondelet*. "Put that in your pocket and never mind the change," yelled one tar as a shot fired. "Look at 'em running," shouted another as he veered through his long glass. "Now they're loadin' their big'en [Lady Polk, Jr.]. Watch out! There she goes." Shouted Captain Walke: "Get out of the way, gentlemen! Let us pay due respects to that fellow. Lie close." Everyone's head went low, but the shot went toward the *Benton*.[32]

At noon the flagship and its two escorts, made fast to each other, moved down the east bank. The three boats produced a "huge volume of coal smoke," according to a newsman. Foote turned to correspondent Albert Richardson and remarked: "You had better take your place with the other correspondents, upon

Fig. 9. The Currier & Ives depiction of the fighting at Island No. 10 (courtesy of the U.S. Naval Historical Foundation)

a transport in the rear, out of range. Should any accident befall you, censure would be cast upon me for permitting you to stay." Richardson persuaded him otherwise, however, and thus became a front-row spectator in the action that was to follow. At 1:20 the three lashed ironclads opened fire, and within fifteen minutes fifty-one rounds had been expended.[33]

At approximately 2:10 that afternoon the Rebels returned fire. The first shot, from Lady Polk, Jr., came on an incredible three-mile trajectory that passed over the Missouri point and struck the USS *St. Louis* just under the side. The gun crew could not see the effects of the shot, however, and, believing that it had gone wild, ceased firing. Shortly thereafter, Trudeau signaled Rucker to commence firing, an order that the redan gunners greeted with loud cheering. Rucker's company had been reinforced with a thirty-man detachment from the 1st Alabama. Normally the 8-inch columbiads in the redan could be operated with a crew of thirteen, but since the men were knee-deep in water, twenty were required. Rucker's 32-pounders remained mute during the long-range bombardment, and he was forced to fight the major engagement of the campaign with only three guns. Mainland Battery No. 2 and the 32-pounder rifle in Battery No. 5 also joined in, and the firing became general. From his headquarters, Trudeau thought the engagement to be "a most significant spectacle." Captain J. J. Neely, commanding a cavalry company, believed that the shelling was "the grandest sight" he ever beheld. "The shell and ball came all around us," he wrote, "ploughing up the ground, some of the men falling flat on their faces and dodging." The 1st Alabama moved up in support, and Steadman was ordered into the redan to assist Rucker. The Federal transports, loaded with troops, could be plainly seen in the distance, their tugboats steaming about. An amphibious assault appeared imminent.[34]

One Northern journalist, amazed at the calmness of the Rebel gunners, wrote: "Quite frankly I observed their men standing all over the works when all about them rained the Federal tempest of iron hail." Among the conspicuous "was a man without any coat, whose white shirt made him a marked object; him I saw a dozen times, now sponging a cannon, now apparently strolling leisurely about the fortifications, or, again standing in full view upon the parapet, waving defiantly a rebel flag in the face of his foes."[35]

The Southern artillery soon got the range and began scoring hits with surprising regularity. The USS *St. Louis* received a glancing shot off its starboard armor. At 2:30 a tremendous explosion rocked the vessel. "A moment later, a dozen men rushed up on the deck, their faces so darkened that they would have been taken for Negroes. Two were carrying the lifeless form of a third," wrote Richardson. One of the crew shouted that an old 42-pounder had exploded, killing and mutilating several men. A head count revealed three dead and a dozen wounded.

The USS *Benton* received three hits. One shot struck the bow "plum in the face," according to an eyewitness, "but, finding it [the armor] too hard to pene-trate, bounced off into the river." An 8-inch shot smashed through the deck, penetrating the half-inch armor plate and five-inch timber near the bow "as if it were paper." It passed through the entire length of the boat—through the ward room, machinery (cutting off a wrought-iron bar), and kitchen—to the extreme stern, where it stopped at the flag officer's desk, crushing the sliding lid. Another shot whizzed within three feet of the head of the *Chicago Tribune* reporter and crashed into the ventilator. Still another missed the rudder by only twenty feet. The USS *Cincinnati* also received a shot through its deck that came very close to dismantling the engine shaft.[36]

At the height of the shelling, Illinois Congressman Elihu Washburne and James Eads, builder of the ironclads, stood beside Foote as he was handed a package of letters. Flag officer Foote selected one, opened it, read a few lines, and then turned to Eads and said: "I must ask you to excuse me for a few minutes, while I go to my cabin. This letter brings me the news of the death of my son, about thirteen years old, who I had hoped would live to be the stay and support of his mother." The death of William, Foote's second son who was living in New Haven with his mother, was totally unexpected; he had been ill only a week. After a momentary absence, the flag officer returned to the deck perfectly composed.[37]

During this period, the USS *Carondelet* and the USS *Mound City*, on the extreme right of the lowest point on the Missouri shore, continued firing. The USS *Pittsburg* came astern of the two vessels, and Lieutenant Thompson boarded the *Carondelet*. Incredibly, he had not been given an assignment during the attack and did not know what position to take. Thompson steered his boat to the other side of the river and sat idle. The other two ironclads continued firing, but the rifled guns could reach the redan only with a nine-degree eleva-tion.[38]

In postwar years, Walke expressed frustration at the inaccuracy of some of the news accounts, believing that the three attacking ironclads, especially the *Benton*, had been given excessive coverage. He insisted that they were never closer than two miles to the redan, which their smoothbores could not possibly reach. Also, the flagship was never "several hundred yards in advance," as claimed by one correspondent. "The *Benton* was never 'within a mile' of the island before its surrender," Walke insisted, "and in this action was nearly a mile farther down from it than the two gunboats [*Carondelet* and *Mound City*] which were *not* mentioned [in news accounts]."[39]

The redan took a tremendous pounding. One columbiad was disabled, a sliver of iron from the gun carriage striking Lieutenant W. M. Clark in the temple and killing him instantly. Seven others in the detachment received wounds. Rucker signaled for relief for his shivering cannoneers. A detachment of twenty-seven men from Hoadley's and Sterling's heavy artillery companies was dispatched, but it would take time for the cannoneers to arrive. In order to fill the void, forty volunteers from the 55th Tennessee waded a mile and a half through ice-cold three-foot-deep water to keep the guns in action. Several Tennesseans attempted to run during the action, but Colonel Steadman drew his revolver and ordered them back.

Captains Harris and Gray of the engineers arrived that afternoon to inspect the damage to the parapet. Water was only a half inch from the gun platforms, and everywhere trees had been hacked down and shattered to pieces. "Mimosa" of the *New Orleans Delta* described the scene: "The parapet was but scarcely three feet high, and with the exception of the planking on which the guns were traversed, the interim of the redan was nothing but a mud-hole in which the men had to work." He added that several hundred blacks were employed in making repairs.[40]

The Confederate steamer *Red Rover*, the tender for the floating battery, also took a hit by a forty-pound shell fragment. The projectile entered the hurricane deck and made a straight line of holes to the bottom. The leak, although dangerous, was quickly plugged, and there were no casualties.[41]

By sunset Foote had had enough and withdrew his three attacking ironclads. "The men [Confederates] at the water battery suppose they have disabled us, and we can hear their cheers, while they sent their shots in pursuit, which fell very close, even at the distance of two miles," commented a *New York Tribune* reporter. It was believed that the redan parapet had been largely blown away and two or three guns disabled. More than a thousand rounds had been expended, 301 from the *Benton* alone. That night Foote got off a telegram to Welles: "This place is even stronger and better adapted for defense than Columbus has ever been; each fortification commands the one above it. We can count forty-nine guns in different batteries, where there are probably double that number, with ten thousand troops." The fuses of the Union shells, many made before the Mexican War, proved worthless and caused premature detonations.[42]

Trudeau was, of course, ecstatic, proudly proclaiming: "The artillery has saved the valley of the Mississippi." He predicted that in the future men would boast, "I was present at the attack upon the redan fort at Madrid Bend." The Southern press quickly singled out Rucker as the hero of the battle. "Capt. Rucker has completely immortalized himself," proclaimed the *Memphis Appeal*. Although the engagement fell short of the decisiveness and intensity of the water battery at Fort Donelson, it was perceived as a great victory at a time when good news was sorely needed from Tennessee.[43]

That evening Wintter's company worked to remount the dismantled columbiad in the redan. Colonel Alexander Brown's 55th Tennessee desperately needed relief, his men "shivering with cold and almost famished with hunger." Colonel John Clark's 46th Tennessee arrived at midnight. The regiment had gotten lost in the murky bottomland and splashed around for several hours, and the colonel and some of the troops returned to camp. Surgeon Caldwell of the 46th was disgusted: "Somebody in high office [Clark] acted very badly that night. I would have been glad to have some few, whose names I will not mention, fall over with a hole through their heads."[44]

Six more mortars joined the Federal flotilla under tow of the *Pike* and the *Dan Wilson*. Mortar rounds were lobbed at the Confederate positions throughout the evening at the rate of one shot on the half hour. Tuesday morning, March 18, dawned sunny and crisp. The Federal gunboats *Benton, St. Louis,* and *Cincinnati* lay together in the towhead throughout the early morning, when at 10:45 the latter two left the flagship for recoaling. The *Benton* and some of the mortars lazily fired a few rounds at both the redan and the island, the latter increasing their rate of fire to one shot per twenty minutes. At 10:20 the *Carondelet* and the *Mound City* began firing at the redan, and at 1:25 the latter succeeded in dismantling a gun. Between 9 A.M. and 6 P.M. some four hundred rounds were expended, and the *Mound City* continued firing until midnight. As for the Confederates, the mainland No. 2 battery fired only two shots in the afternoon. Fatigue parties labored in the redan to strengthen a breach in the parapet.[45]

The first phase of the naval campaign was essentially concluded. Foote had been beaten not so much tactically as he had been mentally on March 17. His gloomy prophecies had become self-fulfilling. The shock of his son's death had plunged him into deep personal depression. He agreed with a fellow officer who stoically advised him: "You ought, flag officer, to rise above your grief, and not dwell so on it." He could hardly restrain himself, however, so great was "the power of [his] grief." The operation now stalled.[46]

8

We Think Foote and His Gunboats a Good Deal of Humbug

ABOUT 7 P.M. ON MARCH 18, a meeting was held aboard the USS *Benton*. Foote called the conference in response to a request by Colonel Bissell, who had arrived that afternoon after a daylong journey through the swamps. On the previous night Bissell had met on the parapet of Fort Thompson with Pope. He listened as the commanding general carefully outlined a plan for two or three gunboats to run the blockade and transport his troops across the river. In a letter to the flag officer, Pope assured him that by this means he could "cross my whole force and capture every man at Island No. 10 and on the mainland." Bissell recalled that neither he nor the general had any doubt but that Foote would comply. The flag officer's response thus shocked and dismayed the colonel. He expressed grave misgivings about such a venture and refused to take responsibility. The details of the consultation that subsequently took place are shrouded in contradictions.[1]

First, there is the question of when the meeting occurred. Foote specifically stated to the secretary of the navy that "today [March 20], for the first time since I have been in command of the flotilla, I called a council of war." In compiling his 1889 history of the 25th Missouri (the engineer regiment), W. A. Neal claimed that the meeting actually took place on the evening of March 18 and that on March 19 Bissell made an expedition to explore a possible backwater approach to New Madrid. Neal's claim might well be dismissed as postwar mixing of dates but for the fact that three correspondents, all aboard Foote's flagship, confirmed in contemporary accounts that the meeting took place on March 18. It is a virtual certainty that Foote's claim of March 20 is incorrect and that he retained certain information at least thirty-six hours or more before notifying Welles. Indeed, Bissell was back in New Madrid on March 20 and was not even with the fleet.[2]

Second, there is the matter of who attended the conference. Foote implied that all his gunboat commanders were present, but such was not the case. Henry Walke noted in his memoirs: "This council appears to have been a secret one, of which we [officers of the *Carondelet*] knew nothing." He was not invited, apparently, because the flag officer knew, or presumed, that Walke's views would differ from his own. This may also explain why the correspondent of the St.

Louis *Democrat,* who was aboard the *Carondelet,* filed no story on the conference.[3]

Exactly what was said and by whom is also in dispute. According to Bissell, the naval officers unanimously agreed that two gunboats should be sent down-river. Foote, however, adamantly insisted that the ironclads were designed for head-on fighting only. He argued that if one or both were captured, they "could be started hard upstream and whip the whole fleet, lying as they did with their unarmored sterns downstream, and that Cairo would be at their mercy." Flag officer Foote told quite a different story. In his letter to Welles, he claimed that he wished to run the blockade himself, in the *Benton,* which, although sluggish, offered more protection than the other boats. He continued: "The officers, with one exception, were decidedly opposed to running the blockade, believing that it would result in the almost certain destruction of the boats." Apparently, the "one exception" of whom Foote wrote was Lieutenant Phelps, although Bissell claimed that "another, I think, was quite as emphatic." Phelps passionately argued that he would not allow his boat to be captured and that he would personally stand in the powder room and blow it out of the water first. A horror-stricken Foote snapped: "That would be inhumane. This council is closed."[4]

Bissell persisted, claiming that he was authorized to make a preemptory demand for the boats, but Foote still refused. Unrelenting, the colonel barked that he would return to Cairo, obtain additional transports, and run them past the Rebel batteries with army crews, thus bypassing the navy. The flag officer adamantly replied that he was in command of all river activity and would not permit any boats to be placed in a position of certain destruction. Bissell jumped up from the table, slammed down his fist, and shouted: "General Pope shall have his boats if I have to take them cross country."[5]

If Bissell's account is correct, Foote called his council of war not to solicit views, but to seek support for a decision already made. If he was not outright deceptive, at the very least, Foote in his letter to Welles failed to capture the intensity of the meeting. His failure to comply with Pope's request was a decision second in importance only to Halleck's not to scrap the campaign. For the next three weeks, Foote settled into the drudgery of a siege.

A month after the campaign, Bissell was still fuming. On May 14, 1862, while at Corinth (then under Federal occupation), he filed a formal letter of complaint with Benjamin F. Wade, the Republican senator from Ohio and a member of the powerful Committee on the Conduct of the War. He stated: "Had Captain Phelps been allowed to try [to run the blockade], as he requested, that island would have been taken nearly four weeks sooner. Fort Pillow at that time had no guns and the opening of the river would have been very easy." What Colonel Bissell did not know, or at least failed to mention, was that Halleck not only fully accepted Foote's decision but also affirmed it. On March

21, Halleck had written the flag officer: "I am very glad that you have not un-
necessarily exposed your gunboats. If they had been disabled, it would have
been a most serious loss to us in the future operations of the campaign, whereas
the reduction of these batteries this week or next is a matter of very little importance indeed. I think it will turn out in the end that it is much better for
us that they are not reduced till we can fully cut off the retreat of their troops."
He concluded, "The reduction of these works is only a question of time and
we are in no hurry on that point. Nothing is lost by a little delay there."[6]

Did Bissell exaggerate the ramifications of the March 18 council? It is easy
for a modern reader to conclude that if Island No. 10 had fallen a month earlier,
Pope's army could have been transferred cross-country to Pittsburg Landing.
Grant's army thus reinforced, the Confederates probably would not have attempted their surprise attack that resulted in the Battle of Shiloh. This idea is
not at all what Halleck had in mind. The theater commander, at that point, had
committed Buell's army to Grant and was determined to maintain Pope's in
the Mississippi River theater of operations. Had Island No. 10 fallen sooner,
Pope's army would not have been sent to Grant, but would have moved on to
Fort Pillow. Also, contrary to Bissell's statement, Fort Pillow was in readiness
by late March 1862.

Rather than have Foote risk another attack or run past the batteries,
Halleck was fully prepared to shift Pope's army. "The main object is accomplished [by the navy] by holding the enemy in position," he wrote Pope on
March 24. "If the idea of crossing is given up send all forces you can spare to
Bird's Point, to be transported up the Tennessee. We can there turn the enemy
and cut off his retreat by land while your guns command the river. If this meets
your views I will also withdraw the forces from Hickman with the same object."
The plan would probably not have worked. Reelfoot Lake and the flooded low-
lands east of Tiptonville would have prevented any investment from that side
until the water level dropped. Pope thus began to explore a third alternative.[7]

From March 19 until the end of the month and beyond, the siege dragged
wearily on. There was little action beyond the monotonous pounding of the
mortars, which on occasion could be heard as far away as Cairo, sixty miles
distant. Usually they were fired at intervals of one shot per fifteen minutes or
on the half hour. On March 22, seventy-four shells were expended, but the next
day the number was cut to thirty-five. During the early morning hours of
March 24, a single mortar fired thirteen rounds, but throughout the remainder
of the day only fifteen rounds were fired from two mortars. On March 25 the
number of rounds rose slightly to thirty, but then dropped again on March 26
and 27 to fifteen and fourteen, respectively. The last two days of the month saw
increased activity with forty-eight and fifty-three rounds. The overall expendi-
ture, however, indicated a leisurely commitment to reducing the Confederate

stronghold. On March 22, *Alps, Wilson,* and *Wisconsin No. 2* came down and towed all but four of the mortars back upriver.[8]

The arching shots of the mortars created a spectacular view. One journalist observed: "Most of the shells would not explode, but when they did so, the effect was always devastating, and one bursting in the trees would send the branches twisted and broken in every direction for fifty or one hundred yards." The scene was most breathtaking at night. Foote informed his wife: "We are throwing mortar shells into the forts at night, which, showing the burning fuse, makes a beautiful sight, like a shooting star in a parabola."[9]

On occasion the gunboats would join in. Very few rounds were fired on March 19 due to a strong upriver wind that churned the water and made accurate firing impossible. During a heavy mist on Thursday morning, March 20, the USS *Mound City* fired several shots at long intervals until 10:50 A.M., when it was signaled by the flagship to cease. The USS *Benton* then picked up the action, although, according to Walke, its shots invariably fell short. On the afternoon of March 22, the *Mound City* fired seven or eight rounds to disperse workmen at the redan. That evening it expended twenty rounds in quick succession at what was termed the "middle battery." One officer claimed that he saw five Rebels killed with a single blast, though his report turned out to be false. On March 27, the *Pittsburg* lobbed a few shells into a house on the Missouri shore believed to be a Confederate picket post. A score of cavalry were sent scampering. On March 28, the *Times* journalist noted to his readers: "For a week the *Benton* has not even lifted an anchor, or scarcely fired a shot—assertions which apply equally to every other boat in the fleet." On the last day of the month the flagship fired three shells, but it was only for show—Assistant Secretary of War Thomas Scott was aboard for inspection.[10]

During this time life on the fleet became routine. "One would be led to judge from the unconcerned and quietlike manner in which we are pursuing this attack, that it was more a trial of gunnery or a Fourth of July demonstration than otherwise. We sit aboard the decks, reading newspapers, magazines, letters, etc. with as much comparative confidence of our safety as though seated at home," Harry Browne described to his cousins. The crews ate supper at 4:00 with lights out at 8:00. Watches were changed every four hours. On Sunday the sailors assembled on deck, dressed in their blues, for religious services. On the flagship Foote stood behind a stool draped with a flag to read prayers and deliver a sermon.[11]

The USS *Conestoga* was charged with the protection of the mortars and transports. Although usually this was a routine task, on the afternoon of March 19, several suspicious skiffs were sighted, giving cause for alarm. Perhaps the Southerners were reconnoitering with a view of setting fire to one of the ammunition transports. About 8:00 that night the officers aboard the vessel were deeply involved in a card game when suddenly one of the gun crews blasted

Fig. 10. A night attack on Island No. 10 (engraving by W. Ridgway after a drawing by C. Parsons; courtesy of the U.S. Naval Historical Foundation)

out a shot. All hands scrambled to their stations as the cannoneers continued to fire onto the Missouri shore. The transport *Judge Torrence* got quickly under way to the middle of the channel, the crew fearful that it was under attack. The entire episode turned out to be only a false alarm—a case of jittery nerves—and calm soon returned.[12]

On Sunday morning, four days later, the monotony was again broken, this time aboard the *Carondelet*. The vessel, moored to the Missouri shore, suddenly received a tremendous jolt. Two immense cottonwood trees had been uprooted on the bank and slammed the port quarter and wheelhouse, breaking its davits and rowboats, and crushing hammock netting and skylights. The freak accident was apparently the result of erosion, caused by the high water and constant shocks of the bombardment. As the crew attempted to extricate the boat, incredibly another tree fell on it. A cottonwood, four feet in diameter, smashed the boat amidship, breaking rigging chains and rocking the vessel. Two sailors were seriously injured and a third killed. At 10 A.M. the *Alps* arrived to tow the vessel out from under the tree that held it fast. The *Carondelet* was taken up-river, and a group of carpenters from Cairo was brought down to make repairs. A week was required to put the boat back into fighting trim, nature having thus accomplished what Rebel batteries had been unable to do.[13]

Two specialty boats joined the Federal fleet. On the evening of March 16, the *Louisiana*, a hospital boat fitted up for three hundred patients, arrived with several female nurses aboard. Toward the end of the month the boat received severe damage when it too was struck by a large cottonwood tree in an accident similar to that experienced by the *Carondelet*. Several days later the *Swallow*, a floating blacksmith shop, united with the fleet. The upper deck was used for sleeping quarters, while the lower had six forges and all the machinery necessary for blacksmiths and boilermakers. On March 28 the *Dickey* brought down four 50-pounder cannon to be swapped with an equal number of guns aboard the flagship.[14]

The Northern "press gang," as it became known, played an increasingly influential role in the campaign. No fewer than fifteen papers had reporters on the fleet, including George P. Upton of the *Chicago Tribune*, Constantine D. Miller of the *Cincinnati Commercial*, Charles Coffin of the *Boston Journal*, Albert D. Richardson and Junius H. Browne of the *New York Tribune*, Francis B. Wilke of the *New York Times*, Frank Chapman of the *New York Herald*, M. C. Misener of the *Chicago Times*, Richard T. Colburne of the *New York World*, William E. Webb of the *Daily Missouri Republican*, and George W. Beaman of the *Daily Missouri Democrat*. Other papers represented included the *Cincinnati Times*, *National Intelligencer* (Washington, D.C.), *Philadelphia Inquirer*, the Associated Press, whose syndicated articles were carried in several papers, and the artists of *Frank Leslie's* and *Harper's*. Besides the fleet journalists, a number of smalltown reporters remained at Cairo.[15]

The overabundance of reporters created two problems. Having little to write about, frustrated journalists resorted to publishing camp rumors, few of which had any basis in fact. Perhaps the most embarrassing of these came on March 18, when a report clicked over the wire to St. Louis that Island No. 10 had been captured. Before checking its validity, Halleck boasted of it to a large crowd as he was serenaded beneath his balcony window at the Planter's House. Compounding the error, several papers eagerly headlined the event. The truth soon became known, and retractions were forthcoming. The *Chicago Tribune* traced the original source to an army communiqué that had come through Pope's headquarters to Halleck on March 17.[16]

The story led to a rather comical reaction aboard the *Carondelet*. Several tars read the headlines of the *Missouri Democrat:* "Island No. 10 Is Ours." Thoroughly believing it, they went running to Captain Walke and inquired about liberty. "What for?" asked the captain. "Why, sir, the papers say that the rebels have all left and we want to get some fresh grub," came the response. Just then a Confederate gun fired, the shot skipping across the water and embedding in the bank just off the port quarter. "There, that don't look much like evacuation, does it?" barked Walke. "Oh, that's nothing. Here is the papers for it," claimed a sailor as he held up a copy of the *Democrat*. "There, General Halleck says they've quit, and he ought to know, being as he's right at headquarters."

A second shot boomed out from the island, this one coming still closer to the ironclad. Walke sneered: "Well, if them chaps has left, they've a damned odd way of showing on't."[17]

Other inaccurate reports surfaced. It was widely claimed that the Confederate ironclad *Manassas* had made an appearance at Island No. 10; the *New York Tribune* reporter admitted, however, that no one had actually seen the vessel. On March 30, a disgusted Symmes Browne wrote his family: "Yesterday we received the Cincinti. 'Times' in which was a statement under the head 'Latest by Telegraph. Island No. 10 Captured—Great loss of life etc.' and even going so far as to name the boats and number of men and officers killed and wounded on each. Such proceedings should be looked upon with perfect contempt by the public."[18]

Even after the Confederates had reduced their forces, various reporters continued to publish wildly exaggerated reports of enemy strength. The *Philadelphia Inquirer* put the number at eleven thousand troops; the *New York Times* and *National Intelligencer*, between ten and twenty thousand; and the *Chicago Tribune*, twenty thousand. Charles Upton of the *Tribune* claimed: "I saw ten regiments at one time on dress parade."[19]

After the quick victories at Fort Henry and Fort Donelson, the nation was not mentally prepared for its first protracted siege. This frustration was aggravated by journalists who had little about which to write. "The siege of Island No. 10 has become as tedious as a twice told tale," commented the *Times* correspondent. "Each day drags on its heavy length more wearily than the one before. The gunboats maintain the same position they did a week ago. [The mortars] booming explosions mark the loss of time."[20]

An observation balloon that arrived received extensive coverage, simply because it presented a novelty to bored reporters. The *Eagle* was piloted by John H. Steiner. When Halleck and Pope proved indifferent to the project, Steiner successfully offered his services to Foote. The German aeronaut's primary mission was to observe the effects of the mortar fire to ascertain whether adjustments were needed. On March 25, Steiner ascended to five hundred feet, but smoke and haze prevented a clear view. The next day cleared, and Steiner, along with Colonel Buford and Captain H. E. Maynadier, commanding the mortars, went afloat. They observed that the mortars were overshooting the enemy batteries, and an adjustment in elevation was ordered. The two-day operation marked the only use of balloon observation in the West during the war.[21]

The press soon began to act as a kind of unofficial lobby to pressure Foote to take decisive action. "This gunboat flotilla should be made subordinate to the command of the land forces," demanded the *Cincinnati Commercial*. The *Democrat* of March 31 claimed: "The siege at Island No. 10 still hangs wearily on, and Commodore Foote's non-combative policy daily becomes the object of criticism." The *New York World* related the question on the minds of many: "If these gunboats are not intended to be marched against fortifications, why were they built?" Nor were the gunboats themselves spared. "The *Benton* is our best protection [from a Rebel fleet], and she is but a trifle better than an unwieldy failure," criticized the *New York Times*. Foote, already buckling under the weight of command, now had additional external stresses placed on him. "The country expects a great deal without appreciating the difficulties of my position, but I must act upon my judgment and independent of popular expression," he was quoted in a St. Louis paper.[22]

The expressed frustration of the press filtered into both the fleet and the army. On March 30, Symmes Browne confided to his wife: "And as for 'running the blockade,' I am sorry that this seems to have been given up entirely. I have been down around the point a mile and a half below our boat and seen the position of all the batteries, breadth and course of the river etc., and I have not the least doubt that in a dark night two or three of the gunboats could run the blockade without receiving any damage. This is also the opinion of our pilots and several of the officers on this boat. But as it has been given up, I should perhaps say nothing of it." Alfred Gilbert frankly believed that the flag officer was motivated by the press coverage that he was receiving. "As it is, they [Confederates] are just laughing at him trying to shell them out." He concluded bluntly: "We think Foote and his boats without land forces a good deal of humbug." An Ohio colonel summed up the progress of the flotilla when he stated: "Oh! It is still bombarding the state of Tennessee at long range."[23]

An associate of fifty-five-year-old Colonel Napoleon B. Buford described him as a "fussy old gentleman, an old granny, but kind and amiable." A railroad president in civilian life, he now commanded the flotilla brigade, a water-borne infantry force whose original function was not amphibious, but rather to garrison Island No. 10 after it fell to the navy. The force consisted of the 27th and 42d Illinois, six companies of Colonel Hans C. Heg's 15th Wisconsin, the famed Scandinavian regiment, Battery I, 2d Illinois Light Artillery, and a company of the 2d Illinois Cavalry. On the night of March 16, the steamer *Nebraska* arrived from St. Louis with the 18th Missouri. On the night of March 21, the 27th Illinois was transferred to the steamer *T. L. McGill.*[24]

Throughout the siege there was little for Buford's troops to do but wait, as they remained tightly crammed together on the transports. As the siege wore on, the misery increased. A severe epidemic of diarrhea struck March 18. "The closets [commodes] on the boat could not meet the demand and holes were cut from the centers of the wheel covers to the deck each way and kept in constant use, and these did not meet the demand," recalled a member. A huge log was partially afloat near the *Nebraska,* and a few men at a time were allowed to go out on it. It proved the only escape from the constant foul odor. A couple of men died and were buried ashore, but the saturated ground quickly filled the graves with water. The caskets had to be stepped on to keep them in place while mud was shoveled on top.[25]

Clearly, something had to be done. On March 23 the troops went ashore, but the rising water level forced a move a mile and a half upriver to the Phillips's plantation. Surrounded by a levee, it made a good campsite, and a nearly level clover field served as a drill ground. The artillery horses were exercised, and the gunners practiced with their James rifles.[26]

On the evening of March 21 Lieutenant Lyman G. Allen of the 27th Illinois took four men from his company to make a raid on the redan in an effort to spike the guns. A few nights earlier he had landed on the Tennessee shore by himself and snatched an artillery marker flag just above the small fort. The party reached the redan but found two hundred men inside, all engaged in building platforms to raise the guns out of the water. Allen brashly marched his squad up to the Rebel sentinel at the lower gun and pretended to be the officer of the guard with a relief. It was a dark and stormy night, and the soldier did not ask questions. Allen's men then spiked an 8-inch columbiad, the Lady Davis, and quickly returned to their landing boat, reaching the transport by midnight.[27]

At the end of March, Buford led a raid on the Confederate garrison at Union City, estimated at fifteen hundred troops. The 27th Illinois and 15th

Wisconsin were joined by Sparrestrom's battery of four 6-pounders and three companies of the 2d Illinois Cavalry at Hickman. The attack came at dawn on March 31; the Rebels had been caught napping. W. H. "Red" Jackson's Tennessee cavalry regiment broke and retreated after two feeble attempts to form a line. Colonel Ed Pickett's 21st Tennessee stampeded to a waiting train at the depot. Buford captured fourteen prisoners, a hundred horses and mules, and a dozen wagons. In the cleanup operation an accidental explosion occurred in which one Federal was killed and another wounded.[28]

The Southern press was prompt with its denunciation. Wrote the editor of a Mobile paper: "There can be no excuse for a surprise. . . . Such affairs are enough to make one's heart sick." Beauregard immediately dispatched an officer to investigate the incident. "We must make an example of those officers who permit their commands to be surprised," he wrote Polk.[29]

9

Be of Good Cheer and Hold Out

As early as February 12, Beauregard had determined that Island No. 10 would be untenable if New Madrid fell. On March 15, the day the Federal fleet made its appearance, the general ordered a withdrawal of most of the garrison and all unmounted guns to Tiptonville, where river transportation would be furnished to Fort Pillow. The remaining garrison would have sixty days' rations and three hundred rounds of ammunition per man. Everything that could not be removed would be destroyed, and transports were to be positioned at Tiptonville as an escape for the remaining troops.[1]

Was Beauregard prematurely pulling out? The indication is that he now viewed Island No. 10 as nothing more than a stall to buy additional time to prepare Fort Pillow. Perhaps the lightning Federal victories at Fort Henry and Fort Donelson, coupled with the loss of New Madrid, made him lose confidence in static defenses. Perhaps he genuinely believed that, considering the geographical advantages of Madrid Bend, eight thousand troops were simply unnecessary. Maybe, as he claimed in postwar years, that was the plan from the outset, that is, to fight the main battle at Fort Pillow. If this were true, why did he leave the majority of his heaviest guns at Island No. 10 to be sacrificed?[2]

If Island No. 10 was intended as nothing more than a holding action, this information was never communicated to McCown. On March 20, Polk wired him that the island was the "key to the Mississippi Valley" and should be held "to the last extremity." Two days later Beauregard sent a dispatch to McCown informing him that Van Dorn planned to attack Pope in reverse at New Madrid. "Be of good cheer and hold out," he encouraged.[3]

Beauregard sent mixed signals. On the one hand he told McCown to hold on, while on the other hand he ordered the withdrawal of the bulk of the garrison to Fort Pillow. This ambivalence echoed again in his message of March 22: "Your [McCown's] command forms the garrison of that key to [the] Mississippi Valley." Yet he obviously was not willing to risk the entire force, even for "the key." He bluntly told him that the position could not be reinforced. It is true that most of the New Madrid forces that were withdrawn were channeled to Corinth for the big fight shaping up in that area. Beauregard, nonetheless, maintained a brigade-size force at Fort Pillow that he refused to release. He admonished McCown: "Country expects you to defend that post of honor

[Island No. 10] to the last or until we can relieve you by a victory here [Corinth]." Perhaps this message was not so much encouragement as a veiled warning that he did not want a repeat of New Madrid. His lack of faith was evident in the final sentence: "Meanwhile, Pillow is being put in fighting order for another stand."[4]

Confusion reigned regarding the number of troops to remain at Madrid Bend. In addition to the heavy artillery companies, Beauregard intended to leave only a single regiment and two field guns on the island and one regiment and four guns on the Tennessee shore. A company of cavalry would remain for scouting purposes. McCown, ever the alarmist, balked because he felt too many troops were being removed. "My experience in that line makes me tremble for the result," he wrote Polk on March 16. Notified of McCown's response, Beauregard, the next day, wired him directly: "In face of exigencies you must exercise your own judgment of force hitherto directed, but cannot understand why you should tremble for the result. What obstacles intervene to withdrawal as instructed?"[5]

Beauregard's order was carried out on March 18, "the need being absolute for a garrison at Fort Pillow, and no other troops then being available," concluded Alfred Roman. McCown actually removed fewer than half the troops at Madrid Bend. Eight transports embarked on March 18, and three more the following morning. The departing outfits included Marks's and Neely's brigades, 5th Tennessee, Point Coupee Artillery, and Neely's squadron of cavalry.[6]

Colonel Walker remained at Madrid Bend with Gantt's and Stewart's brigades (minus the 5th Tennessee); the 40th and 46th Tennessee, the 1st Alabama, Tennessee, Mississippi; the 1st Alabama; Hudson's and Wheeler's companies of cavalry; and J. W. Stewart's heavy artillery company, now equipped with six field pieces. Roman estimated the force at forty-four hundred, which may be a fair estimate of the for-duty strength, although the aggregate probably topped fifty-three hundred (see Appendix 2). A major error had been committed. While Beauregard's projected garrison of only two regiments was arguably too small, McCown's division-size force was clearly too large.[7]

What would have been an appropriate garrison is problematic. There seems little question that the heavy artillery companies, the field battery, and the two cavalry companies were needed. The question revolves around the seven-and-a-half infantry regiments. There were too many to be sacrificed, yet too few to challenge Pope's army if a serious downriver crossing was attempted. As it turned out, Beauregard's original projection of a three-thousand-man force would have held the position as long as the fifty-three hundred subsequently did. If the three Tennessee regiments had been released, it would have given Sidney Johnston an additional brigade at Shiloh.

Not only the numbers but also the quality of the troops raised serious questions. The 46th Tennessee had only 160 of 400 men armed. The 55th Tennessee was short fifty muskets. The 4th Arkansas Battalion reported in as "badly armed," while the 11th Arkansas had "every variety [of] country guns." At the very least the 31st Tennessee, in the rear at Fort Pillow and armed with newly imported Enfield rifles, should have been swapped with, say, the 46th Tennessee.[8]

Israel Gibbons and three other men in the 5th Louisiana Battalion remained with the baggage and the sick of the outfit, with orders to follow as soon as possible. It proved "impossible to get more than one or two [wagon] loads a day hauled over to and below Tiptonville, [therefore] I am staying here saving as much as possible, for the men were marched off with only what they could carry in knapsacks and haversacks." The acting quartermaster of the 4th Tennessee likewise remained, but upon hearing a false rumor that the enemy had crossed below Tiptonville, he abandoned the regimental property. A band of blacks consequently pillaged the camp, smashing trunks and rifling blankets, tents, and personal belongings.[9]

The activity did not go unnoticed by the Federals. On March 19, a Chicago correspondent noted that the number of enemy camps appeared to have diminished and that there were barely enough tents on the island to support the gun crews. Between March 20 and 22, the *New York Times* reporter stated that not as many tents could be detected, that many wagons had been seen leaving the Tennessee shore, and rumors had circulated that the Confederates had evacuated Meriweather's Landing. The Philadelphia correspondent wrote on March 22 that a large number of wagons had been observed in movement and that many men on litters had been removed. It soon became clear, however, that initial optimism for a complete withdrawal was premature.[10]

Exactly who was to command at Island No. 10 remained in question. McCown, assuming he was to withdraw with the troops to Fort Pillow, departed Tiptonville at 10 P.M. on March 17, leaving Colonel Walker in charge. On March 19, however, he received a dispatch from Beauregard ordering him to return to Madrid Bend and congratulating him on his confirmation as major general. McCown and his staff of nine returned the next day and established headquarters on Madrid Bend March 21. Beauregard's congratulations, though, were less than genuine. He continued actively to seek a replacement, and McCown's days were now numbered.[11]

Throughout mid-March the Federal siege of Island No. 10 continued, creating misery for the defenders. A. H. Beauchamp, stationed at the Belmont Battery, wrote on March 22: "The falling shells made my pulse beat double quick the first day but I have [grown] accustomed to them. Some of them fell in three or four feet of me. . . . but they are easily dodged only when the pieces fly in every direction." Three days later he noted: "Our old boys [veterans] that were at Pensacola last year says that [bombardment] was nothing to this." Another member of the 1st Alabama, Samuel Moore, also became acclimated: "My exposure here in mud and water, sleeping on cornstalks, etc. upset me for a time; but I believe I am nearly straight." An Irishman on the island commented about the mortar shelling: "Faith, its diggin' the graves for us they are with the big shells, before they begin to killin' us off with the little ones." The Confederates still maintained a defiant spirit. At the end of March a regimental band stood on the Tennessee shore, in full view of the fleet, and played martial musical.[12]

The Confederate return fire was usually slow and methodical, and on several days no rounds were expended. The shots from the redan invariably fell short, but the Belmont Battery, although scoring no hits, came close on a number of occasions. Some shots from the Lady Polk, Jr. even overshot their mark and caused the Federal transports to move back upriver. A Chicago correspondent noted: "The batteries upon the island have fired many well-directed shots even at their long range, apparently from a 128-pounder rifled gun." The cannon in question was the Lady Polk, Jr., but on March 19 it was discharged for the last time. The huge cannon exploded and shattered into several large chunks, sharing the fate of its twin at Columbus. "One of the pieces weighing five thousand pounds flew over my head. It flew so low that everybody dodged it," wrote Beauchamp. Israel Gibbons added: "Most luckily nobody was hurt. These big rifled guns of ours have turned out to be very big humbugs." On March 28 and 29, the Rebels suddenly broke their silence and opened a vigorous, though harmless, barrage on the Federal fleet.[13]

Constant repairs were made on the redan parapet, sometimes in broad daylight. The flag was shot down on the afternoon of March 22 and not raised thereafter. The Northern press reported that all but two guns in the tiny fort had been disabled. By March 25 the silence of the battery convinced the Federals that it was completely out of commission. Only one gun, supposedly a Quaker, could be seen. Despite the tons of shells rained upon the redan, however, only two guns were ever struck—an 8-inch columbiad hit during the March 17 attack and repaired the next day, and a 32-pounder, which had its trunnion knocked off on March 20. By the end of the month the river had nearly washed away the parapet front.[14]

Some adjustments were made on the island batteries. An 8-inch columbiad replaced the Lady Polk, Jr. at the Belmont Battery. By late March the eight siege guns in Batteries 4 and 5 had been taken downriver, leaving fifteen pieces on the island. The floating battery was considered adequate to cover the main channel.[15]

The Confederates estimated that the Federal flotilla consisted of seven gunboats, each with 120 men, twelve mortars, thirteen transports with five thousand troops, and five tugs. One ironclad, it was believed, had been disabled during the March 17 attack and removed to Hickman, where it sank. The boat may well have been either the USS *Cincinnati* or the USS *St. Louis,* both of which were temporarily taken upriver for recoaling and soon returned. The *Memphis Appeal* later conceded that the report of a sunken ironclad was in error. On March 23 McCown reported that an ironclad had sunk just out of range and the Federals were attempting to raise it. The Southerners were in fact viewing the removal of the USS *Carondelet* after its accident on the morning of March 23.[16]

On March 25 a heavy artilleryman on the Tennessee shore, known only by the initials "R. B. D.," wrote a letter to a friend in Memphis. "They [Federals] are afraid to come in reach of our guns. We have already sunk one of their boats and another would sink if it were in deeper water," he boasted. The latter vessel, he claimed, was struck by a ricochet shot from the redan and then run into a sandbar. Rumors stated that it was the USS *Benton,* but it was actually the tree collision of the *Carondelet.* "One [shell] was thrown at Sterling's battery today, which did not burst." The cannoneer concluded that all the Federal transports had gone back upriver.[17]

Indications are that Confederate casualties were extremely light. By March 18 the Southern command estimated that twenty-five hundred shot and shell (200 on Saturday, 500 on Sunday, 1,400 on Monday, and 400 on Tuesday), requiring 60,000 pounds of powder, had been used by the Federals on their batteries, resulting in no casualties other than those in the March 17 attack. On March 25 a Federal patrol captured several Confederates who said that up until that time 67 men had been killed and 150 wounded, many of whom were slaves. The next day another captured Southerner placed losses at sixty-nine in the redan, twenty-five on the island, and fifty-seven on the Tennessee shore. Neither of these reports can be substantiated, and it was later widely claimed by the Federals that only three men had been killed by mortar fire during the length of the siege.[18]

The rain from the previous night having passed through, March 18 dawned sunny and clear. Hollins's fleet anchored leisurely at Tiptonville as supplies were being unloaded at the dock. About 8 A.M. a number of men could be seen upriver on the opposite bank throwing down a large pile of wood that had been stacked for the use of the transports. As Hollins determined to investigate, a puff of smoke was suddenly seen and a shell came screeching across the river, embedding in the bank.[19]

The force at Riddle's Point was Palmer's division of four Indiana regiments, the 2d Iowa Battery, and two hundred cavalry. During the night the Federals had taken a circuitous backroad, dragging with them a 24-pounder. In the darkness, however, they positioned the siege gun too far upriver and behind a patch of cypress trees that partially blocked the view. The first shot was aimed at an approaching transport. No sooner had that boat escaped than a second packet followed, obviously unaware that the landing was under fire. The Confederate gunboats blew their whistles in warning, but to no avail. The Yankee gunners opened fire, the shot dropping in the water just behind the boat. A second shot came crashing through the bow, but the boat turned about and made it downriver.[20]

His gunboats fortunately already having steam up, Hollins hoisted the signal from the flagship to engage the battery at close quarters. CSS *Marapaus,* a seven-gun sidewheeler that had recently arrived from New Orleans, quickly got under way. It was followed by CSS *Polk* and CSS *Pontchartrain,* with CSS *McRae,* CSS *Ivy,* and CSS *Livingston* bringing up the rear. The squadron made two separate one-hour attacks. Palmer confessed that at times he "thought [his] men would all be killed or driven from the gun but regularly at intervals of two or three minutes it [the crew] kept up its fire." A member of the 46th Indiana described the squadron's maneuvers: "One boat remained in front while the others came around toward the bayou to obtain a cross fire. A sloop [*McRae*] came on an exact line with our trenches. She opened with three guns, throwing ten-inch fuse shells and six- and ten-pound percussion." The riflemen of the 46th kept the boats from approaching too closely, spraying them with musketballs "which killed a great many of their gunners," boasted a Yankee.[21]

Hollins's boats soon began to take hits. A shot passed through the pilothouse of Lieutenant Joseph Fry's *Marapaus,* and another cut its fore and aft chains, setting a small yawl adrift. *Polk* received a hit that passed through from side to side, coming out below the waterline. The captain immediately signaled that he was taking on water and withdrew. Initially, the fleet casualties were placed at one killed—a sailor struck by splinters. A later update revealed three killed and eight wounded.[22]

Despite more than one hundred rounds fired into the Federal position, the enemy had barely been touched. The fleet withdrew "having done us no further damage than to kill one man by the concussion of a shell and to cave in the rifle pit occupied [by] John Statlord and myself," remembered Augustus Sinks of the 46th. Much of their good fortune was due to the near worthless ammunition of the fleet; only one shell in five exploded.[23]

The next day the 63d Ohio arrived with another 24-pounder and three ammunition wagons. The seventy-five-hundred-pound gun had been towed by hand, the roads being too muddy for horses. Having delivered the cargo, the 63d returned to New Madrid. Palmer moved his troops and guns downriver, just south of Tiptonville, where he established his battery of two siege guns and two 10-pounder Parrott rifles.[24]

The *Memphis Appeal* attempted to downplay the consequences of the engagement of the 18th. The *Polk,* it was claimed, was not in as bad a condition as first reported and was afloat with the use of pumps. No amount of favorable press could change the fact that Hollins's squadron, mounting perhaps thirty-

Fig. 11. The CSS *McRae* serves as the flagship of the Mississippi River squadron (courtesy of Frederick Way Jr., Sewickley, Pa., 1941, and the U.S. Naval Historical Foundation)

four guns, had been bested in an exchange with a single siege gun and two field pieces. C. W. Read, executive officer aboard the *McRae,* conceded that the flotilla was "ridiculed by Confederate soldiers and citizens, and treated with contempt by the enemy." On the night of March 18, Hollins withdrew his vessels below Tiptonville. Aboard the last was a good portion of the garrison's provisions.[25]

McCown had no means of communicating with the squadron and, for all practical purposes, wrote Walker, "this bend is entirely cut off." Israel Gibbons noted that he arrived at Tiptonville on March 21 to discover that all the residents had gone and every shanty was filled with sick soldiers. No steamboats were in dock, and the only way to get to the flotilla was via the riverbank road, which remained virtually impassable due to high water, sloughs, and wrecked bridges. The only escape would be for a packet to run the gauntlet. At midnight Gibbons was awakened with good news. The transport *Kentucky* had made it through, escorted by *Pontchartrain* and *Marapaus,* filled with provisions. All lights were extinguished as the sick were quietly loaded aboard. The vessels made it back downriver safely, although Gibbons admitted "some suspense as [they] slipped past the lights of the enemy's lower battery."[26]

For all intents and purposes, Hollins's squadron, with the exception of the floating battery, was no longer a factor in the campaign. The *New Orleans Pica-yune* lamented: "Oh! For a fleet of gunboats to sweep the Mississippi of our invaders! Not miserable wooden concerns, like those which attacked the battery of three guns mounted in a single night opposite Tiptonville under cover of darkness, and occasionally shots were exchanged with the battery."[27]

Perhaps even more disturbing than the poor performance of the gunboats was Hollins's halfhearted support of his present assignment. From the outset, he had strongly asserted that his boats were useless against ironclads and that his squadron should be redeployed to New Orleans, where it would be of more value and oppose wooden Federal vessels. "I wrote several times most urgently to Mr. [Secretary of the Navy] Mallory telling him that I was of no earthly use up there [upper valley]," recalled the commodore. He was not alone in his opinion. "Some of the officers thought that the gunboats would be of better service at the forts below New Orleans, as [David] Farragut was thought to be about ready to make the attempt to pass the forts, and the position at Island No. 10 was so they could not take it," wrote James H. Tomb, an engineer aboard the *McRae.*[28]

Hollins failed to understand that the primary function of the squadron was not to stop the ironclads, which clearly it could not do, but to keep the west bank clear in order to maintain communications with the rear. As early as March 15, Hollins had stated that he had no intention of jeopardizing his boats in a fight with land-based guns. "I feel the preservation of these boats are of last importance to our country, and am therefore unwilling to risk their loss or

Fig. 12. Commodore George Hollins (courtesy of the Massachusetts Commandery Military Order of the Loyal Legion and the U.S. Army Military History Institute)

being crippled by the guns of the land forces of the enemy except in the last extremity," he wrote. To his officers he was even more emphatic. "The Commodore stated that it was useless to fight batteries with wooden gunboats, as the guns on shore were protected by parapets, and that nothing was to be gained even if we did succeed in killing a few artillerymen," Read remembered.

In the event that the ironclads succeeded in passing the island batteries, Hollins promised that he would do his best to stop them; "in that case I will of course run the risk of loss or capture to keep them back." When it came to pass, however, his words would ring hollow.[29]

The position of Hollins proved curiously similar to that of his counterpart Foote. Both considered their flotillas of such value that they could not be risked in serious combat. Each commander understood his role as purely defensive. Both, in fact, wished to be someplace else.

On March 21, Hollins removed eight heavy guns from his boats and sent them via steamboat to New Orleans. These had apparently been requested by the naval commander of that city for the ironclad CSS *Louisiana*, which was nearing completion. The packet carrying the guns stopped at Memphis, at which time the pieces were seized by the army. Hollins loudly protested, and the weapons were finally released, the commodore dispatching the *Ivy* to take them to Crescent City. He further complained that he had ammunition remaining for only a half day's fight, and he feared that the army was preventing his ordnance shipments from getting through. The petty wrangling aside, Hollins remained more attuned to the problems of New Orleans than he did to his own situation.[30]

10

Someone Said Something about a Canal

COLONEL BISSELL LATER conceded that he had used "pretty strong language" in his conference with Foote, as he had vowed to succeed with or without his help. The next day, March 19, reality replaced indignation as he began to explore the riverbanks for options. He was particularly interested in seeing if St. James Bayou, which entered the Mississippi River seven miles above Island No. 8, was connected to St. John's Bayou, which emptied into the river at New Madrid. A man who had rafted lumber down the bayous for years expressed confidence that a tug could get through and reach Pope and that by cutting here and there, a passage could be cleared for gunboats. Accompanied by four journalists, Bissell ascended St. James Bayou on the tug *Intrepid* for five miles, where he discovered a bank that had been formed by the 1858 flood. A sediment buildup now formed an immense levee, separating the stream and the river by at least three-fourths of a mile of solid earth. Bissell's hopes were dashed.[1]

The next morning, March 20, the disappointed colonel stood atop the levee, waiting for a guide and a dugout to take him back to New Madrid. He noticed an opening in the timber directly across a submerged cornfield. "This proved to be an old wagon road extending half a mile into the woods," recalled Bissell. "Beyond and around was dense forest of heavy timber." The guide estimated that it was two miles to the nearest bayou. Pulling out his memorandum book, the colonel asked him to draw a map, "which he did, showing a straight cut to the first bayou and the general route of the bayous to New Madrid." Bissell explored the four-and-a-half-foot slough and arrived at Pope's headquarters that evening.[2]

When told of Foote's refusal to cooperate with the army, Pope openly cursed. He and his staff had just finished supper when, Bissell remembered, "someone said something about a canal." That someone happened to be Brigadier General Hamilton, who later argued that he, not Bissell, authored the canal concept. Pope sneered at the idea, stating that the entire countryside was ten feet under water. Bissell then pulled out his map and claimed that it could be done in fourteen days. The general called him into another room and asked that he explain. The colonel estimated that the canal would be twelve miles in

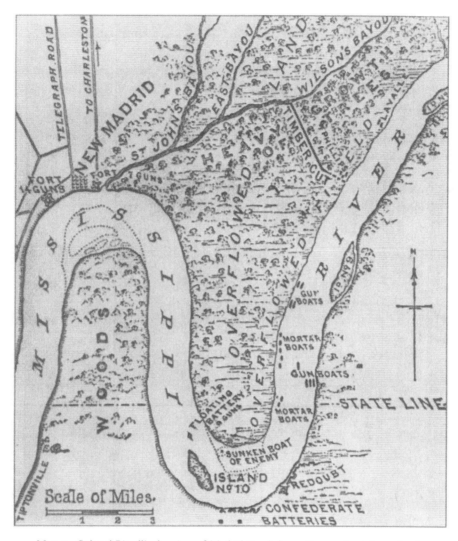

Map 6. Colonel Bissell's drawing of Madrid Bend shows the canal cut from the river to Wilson's Bayou (courtesy of *Battles and Leaders*)

length, two through timber and the balance through crooked and overgrown bayous. Pope, himself a former engineer, was intrigued by the plan and approved the project.[3]

The next morning Captain William Tweeddale and Lieutenant Mahlon Randolph started for Cairo with one hundred men to gather supplies, all of which were collected at Island No. 8. Some six hundred men were assembled, as well as the steamboats *W. B. Terry, Trio, Emma,* and *Hettie Gilmore,* six coal barges, four heavy artillery pieces, axes, saws, tackles, all kinds of tools, and two million feet of lumber.

Phase one began at the Phillips's plantation on March 23. Bissell's later statement that "the way through the submerged cornfield and the half-mile of road was easy enough," somewhat understated the case. A break was made in the levee, but, although barges could get through, it proved too shallow for the steamboat *Terry.* The levee was then cut at an old break a few yards upriver, but so many stumps and logs remained that the boat still could not enter. That night the *Terry* tied up in the rush of water just above the break. Since the Mississippi was two feet higher on the east side, it created a powerful flow of churning water. A near tragedy occurred when Captain Tweeddale and seven men in a small boat were pulled into the undertow, nearly drowning all of them.[4]

The next morning thirty more feet of the levee was cut to raise the water level above the cornfield. Three hundred of Bissell's engineers worked for several hours in cold, waist-deep water, with no hint of complaint. By means of cable lines, the *Terry* was gently lowered into the field. The boat and two barges made it through, although it took all day to go a mere one hundred yards, so numerous were the stumps below the water.

The expedition now reached the flooded forest and began the most difficult task. The entrance was actually a protracted undulation created by the 1811 earthquake and known to the locals as the "sag." It stretched for two miles into a lake (also a result of the 1811 quake) that led to Chepousa Creek and ultimately to Dry Bayou. The term "digging a canal" was thus somewhat of a misnomer, as the primary task was not digging, but cutting stumps and widening a channel that already existed. Tweeddale was assigned the task of cutting, a process that required several stages. First, men on small rafts cut off the large trees eight feet above water level. Another set of men, with boats and lines, dragged away the cut trees by use of a steam capstan aboard the *Terry.* A forty-foot-long raft then moved in with a saw device that cut the stumps four and one-half feet below water level. The saw was in a frame and attached to a pivot and worked like a pendulum, two men pushing and shoving on each end and a fifth guiding the blade. In one stretch, seventy-five trees, each two feet or more in diameter, were cut.[5]

For stumps too close together, three small yawls came forward in lieu of the large raft. Trees a foot or less in diameter presented little trouble. Larger trees proved more difficult, elms being particularly troublesome. They spread out so wide at the bottom that the saw always got pinched. "When the saws ran right we have cut off a stump two feet in diameter in fourteen minutes," described an engineer. "Often it pinched and ran crooked; then a gang would be two or three hours on one of the same size. If there happened to be any

Fig. 13. A way is cleared through the canal for the *W. B. Terry* (courtesy of *Frank Leslie's Illustrated*, Famous Leaders and Battle Scenes of the Civil War, State Historical Society of Missouri, Columbia)

brush under water it added much to the labor; it all had to be fished up and got out of the way." The most obstinate required two and one-half hours for removal. The channel was cleared fifty feet in width, the sternwheelers requiring thirty. It took eight days to clear two miles.[6]

Wilson's Bayou, three miles long, narrow, crooked, and overgrown with trees, now had to be entered. By March 31, the *Terry* was halfway through, and Bissell confidently estimated that he would emerge from Wilson's on April 2. He soon learned just how unpredictable the Mississippi could be. On April 1, the river began dropping at the rate of several inches a day. This meant that stumps cut four feet under the water now had to be cut again. Great heaps of driftwood and debris also washed down, including an occasional swamp oak three feet in diameter. It proved extremely dangerous for men to climb out on the slippery logs in a rushing current and attach cables so that the steam capstan could dispose of them. Lifelines had to be tied so that no one who fell in the water would be sucked down by the undertow. No injuries occurred during the operation, but it was April 6 before Wilson's Bayou was conquered.[7]

While work on the canal progressed, Lieutenant Randolph, with three hundred men, refitted coal barges into makeshift floating batteries. The barges were required because the deep draught ironclads could never make it through the shallow canal. The original plan called for a barge to be lashed to the side of each of three steamboats, the fourth sternwheeler to be kept in reserve. Arrangements were made to pick up some field pieces at New Madrid to add to the four heavy guns they already had. Pope later changed his mind, believing that the lead vessel should be "a fighting boat that could not be disabled." Under the new plan, the lead transport would be lashed with a barge on either side. The barge carrying the guns would have two tiers of cotton bales and barrels packed tightly with cottonwood rails, creating a twenty-four-and-one-half-foot-thick parapet. The steamer was likewise bulkheaded and 150 sharpshooters strategically placed.[8]

On March 31, Pope prematurely informed Halleck that the canal was completed. "The heavy work is done, and it only remains to cut out overhanging limbs and remove driftwood in the bayou," he commented. "Our floating battery is nearly ready, and will carry three heavy guns. There was no indication that the Rebels had made any preparations to counter a downriver crossing. Probably they do not believe it possible to get boats through from No. 8."[9]

If the Confederates had not detected the canal, it was not because the Northern press had failed to supply information. The *New York Tribune* conveniently outlined the four options of the Federals. First, lumber could be sent from Cairo to Bird's Point and transported ten miles by rail and twenty miles by wagon to New Madrid. Flatboats could then be constructed for an amphibious assault. Second, flatboats and skiffs could be sent across the bayous from Island No. 8. Third, one or two tugs could attempt to run past the batteries.

Fig. 14. The ingenious sawing device of Bissell's engineers (courtesy of *Battles and Leaders*)

These vessels were only sixty feet in length and made difficult targets. Since they could reach a speed of fifteen miles per hour, they could be out of range within twenty minutes. Finally, one or two gunboats could attempt a run. The journalist concluded: "The probabilities are that the last-named alternative will be adopted."[10]

Pope became enraged over press leaks. The St. Louis *Republican* and the *New York Tribune* each ran detailed stories on Pope's plan of flanking the island by use of a canal. The latter's crosstown rival, the *Herald,* accused the *Tribune* of treason, but the paper quickly countered that it released no information until a story had appeared in the *Memphis Appeal.* Colonel Gilbert angrily wrote on March 23: "I see a letter in the St. Louis paper of 22d which should cause the writer to be hung for sending it and it is written on Foote's own boat, detailing with minuteness, the plans of Genl Pope in regard to getting troops across the river. . . . This was a profound secret in our camp & the first thing we know a newspaper contains the whole thing. These foolish correspondents of the press do us more harm than the enemy by long odds. Genl Pope is mad today and has a right to be." There is no indication, however, that the Confederates received any pertinent information through the Northern press.[11]

Throughout mid-March and early April 1862, Pope erected a string of batteries along the west bank of the Mississippi, stretching from New Madrid seventeen miles south to Asa Riddle's. The first was established by Plummer's division at Point Pleasant. Shortly after the fall of New Madrid, Plummer was reinforced with the 8th Wisconsin and the 7th Illinois Cavalry. A trooper in the latter noted that nearly every house in the village had been struck by the Confederate battery across the river and one or two dwellings had burned. The main camp was two miles back from the river, and the road leading to it, except for three hundred yards in town, "was a swamp of mud and water to the horse's belly." The Federals had by this time significantly strengthened their position. Two-man rifle pits lined the riverbank for a half mile. The battery consisted of two 10-pounder Parrott rifles and two 13-pounder English rifles.[12]

The Rebels on the opposite bank fired two or three rounds daily from their two 24-pounder siege guns and two 10-pounder Parrott rifles. On Wednesday night, March 26, the shelling lasted for an hour and ten minutes. So ineffective was the fire (the Federals never had a single casualty) that one Yankee acted with contempt: "It is perfectly disgusting the way they waste powder and iron without killing anyone. They have knocked every house in town to flinders, and round shot and shell are lying thick on the ground and yet we haven't a man touched." One day William Smith was in a partially destroyed house when the shelling started. "It [shell] went through the next house to us in which there were several men, but it did not hurt anyone. One man picked up the ball. It was about a twelve pound ball and was fired at a team that was passing, but it was a little too high and ahead of the team. The gunners there said it was a good shot for the distance." On the night of March 27, a group from the 8th Wisconsin crossed the river in an attempt to spike the guns, but the group was fired on by sentinels and returned.[13]

Between March 19 and 21 the Federals established another battery three miles south of Fort Thompson at the Martin Toney house.[14] At sundown on March 19, two hundred men from several batteries at New Madrid went to the location and commenced throwing up an embankment in the shape of a semicircle, ten feet wide with a five-foot trench in front. The next day an additional two hundred men (working in reliefs of a hundred) brought down a 32-pounder from Fort Bankhead. By the next morning, however, the Confederates had constructed a counter battery on the opposite bank, although no guns had been placed. The Yankee gunners fired three practice rounds—one hit the parapet, one struck a house a short distance from the river's edge, and one fell near a horseman in a cornfield. Considering the distance and inexperience of the gunners, "the shooting was quite good," thought William Ball of the 5th Wisconsin Battery.[15]

Down at Riddle's Point, Palmer's gunners continued their periodic exchanges with the gunboats. An old English-style house stood between the two siege guns and two Parrott rifles. Rifle pits stretched for a quarter of a mile along the bank. A gunboat shell that failed to detonate led to a tragedy on March 22. The projectile landed in the front yard of a house a mile back from the river. Several men, considering it harmless, kicked it about for a while. As a soldier of the 47th Indiana attempted to take out the powder with a file, the shell exploded, killing him, the owner of the house, and two of his children.[16]

Palmer's camp was a mile-and-one-half wide strip of land nestled between two bayous. The men stole carpets, stoves, and pictures from nearby abandoned houses to adorn their rifle pits. Palmer believed the locals to be a "queer people." "The men are almost [all] pale & sickly looking while the women are quite as commonly healthy & fat. You will not find in all your acquaintance as many large fat women as are within the circuit of two or three miles here," he informed his wife. On Sunday, March 30, the general heard a few shots from the two Rebel guns across the river. He went down to investigate and found his men taunting them: "Pitch me another," they yelled, and "You damn fools can't shoot worth a damn." He quickly ordered them back to their trenches.[17]

The Federal fort at New Madrid mounted five guns but saw little action. On March 18, two enemy transports came down from the island but turned about and went back. "I suppose they saw with their glasses we were ready for them," suspected Gilbert. Five days later Captain Oscar Pinny, commanding the 5th Wisconsin Battery, jotted to his wife: "We leveled our guns twice yesterday [March 22] at a gunboat [transport] that lies above us. She came around a point but did not get quite close enough to have our guns reach her. When she saw us she pulled back." The Federal cannoneers occasionally took counter battery fire from two small Confederate earthworks across the river, but only one man was ever killed.[18]

The weather from March 24 through early April turned clear and pleasantly warm. At New Madrid, Stanley's division encamped in an oak grove two miles from the river, while Paine's and Hamilton's troops camped further north and east. Pope established his headquarters in the Judge Butler house, three miles from town. On a sunny March 27, the general held a grand review of his New Madrid divisions. Following the review, Pope was heard to say: "I don't care where you go, you can't find a finer looking lot of men than we have got in the army."[19]

Boredom set in as the troops remained idle. A disgusted William Ball wrote: "We have dug entrenchments, hauled cannon, cleaned up forts, wiped regular's as_es and done almost everything that could be thought of that is hard and mean." Morale nonetheless remained high because of regular mail runs. Boasted one soldier: "We get St. Louis & Chicago papers 2 days after publication." Captain Pinny informed his wife on March 28: "The mails here are quite regular now."[20]

"If Island No. Ten falls, we will have to run again, and there is no force between us and Memphis to prevent them from going to that place. The people in Memphis are badly frightened—well they may be, for only six Regiments stand between them and the enemy." Thus wrote Junius Bragg to his wife on March 19. Four days later Surgeon Caldwell of the 46th Tennessee admitted that malingering had become endemic in his regiment. In the previous two days there had been 150 sick requests, only two of which were approved. "Nearly all of them are half scared to death," Caldwell decided. W. T. Avery of the 1st Alabama, Tennessee, Mississippi, posted "12 miles above Aunt Lizzie Meriweather's on the river or a mile back from the river," wrote more optimistically. "I think we will get through safe yet although the enemy are fortifying in great numbers on the other side of the river. Number Ten above is pretty strong and it should [hold]." The arrival of the 1st Alabama, according to member Samuel Moore, had a stablizing effect upon the garrison. "The army was talking about retreating from this point [Island No. 10]. Our presence has acted like a charm."[21]

Because the Confederates had hurriedly evacuated New Madrid, many regiments had no tents or cooking utensils. The infantry now stretched some seventeen miles along the east bank guarding against a Federal crossing. On March 17, the 11th Arkansas camped directly opposite Point Pleasant and had pickets along the river for two miles. On occasion the sentinels would shout at one another, and swaps were even proposed although none occurred. William Mack of the 11th remained encouraged by rumors (false, as it turned out) that Van Dorn's army was coming up on Pope's rear.[22]

On March 24, Colonel E. D. Blake departed Corinth for an inspection tour of Madrid Bend. Arriving in Memphis the next day, he landed seven miles below Tiptonville on March 26. There he boarded one of Hollins's gunboats, which carried him upriver under cover of darkness. Blake found a great deal of sickness. Only two thousand effectives reported for duty, with an additional 1,557 on sick report, the patients being scattered about in private homes. "The sickness was abating; the principal disease, bowel complaint and fever, resulting from exposure," he concluded. On March 17, McCown had boarded five hundred sick on a transport and, under a flag of truce, unsuccessfully attempted to pass the Federal batteries. Pope agreed to accept them as prisoners, but not to let them pass, an offer rejected by McCown.[23]

The food supply remained adequate. Enough flour existed for a 21-day ration and there was bacon for thirty days. Also stockpiled were 18 sacks of coffee (165 pounds each), 100 bushels of rye, and a three-month supply of short rations. Fifty thousand pounds of bacon and fifty thousand bushels of corn could be obtained in Madrid Bend. A gristmill furnished seventy bushels of meal daily.

The Southerners were aware that the Federals could attempt an assault using rafts and skiffs. On March 21, ordnance officer J. T. Trezevant in Memphis wrote Beauregard a letter based on his conversations with several officers who had arrived from Island No. 10. "All rumors say they will throw a force on [the] Tennessee shore from New Madrid landing as far above Tiptonville as they can to elude our gunboats and then move on our rear while [their] gunboats attack us in front. If our gunboats run out of ammunition, as they must in a few more fights or harmless bombardments, this crossing of the river on rafts or launches can be easily effected and all will be lost." The next day the transport *Mears* arrived in Memphis from Madrid Bend, the crew reporting that the Federals were supposedly building rafts for a crossing. When informed of this development in Richmond, attorney general Thomas Bragg enviously wrote in his diary: "What energy they [Federals] display! . . . They will drive us from the island."[24]

The Confederate command apparently did not learn of the existence of the canal until March 29. Scouts indicated that it was being cut nearly opposite Island No. 8, below the mouth of St. James Bayou, and into a small lake connected with St. John's Bayou. Tugs, barges, or flatboats could possibly make it through in high water, it was surmised, but the present water level was "on a stand and may fall."[25]

It seems evident that the Southerners did not take the canal seriously enough; McCown believed it would fail. On April 4, some officers from Madrid

Bend arrived in Memphis and boasted to a journalist: "They [Confederate command] entertain not a particle of doubt of their ability to hold the place." They went on to declare: "It is believed utterly impracticable for the enemy to cut a canal from New Madrid across the bend to a point above the island." The entire country was flooded, and the water would not recede until July. There also remained the matter of the timber: "The trees in the Mississippi bottoms . . . are very large and grow close together, and sent their roots deep into the soil. This growth of our swamps and bayous presents an impenetrable barrier to any such undertaking as that spoken of." After the surrender of the garrison, a Rebel officer was heard to exclaim: "We had heard all about that canal but we did not believe it could be done."[26]

As a precaution, two small, heavy batteries were erected on Watson's Point "to open upon the enemy as well as to prevent the passing up or down of any boat which may possibly force itself through the canal being cut in [St.] John's Bayou." The cannon were positioned as near to the end of the peninsula as the overflowed area allowed. The west battery was about a mile and a half from Fort Thompson and the east battery about the same distance from the mouth of the bayou.[27] (See Table 2 for location, number, and type of weaponry.)

As long as the Madrid Bend vicinity remained flooded, Gray, an engineer, felt no serious concern for the position, believing three to four thousand men capable of holding the garrison. He recommended that a gunboat be placed a mile below Tiptonville to prevent any landing between Point Pleasant and Riddle's Point. "The only landing that could be made by the enemy to affect anything below Point Pleasant must be had in this distance of four miles," he advised. Another boat would also need to be positioned between Doctor Martin Toney's house and Point Pleasant to prevent an amphibious assault.[28]

A curious set of circumstances brought Brigadier General William W. Mackall to Beauregard's headquarters on March 27, 1862. Forty-five years old and a West Point graduate, Mackall was a veteran of both the Seminole and Mexican wars. As a native of Maryland, he believed that he had no constituency to push his fortunes with Jefferson Davis. When he subsequently met with President Davis, he was coolly received and given only a colonel's commission. He was then transferred ("exiled" was the term used by his biographer-son) to the West to be adjutant general to Sidney Johnston, an officer he believed was overrated. Disenchanted and embittered, Mackall quickly fell in line with Davis's archenemy in the West—Beauregard. Through his influence, Mackall received his brigadier's commission in February 1862.[29]

After the fall of New Madrid, Beauregard applied for Mackall to replace McCown. Although the transfer was approved by Johnston, the adjutant general could not be spared until the forces combined at Corinth. On March 27, Mackall finally met with the Louisiana general and received a candid appraisal of the Island No. 10 situation. Matters were considered to be in "a most des-

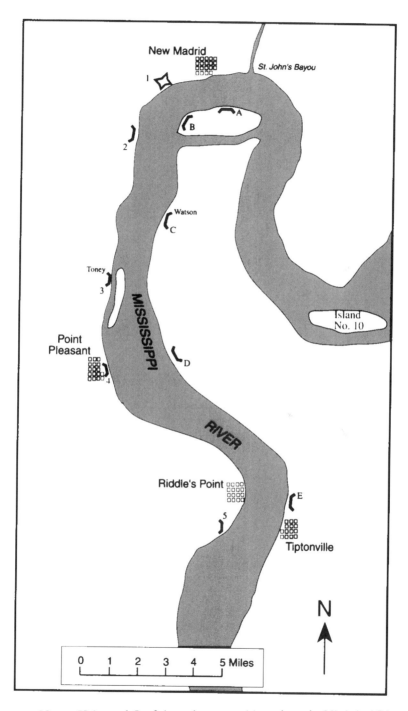

Map 7. Union and Confederate battery positions along the Mississippi River

Table 2. Batteries along the Mississippi

Location	Types
Union	
1. New Madrid	5 heavy guns
2. 1½ mi. above Watson's Landing opposite the slough channel	2 24-pounders
3. Toney House	4 32-pounders
4. Point Pleasant	2 24-pounders
	2 13-pounder English rifles
5. 2 mi. south of Riddle's Point (Andy Riddle)	2 24-pounders
	2 10-pounder Parrott rifles
Confederate	
A. 1½ mi. from and opposite of St. John's Bayou	1 8-inch columbiad
B. 1½ mi. from and opposite of Fort Thompson	2 8-inch siege howitzers
C. Watson's Landing	2 8-inch siege howitzers
	1 32-pounder
D. Opposite Point Pleasant	2 24-pounders
	2 10-pounder Parrotts
E. Aunt Lizzie Meriweather's (Tiptonville)	2 heavy guns

Note: Numbers and letters of locations correspond to those on Map 7.

perate condition" and he would be going "on a forlorn hope." The island had to be held long enough to prepare Fort Pillow properly and to hold back Pope's forces until a strike could be made on the enemy at Pittsburg Landing. Mackall's son later insisted that he accepted the position "with the full knowledge that in all probability he would be compelled to surrender." Beauregard believed that it was imperative that the island hold out twelve days, that is, through April 8. In subsequent conversation with an officer in Memphis, Mackall commented that he had been appointed "into that infernal trap."[30]

The garrison appeared marked for sacrifice. Pope's army had to be held in check long enough for Johnston's army to beat Grant on the Tennessee River. Beauregard admitted as much: "We are in one of those unfortunate positions in war where it becomes necessary to sacrifice a fractional command to save the other and larger portion." It was as close as he would ever come to admitting that his rescue theory of small garrisons had failed. In a real sense, the battle for control of the upper Mississippi was now to be decided on the fields of Shiloh.[31]

Mackall reached Hollins's fleet at 10 A.M. on March 31 and went upriver in a gunboat during broad daylight. It did not take long for him to make his assessment of the flotilla. "I would not give the price of the wood which the boats burn for their present service," he wrote in disdain. The general suggested that the guns and crews be removed to Fort Pillow.[32]

Fig. 15. Major General William W. Mackall (courtesy of *Photographic History of the Civil War*)

Upon his arrival, Mackall boasted that he was "a general made by Beauregard." McCown was asked to remain a day or two, which he agreed to do, but he later changed his mind and abruptly departed. McCown's staff, including Trudeau, left with him, taking virtually all the records of the post. An angry Brigadier General Gantt immediately tendered his resignation, claiming that a junior brigadier had been sent to command. The request was denied. Colonel Walker remained sick in Memphis, and Colonel Steadman was also absent sick. The only information that McCown revealed before his hasty exit was that the enemy numbered thirty thousand, the Federal gunboats could do no harm, and the Yankees were endeavoring to cut a canal but would fail. The position would be safe "until the river fell and no longer."[33]

For the next two days, Mackall's chief engineer, Victor Shelia, proceeded to gather facts. He found fifty-one heavy guns in position, not counting the floating battery. Despite weeks of siege, not a single magazine or bombproof had been constructed on the island, leaving the men entirely exposed. "They imagine themselves safe in some small rooms that have been built in the traverses of Batteries B, Nos. 2 and 3, and which originally were intended for service magazines," Shelia reported. Five kegs of powder had no more protection than a tarpaulin. An adequate amount of solid shot and canister existed, but only enough rounds remained for the columbiads and the rifles for a two-day engagement. The heavy guns could keep the ironclads at bay during the daylight, but whether they would be sufficient if a night run were made remained uncertain. The high-water stage and Reelfoot Lake formed the only protection for the right flank.

Nor did the numbers appear encouraging. There were 2,273 infantry (400 without arms), 1,166 heavy artillery, a field battery, a sapper company, and two cavalry companies. Deducting the necessary guards, it appeared doubtful whether a thousand troops could be assembled within three or four hours as a strike force. There would be little chance of a decisive blow in the event of a serious Federal crossing. "One good regiment would be better than the force which I have," Mackall informed Beauregard. "It [garrison] never had any discipline. It is disheartened—apathetic. So report my best officers. I cannot rely on sentinels or guards."[34]

Obviously, a line from Battery No. 1 to Tiptonville, some twenty-four miles, could not be guarded. No fewer than thirteen possible landing sights existed, besides the four miles on the right flank. Should the enemy feint at one point and land at another, a number of hours would lapse before even a small command could assemble. The position, noted Mackall, could probably not hold ten hours if a downriver crossing were attempted. He ended his message to Beauregard on an ominous note: "When the enemy cross the game is practically up."[35]

11

Success Hangs upon Your Decision

FOR NINETEEN GRUELING days Federal engineers worked on a canal to by-pass the island fortifications. The entire project might not have been necessary had Foote been willing to risk a run past the batteries. The Confederate defenses did not have to be neutralized—only avoided. Even with the canal completed, it became increasingly evident that one or two ironclads were needed downriver to ensure a safe crossing. On March 26, Pope made one last overture. He inquired of the flag officer whether a gunboat could make it through the canal. Such a move was totally unfeasible, but the desperate general was not beyond getting an affirmative answer even to a moot question.[1]

Foote proved unyielding. He saw the army's role as one of support for the navy, not vice versa. His idea was to attack the island defenses (from a distance) simultaneously with a downriver crossing. Assistant Secretary of War Scott, after discussing the issue for hours, was convinced that Foote would not budge. Indeed, there were even rumors of a new Rebel flotilla forming in New Orleans (another small steamboat squadron as it turned out), and Foote believed that his ironclads might have to go on the defensive.[2]

Feeling victory within his grasp, Pope confidently predicted on March 27 that Island No. 10 would fall within a week; "trust me" he assured Halleck. He requested that all naval personnel be removed from two ironclads and replaced with soldiers. While Halleck failed to approve the unorthodox scheme, he did put more pressure on Foote. "Give him [Pope] all the assistance in your power by the use of your gunboats. I think that by a combined operation the object can be accomplished. One or two gunboats are very necessary to protect his crossing."[3]

Halleck, the War Department (vicariously through Scott), and the Northern press were all aligned against Foote. While he stubbornly resisted all pressure, he nonetheless called a second council of war on March 29. Once assembled, the officers were asked to retire and appear individually. In order of rank, Walke was the second officer summoned. Stating that a run past the island batteries was the only way out of the present impasse, Foote inquired whether Walke would volunteer himself and the *Carondelet* for the mission. Walke agreed, but later wrote that he departed with the distinct impression that Foote was simply attempting "to relieve himself of responsibility." The attempt would be made the first stormy or foggy night.[4]

In order to give the *Carondelet* an edge, Foote, in a rare moment of decisiveness, ordered a daring night raid on the redan on April 1. Commanding the attack party was Colonel George W. Roberts of the 42d Illinois. The command consisted of fifty men from the 42d and fifty sailors, ten from each of the ironclads except the *Carondelet*. It had been warm and clear throughout the day, but about 5 P.M. it began to rain. An hour later the men boarded five lifeboats and assembled around the flagship. After dark they were towed downriver by the tug *Spitfire*. Roberts had originally planned to hug the Tennessee shore, but because of a drop in the river and the accumulation of driftwood, this proved impracticable. The boats thus drifted down to the first mortar on the Missouri short and remained in close to the shadows.

At 11 P.M. the expedition got under way. The cutters crossed the river in single file. When the outline of the redan came into view, the boats got into attack formation—three in the first wave and two in the second. The muffled oars allowed the boats to drift to within ten feet of the parapet before a lightning flash divulged their presence. Two sentinels fired and quickly fled. Roberts's men splashed into eighteen inches of water, scaled the parapet, and began spiking the guns. An anxious moment occurred when pickets falsely reported the approach of a Confederate gunboat. The task was completed in half an hour, and by 2:30 Roberts was back aboard the flagship telling of his adventure.[5]

Sometime after 2 A.M. the storm turned ugly, spawning a tornado that struck near New Madrid and worked its way upriver. In the camp of the 7th Illinois Cavalry a tree crashed into a tent, killing a lieutenant and two privates. Seven others were injured, and several horses were killed. The twister continued a swath toward the island, toppling more trees along the way. A lieutenant in Baker's regiment was killed, as well as an officer and a private in the 1st Alabama. The transport *Kenawha Valley* capsized, the cabin being literally ripped from the hull. The violent winds now impartially headed for the Federal transports. *Pike* and *Swallow* lost their smokestacks and drifted helplessly downriver until rescued by *Cincinnati*.[6]

The next morning both sides assessed the damage. The storm had covered a vast front, leaving the Sikeston Railroad under water and the road to Commerce almost impassable. Pope thus directed all supplies to Island No. 8, where they could be loaded on barges and sent through the canal. Scott, meanwhile, urged Foote to launch a general attack. "I resist and am cautious, and they have great confidence in my judgment," the flag officer informed his wife.[7]

Later during the morning of April 2, the Confederate floating battery, relatively quiet throughout the siege, suddenly came to life. She was maneuvered into position to get a shot at the mortars along the Missouri shore. Lieutenant Samuel Averett's crew consisted of a Louisiana company, the Pelican Guards,

Fig. 16. The April 1 night raid of Colonel George W. Roberts on the redan (courtesy of *Harper's Weekly*, April 26, 1862)

and a company of the 1st Alabama. This complement left him shorthanded on two guns, but he had no luck in obtaining infantry volunteers. Averett's shots proved ineffective, and his floating battery retired to its former position.

The Confederates had stirred up a hornet's nest; at noon Foote counterattacked. *Cincinnati, Benton,* and *Carondelet* took up positions along the Missouri shore and, along with the mortars, shelled the floating battery for half an hour. The Rebel vessel was seriously damaged, with several beams displaced and splinters flying in all directions. One shot made a direct hit on the bow, while another dismantled an 8-inch columbiad. Averett's vessel lost its cable and drifted helplessly downriver for some distance, where it was met by the Confederate transport *Ohio Belle* and towed to shore two miles below the island.[8]

Pope had understood that the *Carondelet* was to make its run on the night of April 1. When nothing occurred, he fired off an angry letter to Halleck. "I could tell you many strange and startling reasons given by the commodore for not risking it, such as his grave responsibility to the country for the security of St. Louis, Louisville, etc. He says if the *Benton* were taken by the enemy, or in fact any of his ironclad boats, which (as he says) are invincible fighting upstream, his whole fleet would be routed, and St. Louis and Louisville be at the mercy of the enemy. . . . It is useless to argue against such ideas." His own idea was that an ironclad would not have one chance in a thousand of being damaged, or even seen, in a night run. He estimated that the vessel would not even have to come within three-fourths of a mile of the enemy's guns.[9]

Unconvinced of Foote's resolve, Pope made plans to go it alone. The general noticed on a map that the main road down the bend intersected with the Island No. 10–Tiptonville Road about midway between them. Once that intersection was secured, his forces could move in either direction.[10] He devised a plan whereby the Federal floating battery would be towed at night to the island opposite New Madrid. It would closely follow the shore until it reached the mouth of the slough. From that position the river could be commanded for a mile and one-half, and the Confederate battery at Watson's enfiladed. A division would then be landed and immediately entrench.

In the doubtful hope that Foote would send down an ironclad, a second plan was also devised. The night before the crossing, the gunboats and transports would silently pass down the river, close to the Missouri shore and behind Island No. 11, anchoring opposite Tiptonville. Early the next morning, the force would cross, thus catching the Confederates in a cul-de-sac. The gunboat could easily deal with the Confederate naval flotilla if it dared make an appearance.[11]

The night of April 2, an exasperated Pope informed Halleck that he had given up all hope on Foote's participation. Since the run had been postponed until a rainy or foggy night, it would take too long for the perfect weather conditions. The river was falling several inches a day, possibly allowing the Confederates to escape through the swamps. If the garrison were to be bagged, he must move quickly.[12]

Walke experienced problems of his own. Although the island and shore batteries had little elevation, he remained concerned about his vulnerable hurricane deck. The one-half-inch plating had proven inadequate in repelling 8-inch shot. To solve the problem, he had the deck covered with planks from an old barge wreck. Surplus chain was also coiled at certain vulnerable spots. The exposed pilothouse was completely wound up to the windows with 11-inch cable. Cord wood was piled around the boilers on the exposed port side. A barge loaded with coal and bales of hay was lashed to the port side to protect the magazine and unarmored sections of the vessel. The engineers also rerouted the steam through the pipes aft into the wheelhouse rather than the smokestacks, thus eliminating the puffing sound. The end product, according to Walke, "resembled a farmer's wagon prepared for market."[13]

Hoping for favorable conditions, Walke decided to make his run on the evening of April 4. As the hours ticked away, the commodore grew nervous. The weather gave every indication of a clear night, meaning that the passage would have to be made quite late, if at all. At sunset his fortunes began to change: a haze appeared on the river, the winds shifted, and dark clouds loomed on the northwest horizon. At dusk Buford arrived with twenty-four sharpshooters of the 42d Illinois, who were strategically placed around the boat to harass Rebel gunners. At 8 P.M. the *Carondelet* moved upriver about one mile to have the protective barge attached. The guns were run in, the port doors closed, and all lights extinguished.[14]

Piloting the *Carondelet* would be First Master William R. Hoel, on loan from the *Cincinnati*. With twenty-one years' experience as a river pilot on the Mississippi, Hoel boasted of having made 193 trips to New Orleans. The charted course was a tricky one. There was a large sandbar that forced river traffic to move toward the Tennessee shore and then take a sharp starboard turn to enter the Missouri channel. Yet another possibility was a narrow channel across the bar that was navigable in high water. It was dangerous to negotiate, however, and enfiladed by the Belmont Battery. The little irregular chute next to the Missouri shore had been blocked by the Southerners. To continue down the Tennessee chute was considered near suicidal. The decision was made; it would be the Missouri channel.[15]

At 10 P.M., with a storm looming, the sailors cast off shore lines. So silently did the boat proceed that the crew scarcely knew she was under way. It suddenly began to rain in sheets. The passage went smoothly the first half mile, with no response from the Confederates as the boat passed Donaldson Point. The redan, still out of commission, also remained silent. Some aboard began to remark that the boat might pass totally undetected. As she came abreast with mainland Battery No. 2, however, a five-foot-high flame suddenly shot out of the smoke-stacks. The engineer immediately opened the flue caps, which caused the flames to subside. No alarm sounded.[16]

It is difficult to understand, beyond the poor visibility, why the Southern sentinels did not detect this initial flame burst. For nights they had been anticipating a run, and large log fires had been kept burning along the Tennessee shore, illuminating the river for one hundred yards.[17]

A second flame burst suddenly shot from the ironclad's stacks. Walke demanded to know "why in the hell the flue caps were not kept open." It was later discovered that in rerouting the steam to muffle the noise, an unforeseen problem had been created. The dampness had been removed from the stacks, causing the soot to catch fire. This time the Confederates did take notice, and sentinels sounded the alarm. Five rockets went up from the mainland and from the island, followed by a cannon shot from mainland No. 2.

Having been discovered, Walke had no alternative but to make a run for it. The boat accelerated to full steam ahead. Mainland Batteries 3 and 4 opened fire, but the shooting was five to thirty-five yards high. In the distance *Benton, Pittsburg,* and several mortars offered support fire. *Carondelet* neared the tip of the island, and Hoel had to maneuver around the shoals. A boatswain's mate was stationed on the forecastle with a lead line to determine channel depth. A master's mate stood atop the upper deck to yell information to Hoel, who directed the pilot at the wheel. This proved to be the crucial moment, as the outline of the channel could only be detected by flashes of lightning. Suddenly Hoel shouted "Hard-a-port," as the boat grazed the head of the island.

So close did the ironclad pass the Belmont Battery that during a lull in the thunder a Rebel officer could be heard to shout: "Elevate your guns!" Walke suspected that the barrels had been depressed to keep the rain out. "The [Confederate] officer ordered the guns elevated just in time to save us from the direct fire of the enemy's heaviest fort; and this, no doubt, was the cause of our remarkable escape," he recalled. The attached barge encumbered the *Carondelet,* which was already one of the slowest boats in the squadron. It required half an hour to clear the mainland and island batteries. Contrary to earlier reports, there was no heavy battery at the foot of the island.[18]

It so happened that Lieutenant Colonel W. D. S. Cook arrived on the island with his 12th Arkansas just in time to witness the ironclad pass. Owing to the intense darkness, he reported, the guns "could not be pointed as to disable her." J. M. Grace, a member of the 1st Alabama, Tennessee, Mississippi, was also an eyewitness. "The wind was blowing so hard that I had to hold to a sapling to keep from being blown in the River. It was a raining torrent," he described to his father. Suddenly there was a flash of lightning, and he "saw a huge monster [ironclad] coming down the river."[19]

Fig. 17. The *Carondelet* runs the gauntlet (courtesy of *Harper's Weekly*, April 26, 1862)

The *Carondelet* had emerged unscathed from the shore fire, but the floating battery still remained. A reconnaissance the previous day had located it three miles below the island on the Tennessee shore. A light could be seen burning in the distance as the ironclad bore over to the Missouri shore. The floating battery, still being overhauled from its bruising of the previous day, timidly fired only six or eight rounds, one of which struck the coal barge and another a bale of hay.[20]

In rounding to at New Madrid, a misunderstanding occurred between the pilots and the engineers. The result was that the boat ran hard aground fifty yards from the landing. By moving the forward guns to the stern, the boat was backed off and made secure at 1 A.M. From start to finish the episode had lasted three hours. An estimated forty-nine shots had been fired at the boat, yet it had not been hit a single time. Whiskey was passed among the crew.[21]

In the morning Pope's soldiers eagerly sought to catch a glimpse of the *Carondelet*. The boat appeared quite formidable, thought a Wisconsin artilleryman. "She is of course ironplated and is painted black. . . . [Her crew] are hardy looking fellows with the regular dress of a tar—the usual blue round about and breeches, and a cap without a brim, and with a broad top. . . . They are jolly crews."[22]

Pope sent a messenger up the canal, informing Foote of the safe arrival of the boat. He also urged that a second ironclad be sent down, noting that the enemy transports had constantly passed the Federal shore batteries without harm. His best artillerists, who were Regulars, had informed him that it was utterly impossible to fire with any accuracy at a moving target at night. The risk, he contended, would be much less than ten thousand men crossing a river with inadequate protection. "The success of the operations hangs upon your decision." Scott concurred, and in a message pleaded for a second ironclad to make the run.[23]

The ease with which the *Carondelet* had passed the island had not, however, made a believer of Foote. Perhaps he simply refused to believe that his gloomy predictions had not been fulfilled. More eager to challenge Pope's contentions than the Confederates, the flag officer dictated: "I cannot consider the running of your blockade, where the river is nearly a mile wide and only exposed to a few light guns, at all comparable to running it here, where a boat has not only to pass seven batteries, but has to keep 'head on' to a battery of eleven heavy guns at the head of Island No. 10, and to pass within three hundred yards of thirty strong fortifications." He repeated his long-held contention that the safety of the Midwest rested upon his shoulders. Besides, he argued, there was insufficient time to prepare another barge, and the weather was clearing. He was miffed "to find the expression . . . that 'the success of the operations hangs upon your decision.'" Having ranted on, he nonetheless concluded that he would send another ironclad down if at all possible.[24]

Scott's patience had come to an end. Going over the flag officer's head, he wired Halleck and Secretary of War Edwin Stanton requesting that Foote be relieved "from a responsibility which he is not willing to assume." At 5:15 P.M. on April 6, before a response had arrived from either St. Louis or Washington, Foote's consent message was received, and Scott cancelled his request.[25]

With the promise that another ironclad would be sent down on the night of April 6, Pope postponed his crossing another twenty-four hours. Not content to remain inactive, however, he requested Walke to take the *Carondelet* on a downriver reconnaissance. The ironclad ventured to Tiptonville, exchanging shots with the battery opposite New Madrid along the way. The boat docked at Point Pleasant and picked up Brigadier General Palmer. As the ironclad eased back out into the channel, a few rounds were fired in a vain attempt to draw a response from the enemy battery at Meriweather's Landing. A decision was then made to attack the battery opposite Point Pleasant. The boat turned about and headed back upriver, closely hugging the Tennessee shore.[26]

It proved an unequal contest. The *Carondelet* fired three bow guns at the tiny fort, which had only two light 24-pounders with which to respond. So devastating were the navy guns that the army officers aboard concluded that the boat could neutralize all the downriver shore batteries. The earthwork was manned by the Southern Guards of Memphis. Three or four of the cannoneers were killed, and the others abandoned their guns and fled. A detail of the 27th Illinois went ashore and spiked the guns, hacked apart the carriages and limbers (which had already been damaged during the shelling), and threw the ammunition into the river.[27]

As the landing was taking place, a tall Rebel sniper hiding behind a large cottonwood tree began taking shots at the shore party. For fifteen minutes sharpshooters returned fire, aided by blasts of canister from the gunboat. Even as the Federals approached to within a hundred yards, he continued to stand his ground. Finally he dropped both his muskets and was seen running into the woods. The man was captured the next day, and it was discovered that the tip of his nose had been shot off.[28]

It had taken nearly all day to complete the reconnaissance. Upon Walke's return, Pope informed him that another ironclad was to make the run past the island that evening. He requested that both gunboats move downriver the next day and complete the destruction of the Rebel batteries. The army was also put in motion, Paine's division moving to the New Madrid dock at dawn on April 7.[29]

Even before daylight of April 6, there were those with the fleet who predicted that it would rain before day's end. Second Master Bates of the *Benton* flatly stated that it would come before six bells. Throughout the hot afternoon, Lieutenant Egbert Thompson worked to prepare the *Pittsburg* for the passage ordered for that night. Hoping to repeat its success, the gunboat *Pittsburg* would follow the same course of the *Carondelet*. A barge piled with three tiers of baled hay would be lashed to the portside and piled to the upper deck.[30]

Dark clouds blotted out the moon that night, with distant flashes of lightning on the horizon. At 2 A.M. the *Pittsburg* quietly eased into the channel. Rain began to fall heavily, and within minutes there was a deluge, uncannily mirroring the *Carondelet's* experience. The redan offered no resistance as the boat passed. Three shots suddenly rang out. A journalist aboard the flagship described what then transpired: "Lights gleamed one after the other [on the mainland], and we knew then that the whole [Confederate] force were at their guns. There was a mysterious silence, which only made us the more anxious. It was soon broken."[31]

The enemy now opened fire in earnest. At times there was only a solitary shot, but then followed by five or six consecutive blasts. A total of seventy-three rounds was expended, all failing to strike the target. The stern of the flagship remained crowded with spectators, despite the downpour. "Half the crew was soon in a stir to see the fun and was soon on the afterpart of the deck watching the enemy fire on the '*St. Louis*,' [*Pittsburg*] for by this time she was opposite their batteries, and the flashes of their guns and roaring was almost incessant," observed a sailor.[32]

Within forty-five minutes the ironclad had passed the island, but the enemy continued firing, apparently believing that another boat was attempting a passage. Volleys of musket fire could be heard from the island until daylight. At 5 A.M. the *Pittsburg* docked safely at New Madrid. The way had been prepared for the final phase of the campaign.[33]

At dawn on April 7, Walke sent an officer aboard the *Pittsburg* with instructions to follow the *Carondelet* into action. To the commodore's disgust, Lieutenant Thompson replied that he was not ready for service and gave no indication when he would be. The army's transports were already beginning to emerge from the canal, and in the daylight they would be exposed to the fire of the enemy's guns. Walke could wait no longer. At 6:30 A.M. the *Carondelet* moved to the attack, Walke signaling the *Pittsburg* to "follow my motions." A half hour elapsed before the boat responded.[34]

The ironclad moved slowly downriver to Watson's Landing and engaged the small fort there, "feebly assisted by our batteries on shore," Walke contemptuously reported. The earthwork, about an acre in size, mounted two 8-inch siege howitzers and a 32-pounder—heavier guns than those opposite Point Pleasant, but still no match for an ironclad. Walke fired slowly, and he frequently ordered a ceasefire to let the smoke clear. One shot from the fort struck the *Carondelet's* bow armor, but bounced off. Another shot destroyed the lifeboats and rearranged the steering gear. After repairing the gear, Walke moved in for

Fig. 18. The *Carondelet* and the *Pittsburg* engage the Confederate battery at Watson's Landing (courtesy of *Battles and Leaders*)

the kill. By this time the *Pittsburg* had belatedly joined the fray and was firing shells dangerously close over the *Carondelet's* bow. The Rebel 32-pounder was soon capsized by a direct hit on the muzzleface, and the other pieces dismounted. As the Southern gunners ran for their lives, three men from Walke's gunboat went ashore and spiked the guns.[35]

The two ironclads now moved upriver and attacked the Confederate batteries on the upper peninsula. The first earthwork, about one-half mile above Watson's Landing, consisted of two 8-inch siege howitzers. One piece was quickly dismounted and abandoned by its crew. A quarter of a mile upriver was the northernmost battery, at what the locals sometimes called Water's Point. This work contained a single 8-inch columbiad mounted on a naval pivot carriage. According to a Chicago journalist, the Confederates fired a shot, after which there was a huge explosion from an unknown cause, and men could be seen running in all directions. "Observing the enemy retreating . . . we fired on them as they ran," noted Walke. A considerable amount of ammunition was found at both works.[36]

Back at New Madrid, troops lined the bank to watch the two-hour engagement. "The four companies of artillery stationed here and the companies of regulars were spectators of the battle. They stood on the bank of the river by our camp and watched. . . . They [gunboats] were about ten miles below us, in plain sight. We could see the bright flame and white smoke leap from the cannon's mouth," William Ball described.[37]

Four transports and five barges now exited the canal. Paine's division constituted the first assault wave, the troops having anxiously waited for hours. At 4 A.M. on April 7, Private William D. Hynes wrote his father: "The orderly passed through the regiment at 3:30 waking us all up to get breakfast and be ready to start by five. So I suppose we are going at last." Three thousand troops boarded at 10:30, including four Illinois regiments, Houghtaling's Illinois Battery, and two companies of the 1st Illinois Cavalry. One soldier not involved in the crossing expressed grave concerns about the prospects: "We may have another Ball's Bluff affair—as the rebels are pretty strong."[38]

The steamers moved out at 11 A.M. Having received a report from a spy, Pope cancelled his original instruction to Paine and ordered his troops not to entrench but to move inland. As the transports pulled in at Watson's Landing, the regiments began debarking "amid the cheers of the men," wrote Paine. Stanley's and Hamilton's men watched apprehensively from the west bank. "We were expecting every minute to hear the enemy open," an officer expressed to his wife. Paine's men quickly passed the remains of the Rebel fort.[39]

There was little at the landing other than the home of Daniel Watson, which an exaggerated New York news column called a "Tennessee plantation." A black person came up and reported that "Massa Watson" had gone into the swamps "scared to death." A Rebel captured at the landing led the column to

Fig. 19. The Federal debarking at Watson's Landing on April 7, 1862 (courtesy of *Frank Leslie's Illustrated*, May 3, 1862)

Tiptonville. Colonel James D. Morgan's brigade spearheaded the march, followed by G. W. Cumming's brigade. As the Federals advanced, a frantic woman ran up to Paine and exclaimed: "They [Northerners] are stealing all my chickens, General. I sha'n't have one left." Paine replied: "I am exceedingly sorry, ma'am, but we are going to put down the rebellion if it takes every chicken in the state of Tennessee."[40]

The transports quickly returned to New Madrid to board the second assault wave—David Stanley's division of four Ohio regiments and Dee's Michigan Battery—about three thousand troops. "My company was in the bow of the steamer and I was the first man to go up the bank [at Watson's]," boasted Captain Jackson. Stanley had orders to hold his division at the beachhead until the arrival of the third wave, and then follow Paine's division to Tiptonville.[41]

As the division came ashore, Stanley shouted congratulations to Walke. The commodore was very affable and invited him and several other officers aboard for a drink. About this time the *Pittsburg* came up, and Lieutenant Thompson likewise shouted his congratulations. "Damn you, I don't congratulate you," shouted Walke in reply. "You skulked behind my boat and fired shots over my deck. Damn you, if you ever do such a thing again, I will turn my batteries on you and blow you out of the water." Stanley was pained to see such an outburst, but the officers "considered it a naval affair and [they] turned away."[42]

Hamilton's division did not cross until after sunset. The 26th Missouri was the last of the regiments to debark, and Pope happened to be aboard the transport. As the boat pulled into the landing, it nearly collided with the Federal floating battery. An enraged Pope accused the pilot of the steamer of trying to kill them all. The infantry having crossed, the Federal ironclads proceeded downriver to Tiptonville. The trap was now effectively closed.[43]

12

The Only Point of Exit

DESPITE THE DRAMATIC engagement with the *Carondelet,* Brigadier General Mackall continued to believe that a gunboat had not penetrated his defenses. On the morning of April 6, Confederate scouts spotted a double-deck boat in St. John's Bayou, convincing the general that only a transport had passed. The vedettes had actually sighted the Federal steamboats hiding in the bayou. Mackall should have deduced this, for only two days earlier a spy had reported that transports were passing through the canal.[1]

At noon the ominous sounds of gunfire could be heard downriver. At 12:30 a courier advised Mackall that an ironclad had, indeed, slipped past the island. The general still believed that all was not lost. Unaware that Federal transports were waiting to emerge from the canal, Mackall surmised that the gunboat could not cross more than five hundred infantry at a time. If the first assault wave could be repulsed before the troops had a chance to dig in and establish a beachhead, the day might yet be saved. He planned to assemble the division at dark and move to the center of the bend. From there he would be within four or five miles of any landing point. Captain Andrew Jackson, Jr. was directed to remain behind to command the shore batteries. The big guns on the island would be manned by a battalion of the 1st Alabama, 350 strong, supported by the 12th Arkansas, 300 muskets. Jackson was to hold as long as possible and then spike the guns and escape toward Reelfoot Lake.[2]

Mackall assembled his mobile column at Madrid Bend. Included were twenty-five hundred infantry, Stewart's battery of light artillery, and about 150 cavalry. The infantry comprised five regiments and two battalions—the makings more of a brigade than a division. The troops arrived at Watson's Landing about 2 A.M. amid a light rain and formed a line of battle.[3]

Early on April 7, Mackall hurriedly summoned his regimental commanders. "Gentlemen, I have some good news to communicate at last," he reported. Another ironclad (*Pittsburg*) had attempted to pass the island during the evening, but had been repulsed. There was great relief, but it was shortlived; the information again proved to be faulty. Within hours the truth became known, and at noon a council of war was called. Intelligence now indicated that two gunboats and as many as five transports were below the island and that the Federals were landing five thousand men at a time at Watson's, only three miles distant. In a unanimous decision, the division was ordered south toward Tiptonville.[4]

Mackall's actual intention has been questioned by historians. It has been suggested that his plan was "either to be met at some point on the bank by transports or to follow high ground to Reelfoot Lake where he would attempt a crossing on rafts to safety." Baker, however, mentioned "making for that narrow and partially overflowed bridge of land between the lake and the river, which was the only point of exit." Mackall wrote of escaping via "a sluice, which here [Tiptonville] emptied into the river, and then by the bank of the river. . . . This was practicable, if the gunboats did not interfere."[5]

Meanwhile, the Federal advance from Watson's made significant progress. Scouting the road north, Colonel Cumming's brigade of Paine's 4th Division uncovered an abandoned artillery camp and soon came "in full view of the famous Island No. 10." A half dozen captured Rebels claimed that only five men remained on the island. Colonel Morgan's brigade pushed south, encountering signs of a hasty Confederate retreat—a road strewn with equipment. The troops suddenly encountered the entire Confederate force, nine miles from the landing. Morgan deployed his men, but after exchanging a few shots, the Confederates mysteriously withdrew.[6]

Morgan cautiously advanced, with Cumming's brigade a mile and a half in his rear. By late afternoon the Federal spearhead was just south of Tiptonville. Peering over a high board fence, Morgan saw the main Confederate encampment. When two companies of the 16th Illinois advanced as skirmishers, the Southerners again fled. The sight of so many of the enemy fleeing before so few Federals elicited wild cheers from Morgan's men.[7]

Pope's remaining units brought up the rear. Stanley's division rounded up forty prisoners in the process, most of whom were sick. The troops camped within a quarter of a mile of Tiptonville, with Hamilton's division three miles in the rear of Stanley. Plummer's division remained at the landing, and Pope spent the night in the Watson house. At 7 P.M. he wired Halleck: "Think we shall bag the whole force, though not certain. No escape below Tiptonville, except by wading shoulder-deep in swamp." About a hundred prisoners had already been taken. Buoyed by his own enthusiasm, Pope boasted that he would be in Memphis in seven days.[8]

For Mackall, all was lost. At Tiptonville his troops could see the smokestacks of the ironclads. The men spent the night in a cypress swamp. Realizing that they were caught in a trap, the demoralized Confederates anticipated an enemy attack at daylight. Some 359 deserters crossed the line that evening and surrendered. At 2 A.M. on April 8, Mackall tendered the unconditional surrender of his command.[9]

Some of his troops decided not to wait for the inevitable and attempted to make it out through the swamps. Stragglers from Henderson's, Clark's, and

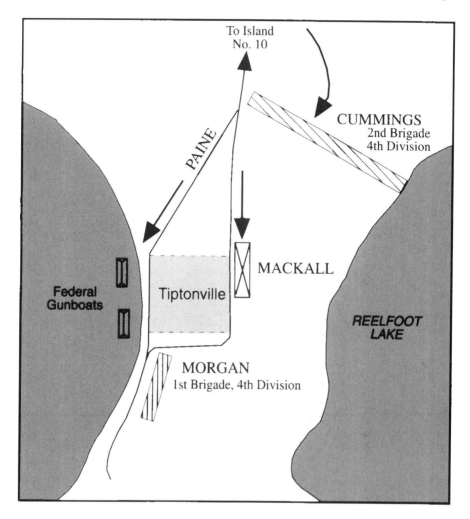

Map 8. Capture of Confederate forces, April 7, 1862

Brown's regiments waded around the Federal flank and moved north to link up with the Confederate force at the island. At times they were knee deep in water, and in other places water was over their heads. A guide was finally found who, for a bribe, led them out. Doubtless a few men attempted to filter out by taking the more treacherous southern route, but only one such party is documented. Four Confederates made a raft and floated in the swamps for a considerable distance. They suddenly found themselves drawn into the Mississippi River, being pushed along in the choppy waters. The group finally attracted the attention of a farmer, who then got a skiff and rescued them. The four eventually made it to Memphis.[10]

Throughout the afternoon of April 7, couriers arrived at Jackson's head-quarters. They informed him that the Yankees had effected a landing, driven Mackall's division back toward Tiptonville, and occupied the ground between the divided Confederate forces. That afternoon Lieutenant Averett reported that an enemy force had come up in the rear of his floating battery and moved to within one mile of the island, capturing several of his men. Averett responded by opening all the valves, partially submerging the *New Orleans* and all its guns. An immediate evacuation was made of the island and shore batteries.[11]

Hoping that a sunken fleet might effectively plug the river channel, the Confederates set about to destroy the transports positioned two miles south of the island. The *Prince* was scuttled, the *John Simonds, Mohawk, Grampus,* and *Yazoo* sunk, and the *Desoto, Red Rover, Mears,* and *Ohio Belle* partially sunk, the latter floating down to New Madrid. Two boats, the *Winchester* and the *Kenawha Valley,* had been previously destroyed, the latter by a storm. The hospital boats *Champion* and *Admiral* remained intact, as did the wharf boat.[12]

The heavy artillery companies that made it out departed at 6:30. The column, with seven companies of about three hundred men, took the twenty-mile road through the swamps to Stone's Ferry on Reelfoot Lake. Hudson's cavalry company spearheaded the second column, consisting of the 300 troops of the 12th Arkansas, 150 of the 1st Alabama, a few men of the 11th Arkansas, and some stragglers from three regiments of Mackall's command, including 140 men of the 46th Tennessee. The number of escapees totaled about one thousand.[13]

The extremely dark night and rugged terrain made for a chaotic march. Some of the men became separated and stumbled into enemy lines. The first column arrived at the lake at noon on April 8, only to find three flats and a few canoes and skiffs available. It is difficult to understand why a greater effort was not made to evacuate via the lake. As early as March 9, Polk had dispatched an officer to examine the ferries as a possibility for a future evacuation "in case [McCown] could not do so by the river." In late March Lieutenant Colonel Blake had declared the lake impassable to either flats or rafts. He was referring to a possible Federal crossing, but obviously he was incorrect, for the Confederates used this route to escape.[14]

Mackall's evacuation plan more properly should have been north, toward the lake, rather than south toward Tiptonville. Escape at the latter was nearly impassable because of high water. A defensive line should have been constructed south of the island, from the river to the lake, as had been done north of the island. There were a number of unmounted 24- and 32-pounders lying about (useless against ironclads) that could have been mounted to add muscle to this line. A staunch rear guard action might have held long enough for the balance of the garrison to escape.

Jackson's men completed their crossing by sunset on April 8. The infantry arrived sometime late that afternoon and found Hudson's troopers waiting in line. Chaos soon broke out. The cavalrymen persistently continued to load their horses, even though a number of infantrymen waded into the water in hopes of being boarded. Lieutenant Colonel Cook directed that all horses be left until his men had crossed, but the order was ignored. The troopers kept their boats far out in the water, and one even took an ax and threatened to sink a canoe if anyone other than his company members approached. One boat was so damaged by horses that it sank. Cook did form a ragtag battle line in the event of a Federal pursuit. Some of the men busied themselves by fashioning makeshift rafts. At best, the crossing would be precarious, the lake at that point being a mile wide, with a rapid current and a maze of cypress brakes. A driving rain that night ceased all activity. Many of those remaining suffered from measles and mumps.[15]

A bitter cold front came through the next morning, accompanied by a light snow. Once across the lake, the troops used a ferry to cross the Obion River and make their way to Dyersburg, where they were warmly received by the populace. From there the column moved to Bell Station (northeast of Brownsville) on the Memphis & Ohio Railroad, arriving on April 11. Two days were spent regrouping and waiting for stragglers. After days of "unparalleled suffering and exposure," the men finally made it out to Memphis and safety. "We are without clothing, tents, and other comforts, but hope soon to be able to take the field again," reported Cook. Surgeon Jennings wrote more candidly: "The 12th [Arkansas] Regiment is *entirely* demoralized."[16]

A little before 9 P.M. on April 7, an unidentified vessel was sighted in the darkness coming astern of the flagship. The call to quarters sounded, and all hands scrambled to their posts. The oncoming boat sounded four shrill whistles, obviously attempting to communicate. Investigating the waters ahead, the tug USS *Dauntless* discovered the Confederate transport *Desoto,* bearing a flag of truce. On board were two lieutenants, George S. Martin and E. S. McDowell, who wished to address Foote.[17]

Once aboard the flagship, the officers stated that the island had been abandoned and that they wished to discuss surrender terms. The flag officer responded mildly, but firmly, that no conditions were acceptable but unconditional surrender. The officers stated that they must return and confer with their superior, Captain W. Y. C. Humes. Captain Phelps of the *Benton* accompanied the lieutenants to clarify matters. The island and shore batteries were formally surrendered at 3:25 A.M. Foote directed Buford to occupy the Rebel works in the morning.[18]

Shortly after 6 A.M. seven companies of Colonel Heg's regiment took possession of the island, the colonel being the first to raise the stars and stripes. "Their Camp was scattered over five miles in length [on the Tennessee shore], tents standing, and most of their trunks and Baggage was scattered all over," he wrote. One trooper observed that "they left in such a hurry that they scattered their coats, blankets, dishes, and everything else along the route. I think they are about gone up." A *New York Times* correspondent, investigating the mainland, found the ground completely plowed up from the shelling. Something else attracted his attention—a camp of fifteen to twenty Memphis women, dressed in a cosmopolitan fashion. "It required no penetrating optics to determine their position and calling," he concluded. Indeed, they proved just as willing to offer their services to the Federals.[19]

The list of the captured included 17 officers, 368 men, 100 sick, and 100 sailors who formerly worked the transports. George Boomer considered them "the most insulting lot of men I ever saw, especially those from Alabama." One journalist admitted that the officers, generally ages 28 to 35, were "quite spunky even in front of us." Many of the Tennessee cannoneers were Irishmen from Memphis and Nashville and had had quite enough of the war. The story was told that virtually all of Humes's company, with the exception of the officers, comprised Irish laborers who had come to Memphis from Chicago a year and one-half earlier seeking employment. Indeed, a member of the 27th Illinois found his brother among them. All claimed that they had been impressed into service and hated their officers. The officers were clearly of a different breed— educated but militarily inexperienced, well dressed with gray uniforms trimmed in red, and quite willing to talk politics. One captive was Lieutenant Rufus J. Polk, nephew of the general.[20]

A huge store of food and ordnance fell into Federal hands. "My Boys captured 4 Secesh Flags of very elegant silk, and very large on one of them is inscribed, 'Mississippi Devils—presented by the Ladies,' " commented Heg. Another read: "Equal Justice To Each New Member in the New Firm." The Northern press grossly exaggerated that fifty thousand artillery rounds had been taken, but Confederate reports placed the number below twenty thousand. The captured wharf boats *J. K. Robbins* and *J. M. Smith* were loaded with sugar and molasses, and a large store of commissary supplies lined the shore.[21]

That evening the Confederate floating battery drifted downriver toward New Madrid. Not realizing that it had been abandoned, the upper Federal battery at the town opened fire. Receiving no response, the gunners ceased, but not before a shell prematurely exploded, killing a cannoneer. The vessel eventually lodged on the Missouri shore below town. On board were eighty torpedoes, hundreds of skyrockets, and a couple of submarine batteries.[22]

At daylight on April 8, Colonel Washington Lafayette Elliott of the 2d Iowa Cavalry took two companies and swept north from Watson's toward the island. About a mile and one-half below the island, at Harris's Meadow, an earthwork was found with an abandoned field piece. A half mile above was another work, this one with no guns but with a large amount of ammunition in a nearby ravine. "Before reaching this ravine I had placed a guard over steamboats, wharf-boats, and prisoners, consisting of soldiers, deckhands, and laborers employed on the fortifications of the enemy," Elliott wrote. Soon he observed a Federal transport moving downriver from the island. The linkup was complete.[23]

At 8 A.M., without waiting for Pope, Paine conducted his own surrender ceremony at Tiptonville. The town, according to a journalist, was nothing more than a collection of dilapidated shanties. The troops were formed on three sides of an open-ended square, with Houghtaling's battery in front, the 22d Illinois on their right, and the 51st Illinois in the rear and to the left toward the timber. At the appointed time the Rebels marched in close-line formation. For a moment all was silent, and then, spontaneously, they raised their hands and were ordered to stack their arms. As Mackall surrendered his sword, Gantt was overheard reminding the general that in Memphis he had sworn that he would rather die a thousand deaths than surrender his sword.[24]

For the first time the Federals got a close view of their opponents. Most of the Southerners were wrapped in dirty white blankets, and they stood around shivering with chattering teeth. Armed mostly with squirrel rifles and old flintlocks, they did not have the appearance of a disciplined army. Gilbert later wrote that he "never saw so motley [a] crowd[;] good-looking stalwart men too."[25]

The color of the Confederate clothing was nondescript, but butternut predominated. Only one battalion was outfitted in gray. "They were dressed mostly in coarse clothing of every color and make. No two dressed alike, officers or men. Their build is different from us. There was hardly a chubby one among them. Nearly all were lank, lean, bony," observed a Federal, David McLean. "Some of them tall, some poor fellows had had but one meal since Sunday. I saw a good many boys not over 12 or 13. It was the most miserable looking set of men I ever saw collected together, physically and mentally. I talked with a good many. Some said they would have been drafted or forced into service if they had not volunteered."[26]

Demoralized from weeks of siege, many of the Confederates openly expressed their discontent. "The rebels seem to be entirely discouraged and are glad to be taken prisoners. They say they are not afraid of Eastern soldiers but cannot stand the Western boys," wrote David McLean of the 8th Wisconsin. The prisoners also complained of lack of pay and irregular mail deliveries. Dan Smith noted: "They expressed themselves tired of the war and of being badly treated by their officers, made to work too hard and poorly fed and clothed and much poorer paid." Some prisoners, however, remained " 'dyed in the wool' Secesh." Lieutenant Matthews of the 10th Illinois had a conversation with an artillery officer and stated: "He was courteous, intelligent, undismayed by their

Fig. 20. The Confederate surrender at Tiptonville on the morning of April 8, 1862 (courtesy of *Frank Leslie's Illustrated*, May 3, 1862)

ill fortunes, and had a rock-rooted faith that the South would never be overcome!"[27]

Brigadier General Stanley found Captain Henry B. Davidson, an old friend and West Point classmate, among the prisoners. Stanley sent him over to the high-ranking Southern officers to extend an invitation to dine with him. Mackall, Stanley later wrote, "very high and mighty, declined." When Davidson whispered about that Stanley had some whiskey to share, several officers did come over. One of them, Gantt, expressed gloom over the South's prospects of winning the war.[28]

Hamilton's division, and Cumming's brigade of Paine's 4th Division, guarded the prisoners until they could be loaded aboard transports. Morgan's brigade swept east toward the lake, rounding up two hundred stragglers and two brass field pieces. Stanley's division moved north toward the island, combing Madrid Bend for stray Rebels. Only forty were found, but all the houses were filled with sick soldiers. Major J. M. Coarse, Pope's inspector general, discovered a crowd of Southerners hiding in a cornfield. Although alone at the time, he decided to bluff. He removed the rails surrounding the field and demanded that they come out. They quickly obeyed and stacked arms, just as a Federal guard appeared.[29]

13

Island Number Ten Is Ours!

Although preempted to a large extent by the shocking battle reports coming out of Pittsburg Landing, Tennessee, Island No. 10 was nonetheless hailed as a great victory throughout the North. "Island Number Ten Is Ours!" read the headlines of the *New York Times*. The paper contended that it was second only in importance to Fort Donelson, "if, indeed, it is second to that achievement." Even though Donelson had netted more prisoners, it had come at the cost of three thousand Federal casualties. Island No. 10 had netted far more heavy guns, and, more important, there had not been a single Northern casualty during the final phase of the campaign. On the evening of April 8 a large crowd, accompanied by Frank Boehm's silver cornet band, appeared at the Planter's House in St. Louis. A jubilant Halleck announced: "We have glorious news today. I have opened the Mississippi Valley to the commerce of St. Louis and trust it will not be long before the city will have communications with the ocean!" The crowd cheered wildly as the band struck up to "Yankee Doodle."[1]

The celebration continued for days. One-hundred-gun salutes marked the victory in Boston and Providence, Rhode Island. Letters of congratulation came from congressional leaders, Halleck, and the Secretary of the Navy. Thomas Scott confidently predicted that Memphis would fall within ten days. Pope's troops, likewise, reveled in the victory. Illinois infantryman Lyman Needham believed the campaign to be "the greatest victory that has yet been achieved." Cavalry trooper James H. Wiswell concurred: "Genl. Pope is the luckiest Genl. that I ever saw or heard of. This is his third great capture without having scarcely any fighting."[2]

The number of killed and wounded during the second phase of the campaign had been astonishingly low. In the Federal army, as Table 3 indicates, accidental deaths surpassed combat deaths. The number of Federal casualties, both army and navy, from March 1 to April 8, 1862, did not exceed one hundred.[3]

Almost before the cheering died down, a controversy arose over the number of Confederate prisoners. A *Chicago Times* reporter curiously noted that the figure given to the press on April 8 was 7,000; on April 9, 2,789; and on April 10, 5,300. Some papers detailed 222 officers and 4,400 privates and non-commissioned officers. When Pope submitted his report, however, he placed

COMMODORE FOOTE'S GAME OF TEN PINS WITH BEAUREGARD.

Fig. 21. A Northern cartoonist taunts the victory at Island No. 10 (courtesy of *Harper's Weekly*, April 26, 1862)

Table 3. Federal casualties for the second phase of the Island No. 10 campaign

	Killed	Wounded	Missing	Total
Accidental explosion on the *St. Louis*	2	12		14
Tree crash on the *Carondelet*	1	2		3
Accidental shell explosions	2			2
Missing on picket duty			4	4
Killed by Confederate artillery fire	2			2
Total	7	14	4	25

the figure at 6,973. The discrepancy did not go unnoticed. Mrs. Ulysses S. Grant, jealous of Pope's good press at a time when her husband was being raked by reporters, expressed anger at "greatly exaggerated" prisoner counts. "Never mind, Mrs. Grant," laughed John Rawlins, Grant's chief of staff. "They will find out how many prisoners were captured when they come to draw their rations."[4]

It is difficult not to conclude that Pope's figure of seven thousand was sheer fabrication. The actual number probably did not exceed 4,538 (see Appendix 3). Certainly the general had every reason to manipulate the figures. For the nation to learn that thirty-five hundred Confederates (not counting the sick) had held a powerful ironclad flotilla and a twenty-four-thousand-man army at bay for three and one-half weeks might have significantly lessened the jubilation and even created a backlash. There is evidence that only a month after the fall of the island, Pope again attempted to manipulate numbers. In May 1862, it was learned that he had grossly inflated his prisoner count as the Confederate army fell back to Corinth.[5]

Other claims were similarly exaggerated. Pope reported seven thousand arms taken, tents for twelve thousand men, and hundreds of horses and mules. Yet all Northern correspondents agreed that the number of arms did not exceed five thousand, and it is possible (based on Southern accounts) that the actual number was much smaller that that. In terms of horses, mules, and wagons captured, only press accounts offer specifics. The *Cincinnati Commercial* listed 125 horses and 600 mules; the Philadelphia and St. Louis papers, 1,200 horses and 625 mules. All three placed the number of captured wagons at 400. A. T. Gay, a Southerner captured at the island, wrote bluntly that if more than one hundred horses were taken, "they got them from the surrounding countryside."[6]

A discrepancy in the number of cannon also occurred. Pope boasted of 123 heavy guns and 35 field pieces. Detailed news accounts and an actual survey conducted by Brigadier General Cullom revealed only 80 big guns, including 27 dismounted pieces and two small mortars, one of which had a "George II" stamp. To this number could be added the nine guns of the floating battery, a dozen heavy guns in downriver positions, the six field pieces of Stewart's battery, and two field guns aboard the *Grampus,* bringing the actual number to 109, not 158.[7]

After Pope's ignominious defeat at Second Manassas, the image that emerged of him among historians was one of an inept braggart. His inflated capture figures at Island No. 10 seem to confirm the conventional view. In truth, his exaggerations were not only unfortunate, but also unnecessary. The campaign had been a brilliant success in its own right and had brought great reward to the North. Pope's personal failings aside, there was legitimacy to his victory and his subsequent promotion.

The *Memphis Avalanche* was the first Southern paper to break the story of the defeat in the upper Mississippi Valley. "As the day approached meridian there came vague rumors that Island Number 10 had been surrendered, and the gloom that overspread every face became more intense and dark. It was not long before rumor became conviction, although many hoped against hope," the paper stated on April 7. Both the *Avalanche* and the *Memphis Appeal* assured the public that Fort Pillow was in battle readiness. The Memphis correspondent of the *Mobile Register* remained pessimistic: "The reduction of Island No. 10, though anticipated, is a very serious blow, and will be followed soon, I fear, by the fall of Fort Pillow."[8]

Reaction came slowly in other cities. On April 10, the *New Orleans Picayune* printed in bold type, "Island No. 10 Still Held," putting to rest the "false rumors" spreading throughout the city. The next day, however, a copy of the *Avalanche* was obtained, and the truth became known. The *Richmond Enquirer,* three days after the surrender, still insisted that the news from Island No. 10 "is of the most gratifying character." Not until April 19 did the capitulation become known. The news did not reach Charleston, South Carolina, until April 17, and then only because a copy of the *New York Herald* had been secured.[9]

Recriminations were soon forthcoming. The *Avalanche* advised: "It is not time to lament, or, indeed, to criticize the ineptness, or neglect, or incapacity that led to the catastrophe," although the editor went on to state that "comment on the street is very free, and not altogether complimentary." Hollins and his gunboats received the sharpest attacks. "What are the gunboats made for?" questioned the *Memphis Argus.* "Will someone inform us of a single benefit resulting to the Confederacy from the fleet which passed Memphis with pomp and parade before the disgraceful hullabaloo at New Madrid." The Natchez, Mississippi, paper was stunned to learn that the flotilla had withdrawn without consulting the advance of the Federal vessels and labeled Hollins's squadron "make-believe gunboats."[10]

In reflecting on the loss, postwar historian Edward Pollard stated that the Southerners had been constantly assured that Island No. 10 was impregnable. The loss of the "Little Gibraltar of the Mississippi," as some referred to it, proved demoralizing and "almost irreparable." He disgustedly concluded: "We have saved none of our cannon or munitions; we have lost our boats; our sick have been abandoned; there can be no excuse for the wretched mismanagement."[11]

Panic spread at home and abroad. Martial law was declared in Memphis and the hard currency in the city banks removed to safety. Many inhabitants fled, and some threatened to lay the city in ashes rather than endure capture. Mayor John Park put an end to the loose talk when he declared that anyone attempting to fire a house, whether his own or a neighbor's, would be hanged. In an effort to allay the fears of a London diplomat, Secretary of State Judah Benjamin declared that although the loss of the island was harmful, "it is far from having given the enemy control of the river or the ability to descend Memphis."[12]

For the captured of Island No. 10 the misery was only beginning. Transports worked throughout April 8 to move the prisoners to New Madrid. The ironclads *Mound City* and *St. Louis* even dropped down to pick up three hundred of the captured. The officers were sheltered in homes, but all others remained huddled along the bank, shivering in the rain. On the morning of April 9 and throughout April 10, the captives embarked for Cairo. Arriving there throughout April 11 and 12, they were transferred to railroad cars—the officers in passenger cars and the men in cattle cars.[13]

The captives were farmed out to prison camps throughout the North. Some twenty-five to thirty officers reported to Fort Warren in Boston and the balance to Johnson's Island at Sandusky, Ohio. About fifteen hundred of the captured arrived at Camp Douglas, near Chicago; one thousand at Camp Butler at Springfield, Illinois; and the remainder at Columbus, Ohio, and Camp Randall at Madison, Wisconsin. A few of the men took the oath of allegiance, but a far greater number died of disease during their captivity. Some 140, mostly of the 1st Alabama, died and were buried at Camp Randall. On September 8, 1862, the enlisted men were transported to Cairo and thence by steamer to Vicksburg for their exchange, which occurred on September 23.[14]

As in all military campaigns there are winners and losers, and Island No. 10 was no exception. The clear winner proved to be Pope, who, having already been promoted to major general of volunteers on March 22, 1862, now boldly requested through his political contacts in Illinois a similar commission in the Regular Army. Lincoln was quick to reply with his inevitable wit: "I fully appreciate Gen. Pope's invaluable results; but you must know that Major Generalships in the Regular Army are not as plentiful as blackberries." Pope's near bloodless exploits, coming on the heels of Grant's staggering losses at Shiloh, did, nonetheless, catch the attention of the president. General Pope was given command of an army in Virginia, where, at Second Manassas, he was soundly defeated by Robert E. Lee. His Civil War career ended in relative obscurity, fighting Indians in Minnesota.[15]

Foote was promoted to the new grade of admiral. Due to ill health, however, he proved unable to continue his duties and was placed in charge of the navy's recruiting bureau in Washington. Longing to return to the blue-water fleet, he was finally given a position with the South Atlantic Squadron. He died on June 26, 1863, of Bright's disease, while en route to his new command.[16]

While there were no winners on the Confederate side, McCown emerged as the clear loser. He assumed a division command in the Department of East Tennessee and later in the Army of Tennessee, now under Braxton Bragg. The specter of New Madrid continued to haunt him. Bragg considered McCown his worst division commander and, following the Battle of Stones River, charged him with disobedience of orders. McCown countered that, unless Bragg were removed from command, he would resign from the service and raise potatoes on his four-acre Tennessee farm. A subsequent court-martial ruled against McCown, and his career was finished. Thoroughly embittered, he openly called the Confederacy "a damned stinking cotton oligarchy . . . gotten up for the benefit of Isham G. Harris and Jeff Davis and their damned corrupt cliques."[17]

Mackall was imprisoned for a few months at Fort Warren. He returned to Richmond after his exchange and submitted his report to the Secretary of War. President Davis's displeasure was apparent in his endorsement: "Read. Unsatisfactory.—J. D." In December 1862, Davis at long last acted and assigned him to command the Department of the Gulf, with headquarters in Mobile. He eventually became chief of staff of another critic of the Davis administration, Joseph E. Johnston.[18]

As for his part, Beauregard continued to support Mackall, saying that Mackall had done the right thing at Island No. 10 and insisting that a court of inquiry was unnecessary. His only regret was that he had not sent him there several weeks earlier "to enable [him] to make [his] own preparations for its prolonged defense." Even in postwar years, Beauregard never waned in his convictions. He assured Mackall in 1878 that no one had condemned him for the loss except Davis, whose remarks "ought not to have been considered by you as entitled to any weight."[19]

It is difficult to see how Mackall, in less than two weeks, could have accomplished more than he did. The fate of the island had been virtually sealed by the time of his arrival. Indeed, had it not been for a timorous Federal naval commander, the position might well have fallen weeks earlier. The fact nonetheless remains that Island No. 10 withstood twenty-three days of siege, while Port Hudson, on the other end of the Mississippi, with a similar one-to-four disparity in troop strength, held for forty-seven days.

There were two military disappointments during the campaign. One was the complete ineffectiveness of long-range shelling, except as a factor affecting morale. The other was the total ineptness of the Confederate flotilla. Hollins's preoccupation with New Orleans and his lethargic response in beating back the Federal batteries on the west bank cost him dearly. He never again received an active command, and he spent the remainder of the war giving tests to midshipmen in Richmond.[20]

Gantt's career took a political twist. He came under undeserved criticism for the New Madrid debacle, although his hometown newspaper, the *Washington Telegraph,* continued to support him. After his prisoner exchange, he returned to Arkansas, where after an unexplained absence in the fall of 1863, he suddenly turned up in Little Rock as a Federal sympathizer. He subsequently wrote an anti-Confederate pamphlet, toured the North denouncing the Confederacy, and in postwar years became involved in the reconstruction government of Arkansas.[21]

The great tactical lesson of the campaign regarded the Federal navy. Foote's overly cautious nature made him view his ironclads as the North's best defensive weapon, when in reality the boats represented the most effective offensive weapon in the Federal arsenal. The passing of the Island No. 10 batteries by the *Carondelet* was hailed as a great and daring accomplishment, but in retrospect it was much less so. In the years ahead such a tactic "became almost commonplace on the western rivers," observed William Fowler. Foote failed to recognize "how much technology had changed the rules" and did not "appreciate the mobility and strength offered by steam and armor."[22]

The surrender of the island proved a serious defeat for the Confederates, but it was not a catastrophe on the scale of Fort Donelson. Within five months the captured units had been exchanged and, although depleted, were back fighting again. The heavy guns were more difficult to replace, but even that loss was mitigated by the fact that all but thirty-seven were ineffective against ironclads. Never again, however, did the Rebels marshal such an impressive array of heavy guns in the West. Even the extensive Vicksburg defenses mounted only fifty-three big guns.[23]

In several respects Island No. 10 was a blueprint for the capture of Vicksburg, although there is no indication that Grant made such a comparison. The canal in that instance proved unsuccessful, but the city was similarly taken in reverse. Ironclads and transports simply passed the river batteries at night. Once downriver, Grant easily ferried his troops across the Mississippi River.

The loss of the Island No. 10 garrison might, of course, have been viewed as acceptable had Shiloh been a smashing Southern victory. After all, a division had held in check the equivalent of an entire corps during the critical period of Confederate concentration at Corinth. The failure of the Confederate offensive meant that the fight for the upper valley was concluded. There was no reason for the Federals to attack Fort Pillow, which could now be outflanked from the east, so Pope's army was withdrawn and sent to join Grant's and Buell's at Pittsburg Landing. The Southerners abandoned Fort Pillow and Fort Randolph to their fate on June 5, 1862, and Memphis fell the following day after a brief naval engagement.[24]

The Confederate leadership in the West never came to grips with the salient issue. The *Appeal* stated it clearly: "It is plain we must encounter his [Foote's] gunboats successfully or abandon navigable water courses. Which shall we do?" Unable to do the former, the Davis administration refused to do the latter. The politics of yielding the rivers and their cities simply made this option unacceptable. Thus, failing to devise an alternative strategy, the Southerners committed the same mistake over and again. Between February 1862 and July 1863, the fixed fortifications at Fort Donelson, Island No. 10, Arkansas Post, Port Hudson, and Vicksburg all fell and, with them, their garrisons of 64,400 troops—some nine divisions. This failed strategy proved a significant factor to Confederate defeat in the West.[25]

Appendix 1: The Opposing Forces*

March 4, 1862
Army of the Mississippi
Maj. Gen. John Pope
First Division
Brig. Gen. D. S. Stanley

First Brigade, Col. John Groesbeck
    27th Ohio
    39th Ohio
Second Brigade
    43d Ohio
    63d Ohio

Second Division
Brig. Gen. Schuyler Hamilton

First Brigade, Col. W. H. Worthington
    59th Indiana
    5th Iowa
Second Brigade, Col. J. B. Plummer
    26th Illinois
    47th Illinois
    11th Missouri

Third Division
Brig. Gen. J. M. Palmer

First Brigade
    34th Indiana
    43d Indiana
Second Brigade
    46th Indiana
    47th Indiana

*All information in Appendix 1, unless otherwise indicated, comes from a compilation of sources in *Official Records of the Union and Confederate Armies,* VIII.

Army of the Mississippi
Maj. Gen. John Pope
March 31, 1862
First Division
Brig. Gen. D. S. Stanley

First Brigade—Col. John B. Groesbeck
    27th Ohio—Col. John W. Fuller
    39th Ohio—Maj. Edward F. Noyes
Second Brigade—Col. J. L. Kirby Smith
    43d Ohio—Lieut. Col. Wager Swayne
    63d Ohio—Col. John W. Sprague

Second Division
Brig. Gen. Schuyler Hamilton

First Brigade—Col W. H. Worthington
    5th Iowa—Lieut. Col. Charles L. Matthies
    59th Indiana—Col. J. J. Alexander
Second Brigade—Col. Nicholas Perzel
    10th Iowa—Lieut. Col. William Small
    26th Missouri—Col. George B. Boomer
Artillery—11th Ohio Battery—Capt. Frank C. Sands

Third Division
Brig. Gen. John M. Palmer

First Brigade—Col. James R. Slack
    34th Indiana—Col. Townsend Ryan
    47th Indiana—Lieut. Col. Milton S. Robinson
Second Brigade—Col. Graham N. Fitch
    43d Indiana—Col. William E. McLean
    46th Indiana—Lieut. Col. Newton G. Scott
Cavalry—7th Illinois Cavalry—Col. William P. Kellogg
Artillery—G, 1st Missouri—Capt. Henry Hescock

Fourth Division
Brig. Gen. Eleazor A. Paine

First Brigade—Col. James D. Morgan
    10th Illinois—Lieut. Col. John Tillson
    16th Illinois—Col. Robert F. Smith

Second Brigade—Col. Gilbert W. Cumming
    22d Illinois—Lieut. Col. Harrison E. Hart
    51st Illinois—Lieut. Col. Luther P. Bradley
Sharpshooters—64th Illinois (Yates's Sharpshooters)—Lieut. Col. D. E. Williams
Cavalry—1st Illinois Cavalry (Co. H and Co. I)—Maj. P. D. Jenkins

Fifth Division
Brig. Gen. J. B. Plummer

First Brigade—Col. John Bryner
    8th Wisconsin—Col. R. C. Murphy
    47th Illinois—Lieut. Col. Daniel Miles
Second Brigade—Col. John M. Loomis
    26th Illinois—Col. H. Dougherty
    11th Missouri—Lieut. Col. William E. Panabaker
Artillery—M, 1st Missouri—Capt. Albert M. Powell

Cavalry Division
Brig. Gen. Gordon Granger

2d Michigan Cavalry—Lieut. Col. Selden H. Gorham
3d Michigan Cavalry—Col. John K. Nusener

Artillery Division
Maj. Warren L. Lothrop

2d Iowa Battery—Capt. N. T. Spoor
5th Wisconsin Battery—Capt. Oscar F. Pinny
6th Wisconsin Battery—Capt. Henry Dillons
7th Wisconsin Battery—Capt. Richard R. Griffiths
C, 1st Michigan—Capt. A. W. Dees
H, 1st Michigan—Capt. S. DeGolyer
C, 1st Illinois—Capt. C. Houghtaling
F, 2d U.S.—Lieut. J. Darling

Unassigned Troops

Engineer Regiment of the West (25th Missouri)—Col. Josiah W. Bissell
22d Missouri—Lieut. Col. John D. Foster
2d Iowa Cavalry—Col. Washington L. Elliott
2d Illinois Cavalry (4 Companies)—Lieut. Col. H. Hogg
4th U.S. Cavalry (3 Companies)—Lieut. M. J. Kelley
1st U.S. Infantry (6 Companies)—Capt. G. A. Williams

Flotilla Brigade
Col. Napoleon B. Buford

27th Illinois—Lieut. Col. F. Harrington
42d Illinois—Col. George W. Roberts
15th Wisconsin—Col. Hans Heg
G, 1st Illinois—Capt. A. O'Leary
I, 2d Illinois—Capt. F. Sparrestrom

Army of the Mississippi
March 31, 1862

| | Present for Duty | | |
Command	Officers	Men	Aggregate
1st (Stanley's) Div.	122	1,535	3,330
2d (Hamilton's) Div.	121	2,428	2,972
3d (Palmer's) Div.	151	3,131	3,790
4th (Paine's) Div.	142	2,832	3,447
5th (Plummer's) Div.	97	2,408	2,998
Cavalry (Granger's) Div.	75	1,341	2,026
Artillery (Lothrop's) Div.	29	782	972
Engineer Troops	9	96	802
Unattached	50	1,238	1,478
Bird's Point, Mo.	36	775	842
Sikeston, Mo.	6	143	151
TOTAL	838	17,709	22,808
Flotilla Brigade			2,251
			25,059

Confederate Forces at New Madrid
March 3–14, 1862
Brig. Gen. Alexander P. Stewart

Fort Thompson—Brig. Gen. Edward W. Gantt
    11th Arkansas—Col. Jabez M. Smith
    12th Arkansas—Lieut. Col. W. D. S. Cook
    Upton's Co. Heavy Artillery
    Stewart's Co. Heavy Artillery—Capt. J. W. Stewart
Fort Bankhead—Col. Lucius M. Walker
    5th Tennessee—Col. William E. Travis
    40th Tennessee—Col. C. C. Henderson
    1st Alabama, Tennessee, Mississippi—Col. Alpheus Baker
    Bankhead's Tenn. Battery—Capt. Smith P. Bankhead

Mississippi Flotilla
Commo. George N. Hollins

McRae (flagship)—Lieut. Thomas B. Huger	8 Guns
Livingston—Commo. R. F. Pinkney	6 "
Polk—Lieut. Commo. J. H. Carter	5 "
Pontchartrain—Lieut. Commo. John W. Dunnington	7 "
Marapaus—Lieut. Joseph Fry	5 "
Jackson—Lieut. F. B. Renshaw	2 "
Ivy [not given in records]	2 "
New Orleans (floating battery)—Lieut. S. W. Averett	9 "

Confederate Forces, Madrid Bend
Late February 1862
Brig. Gen. John P. McCown

Gantt's Brigade—Brig. Gen. E. W. Gantt
    11th Arkansas—Col. Jabez M. Smith
    12th Arkansas—Lieut. Col. W. D. S. Cook
    Stewart's Co. Heavy Artillery—Capt. J. W. Stewart
    Upton's Co. Heavy Artillery
    Missouri Cavalry (1 Company)
Neely's Brigade—Col. R. P. Neely
    12th Louisiana—Col. Thomas M. Scott
    4th Tennessee—Col. R. P. Neely
    31st Tennessee—Col. W. M. Bradford
Marks's Brigade—Col. S. F. Marks
    11th Louisiana—Col. S. F. Marks
    5th Louisiana Battalion—Col. J. G. Kennedy
    Bankhead's Tennessee Battery—Capt. Smith P. Bankhead
Stewart's Brigade—Brig. Gen. Alexander P. Stewart
    4th Arkansas Battalion—Maj. M. M. McKay
    5th Tennessee—Lieut. Col. F. A. Terry
    55th Tennessee—Col. Alexander J. Brown
Tennessee Heavy Artillery Corps
    Jackson's Co.—Cap. Andrew Jackson, Jr.
    Sterling's Co.—Cap. Robert Sterling
    Humes's Co.—Capt. William Y. C. Humes
    Hoadley's Co.—Capt. Frederick W. Hoadley
    Jones's Co.—Capt. W. C. Jones
    Dismuke's Co.—Capt. Paul T. Dismuke
    Fisher's Co.—Capt. James A. Fisher

Not Brigaded
  1st Alabama, Tennessee, Mississippi—Col. Alpheus Baker
  40th Tennessee—Col. C. C. Henderson
  46th Tennessee—Col. John M. Clark
  Johnson's Siege Battery (Southern Guards)—Capt. Thomas Johnson
  Rucker's Co. Heavy Artillery—Capt. Edward W. Rucker
  Haywood's Cavalry Co.
  Hudson's Cavalry Squadron
  Neely's Cavalry Co.
  Wheeler's Cavalry Co.
  Pointe Coupee Artillery—Capt. R. A. Stewart

| | | Effective Strength | | | |
Command	Infantry	Heavy Artillery	Light Artillery	Cavalry	Aggregate
Gantt's Brigade	1,036	120		100	1,256
Marks's Brigade	887		132		1,019
Neely's Brigade	1,714				1,714
Stewart's Brigade	1,163	441			1,604
Not Brigaded	1,271	95	173	300	1,839
	6,071	656	305	400	7,432

April [?], 1862*
Brig. Gen. William W. Mackall

First Brigade, Brig. Gen. L. M. Walker
  40th Tennessee   Lieut. Col. C. C. Henderson
  4th Tennessee   Col. John M. Clark
  1st Alabama   Col. I. G. W. Steadman
  1st Ala., Tenn., Miss.   Col. Alpheus Baker
Second Brigade, Col. E. W. Gantt
  12th Arkansas   Col. E. W. Gantt
  11th Arkansas   Col. Jabez M. Smith
  4th Arkansas Battalion   Lieut. Col. F. A. Terry
  West Tenn. Battalion (55th Tenn.) Col. Alexander J. Brown
  10 Companies Heavy Artillery Brig. Gen. James Trudeau

*Source: P. G. T. Beauregard Papers, LC

Appendix 2: Strength of Confederate Forces, Madrid Bend

April 1, 1862

SHORTLY AFTER THE fall of New Madrid, a significant portion of the Confederate garrison at Madrid Bend was withdrawn. Estimating the number of remaining troops is, at best, tricky. It involves piecing together two tabular returns, coupled with some guesswork. It is noted that the difference between the present-for-duty strength and the aggregate strength of six units on March 21, 1862 was 37 percent. Where the aggregate strength is missing for some units, that figure is added to form an estimate.

Unit	Present for Duty	Aggregate
1st Alabama	468 (A)	683
1st Alabama, Tennessee, Mississippi	415 (A)	536
40th Tennessee	471 (A)	668
46th Tennessee	375 (A)	531
55th Tennessee	327 (A)	402
11th Arkansas		
	1,036 (B)	1,419 (C)
12th Arkansas		
4th Arkansas Battalion	250 (D)	342 (C)
Heavy Artillery	330 (A)	455
Stewart's Battery	120 (A)	164 (C)
Hudson's and Wheeler's companies	80 (D)	110 (C)
Sapper company	40	40
Total	3,912	5,350

A = March 21, 1862
B = Effective Strength, February 28, 1862
C = 37 percent added to form an estimate
D = Estimate

Another way of computing the number is to start with Captain Shelia's report of April 3, 1862, in which he states that there were 2,273 infantry and 1,166 artillery, a total of 3,436. To this number must be added Stewart's battery, two companies of cavalry, and the sapper company, say 250 men. On March 26, 1862, Lieutenant Colonel Blake placed the number of sick at 1,557. The combined number of the two reports would thus be 5,243—very close to the previous estimate.

Source: *Official Records of the Union and Confederate Armies,* VIII.

Appendix 3: Dispute over Prisoner Returns

W HILE POPE'S PRISONER report of nearly seven thousand was hardly creditable, Confederate estimates proved little better. The *Memphis Avalanche*
initially placed the number at twenty-five hundred, but the *Appeal* lowered the
figure to two thousand. On April 24, 1862, the Atlanta *Southern Confederacy*
disregarded accounts of a large-scale capture: "We did not believe the first [Un-
ion] reports about 5,000 or 6,000 of our troops being captured, and do not
believe it now." Edward A. Pollard, editor of the *Richmond Examiner,* wrote
in 1863 that the number of prisoners was "not less than two thousand."[1]

The controversy continued in postwar years. Southerners Daniel Smith and
A. T. Gay stated that the number of captives did not exceed three thousand.
Even some Northern writers began to raise doubts. Thomas Knox, a New York
correspondent, wrote: "General Pope reported his captures somewhat larger
than they really were, and received much applause for his success." Walke lowered the number to five thousand without comment. Charles W. Davis, admitting that the figure was in dispute, placed the number at "less than 4,000."
Brigadier General R. D. Drum, adjutant general of the United States Army,
stated that he had seen a document in the army archives on several occasions
in which Pope ultimately adjusted the number upward to ten thousand. Pope
adamantly denied this, and a subsequent search of the archives failed to uncover
such a document.[2] Perhaps even more disturbing is the fact that most modern
historians have accepted Pope's report at face value. Thus, for better or for
worse, the number that has gone down in history is seven thousand.[3]

As previously stated, McCown, after the division of his forces, had an aggregate present of about 5,350. Even if this is low by one or two hundred, it is
known that some sick did get out on transports throughout the latter part of
March 1862, thus making an offset. To the aggregate present must be added
one hundred civilian transport workers and, probably, 128 Irish laborers who
were present in the fall of 1861 and apparently at the surrender. Placing the
number of escapees at one thousand, the captured probably totaled in the range
of 4,410 troops and 228 civilians, making 4,538.

---

1. *Memphis Avalanche,* April 7, 1862; *Memphis Appeal,* April 11, 1862; *Southern Confederacy,* April 24, 1862; Edward A. Pollard, *First Year of the War* (London: George Phillips & Son,
1863), 285.

2. Daniel P. Smith, *Company K First Alabama Regiment or Three Years in the Confederate Service* (Gaithersburg, Md.: Butternut Press, 1984), 17; A. T. Gay, "Correct History Wanted," *Confederate Veteran* 11 (November 1893): 337; Thomas Knox, *Camp-Fire and Cotton-Field: Southern Adventure in Time of War* (New York: Da Capo Press, 1969), 170; Henry Walke, "The Western Flotilla at Fort Donelson, Island Number Ten, Fort Pillow, and Memphis," *Battles and Leaders of the Civil War,* ed. Robert C. Johnson and Clarence C. Buel, vol. 1 (New York: Thomas Yoseloff, 1956), 447; Charles W. Dean, "New Madrid and Island Number Ten," *Military Order of the Loyal Union of the United States: Illinois* 1 (1891): 91; James M. Morgan, *Recollections of a Rebel Reefer* (Boston: Houghton Mifflin Co., 1917), 70.

3. See, for example, Shelby Foote, *The Civil War: A Narrative,* vol. 1 (New York: Random House, 1956), 313; James M. McPherson, *Battle Cry of Freedom: The Civil War Era* (New York: Oxford University Press, 1988), 415; Stanley F. Horn, *The Army of Tennessee* (Indianapolis: The Bobbs-Merrill Company, 1941), 145; Thomas L. Connelly, *Civil War Tennessee: Battles and Leaders* (Knoxville: University of Tennessee Press, 1979), 51; Steven E. Woodworth, *Jefferson Davis and His Generals: The Failure of Confederate Command* (Lawrence, University of Kansas Press, 1990), 109; Charles L. Dufour, "The Conflict of the Mississippi," *The Image of War 1861–1865,* vol. 2 (Garden City, N.Y.: Doubleday & Co., Inc., 1982), 263.

Two exceptions are Patricia L. Faust, ed., *Historical Times Illustrated Encyclopedia of the Civil War* (New York: Harper & Row, 1986), 386, which gives the prisoner count as 3,500, and Time Life, *The Road to Shiloh* (Garden City, N.Y.: Doubleday & Co., Inc., 1982), 166, which places the total at 5,000.

Notes

.

Abbreviations

ADAH	Alabama Department of Archives and History
CHS	Chicago Historical Society
DU	Duke University
ILSHL	Illinois State Historical Library
INHS	Indiana Historical Society
INSL	Indiana State Library
IOSHS	Iowa State Historical Society
LC	Library of Congress
MOHS	Missouri Historical Society
MSU	Michigan State University
MUO	Miami University of Ohio
NA	National Archives
NMHM	New Madrid Historical Museum
OR A	Official Records of the Union and Confederate Armies
OR N	Official Records of the Union and Confederate Navies
SHC	Southern Historical Collection
TSLA	Tennessee State Library and Archives
TU	Tulane University
UALR	University of Arkansas at Little Rock for Medical Sciences
UM	University of Mississippi
UMI	University of Michigan
UW	University of Wisconsin
US	University of the South
USMHI	United States Military History Institute
WSHS	Wisconsin State Historical Society

1. The Finest Strategic Position

1. Richard Beringer, Herman Hattaway, Archer Jones, and William S. Still, *Why the South Lost* (Athens: University of Georgia Press, 1986), 118; Herman Hattaway and Archer Jones,

How the North Won (Urbana: University of Illinois Press, 1983), 60; Benjamin F. Cooling, *Forts Henry and Donelson: The Key to the Confederate Heartland* (Knoxville: University of Tennessee Press, 1987), 4, 9–10.

2. *The War of the Rebellion: A Compilation of the Official Records of the Union and Confederate Armies* (Washington, D.C.: U.S. Government Printing Office, 1880–1901), Series 1, III, 619 (hereafter cited as *OR A;* unless otherwise indicated, all citations are in Series 1).

3. Ibid., 617–18; Thomas L. Connelly, *Army of the Heartland: The Army of Tennessee, 1861–1862* (Baton Rouge: Louisiana State University Press, 1967), 48–49; Richard M. McMurry, *Two Great Rebel Armies: An Essay in Confederate Military History* (Chapel Hill: University of North Carolina Press, 1989), 78–79; Steven E. Woodworth, *Jefferson Davis and His Generals: The Failure of Confederate Command* (Lawrence: University of Kansas Press, 1990), 30–31.

4. Woodworth, *Davis,* 26–28, 30–31; Joseph Parks, *General Leonidas Polk, CSA, The Fighting Bishop* (Baton Rouge: Louisiana State University Press, 1962), 34–37; *Memphis Appeal,* July 23, 1861.

5. M. Jeff Thompson, *The Civil War Reminiscences of General M. Jeff Thompson* (Dayton: Morningside, 1988), 7–8, 28–32, 75–83; *OR A,* III, 613, 654–57, 681; *Memphis Avalanche,* September 3, 1861; *Nashville Daily Gazette,* December 11, 1861.

6. *OR A,* III, 617–19, 654.

7. Jay C. Mullen, "Pope's New Madrid and Island Number 10 Campaigns," *Missouri Historical Review* 59 (April 1965): 328; *OR A,* III, 630, 686–87; *Memphis Appeal,* August 4, 6, 13, 1861; *Official Records of the Union and Confederate Navies in the War of the Rebellion* (Washington, D.C.: U.S. Government Printing Office, 1894–1927), XXII, 299 (hereafter cited as *OR N*).

8. Connelly, *Army of the Heartland,* 21; *Memphis Appeal,* April 19, 28, May 1, 2, 3, July 20, August 2, 1861, February 19, 1862; William H. Russell, *My Diary North and South* (Boston: Harper, 1863) 310–13; *OR A,* IV, 251.

9. Shelby Foote, *The Civil War: A Narrative,* 3 vols. (New York: Random House, 1958–1974), 1: 307; James T. Poe, *The Raving Foe: A Civil War Diary and List of Prisoners* (Eastland, Tex.: Longhorn Press, 1967), 18; M. F. Force, *From Fort Henry to Corinth* (Wilmington: Broadfoot Press, 1989), 67; Lonnie J. White, "Federal Operations at New Madrid and Island Number Ten," *West Tennessee Historical Society Papers* 17 (1963): 47; *OR A,* VIII, 141–42; *New Orleans Crescent,* March 26, 1862; *New York Tribune,* April 14, 1862; *Chicago Tribune,* April 11, 1862; *New York Times,* April 3, 1862; Walter J. Buttgenbach, "Coast Defense in the Civil War: Island Number Ten," *Journal U.S. Artillery* 39 (May–June 1913): 333–34.

10. *New York Herald,* March 8, 18, 1862; Force, *Fort Henry,* 67; Mullen, "Pope's New Madrid," 330.

11. The *New Orleans Delta* referred to New Madrid as "the weak point of our defense."

12. *OR A,* III, 661; VIII, 141–43.

13. Ibid., III, 653, 658, 660, 662–63, 666, 688; LII, pt. 2, 123; *OR N,* XXII, 747–48.

14. *OR A,* III, 685.

15. Woodworth, *Davis,* 37–39; Connelly, *Army of the Heartland,* 51–52; *OR A,* III, 683, 687; Stanley F. Horn, *The Army of Tennessee* (Indianapolis: The Bobbs-Merrill Company, 1941), 44; Nathaniel C. Hughes, Jr., *The Battle of Belmont: Grant Strikes South* (Chapel Hill: University of North Carolina Press, 1991), 5; Pillow to Magoffin, May 13, 1861, Isham G. Harris Papers, DU.

16. Connelly, *Army of the Heartland,* 51–52; Woodworth, *Davis,* 39–41; McMurry, *Two Great Rebel Armies,* 11–12; *OR A,* IV, 191.

17. Polk to wife, September 18, 1861, Leonidas Polk Papers, US; David D. Porter, *The Naval History of the Civil War* (Secaucus, N.J.: Castle, 1984), 163; *Chicago Tribune,* January

24, 1862; Rowena Reed, *Combined Operations in the Civil War* (Annapolis: United States Naval Institute, 1978), 244, 265; *OR N*, XXII, 808; *OR A*, VIII, 141–43.

18. *OR A*, VII, 730; VIII, 141–43, 160, 811.

19. Ibid., VII, 720–21; VIII, 805–06.

20. Ibid., VII, 629; VIII, 689, 753; Poe, *Raving Foe*, 15–16.

21. Poe, *Raving Foe*, 17–18; I. J. Gaughen, ed., *Letters of a Confederate Surgeon* (Camden, Ark.: The Hurley Co., Inc., 1960), 21; "Account of John K. Craig Taking Food to Island Number Ten," NMHM.

22. *OR A*, III, 740–41; VIII, 691; Thompson, *Reminiscences*, 122–23; Oscar Pinny to wife, March 23, 1862, Oscar Pinny Letters, WRHS; *Cincinnati Commercial*, March 19, 1862.

23. Michael B. Dougan, *Confederate Arkansas: The People and Politics of a Frontier State in Wartime* (Tuscaloosa: University of Alabama Press, 1976), 21, 57, 66; *Arkansas Gazette*, June 11, 1874; Roscoe A. Jennings to brother, December 6, 1861, Roscoe A. Jennings Letters, UALR; *OR A*, VII, 826.

24. *OR A*, VIII, 707–09, 717, 723; *Memphis Appeal*, February 5, 1862.

25. *OR A*, VII, 689, 853–54; VIII, 698, 717, 759.

26. Ibid., VII, 690, 708, 731, 773–74, 808, 824, 828, 835, 837, 848, 852.

27. *OR N*, XXII, 817, 819–20.

28. *Chicago Tribune*, January 24, 1862; *Philadelphia Inquirer*, February 20, 1862; Reed, *Combined Operations*, 85; David Roth, "Civil War at the Confluence," *Blue & Gray* 2 (July 1985): 11; Charles B. Dew, *Ironmaker to the Confederacy: Joseph R. Anderson and the Tredegar Iron Works* (New Haven: Yale University Press, 1966), 135; *Frank Leslie's Illustrated*, February 22, 1862; William G. Stevenson, *Thirteen Months in the Rebel Army* (New York: Barnes, 1864), 64–65, 76; *OR N*, XXII, 791.

29. *OR A*, LII, pt. 2, 215; Alpheus Baker, "Island No. 10," 1 (1882–1883): 55.

30. *OR A*, VII, 708–09, 728–729; *Cincinnati Commercial*, March 14, 1862.

31. *Ibid.*, LII, pt. 2, 215; Cooling, *Forts Henry and Donelson*, 53, 56.

32. Roth, "Civil War," 7, 11; Charles L. Dufour, *The Night the War Was Lost* (Garden City, N.Y.: Doubleday & Co., Inc., 1960), 268–69; *Daily Missouri Democrat*, January 7, 1862; Stevenson, *Thirteen Months*, 59, 66; "Obstructing Federal Gunboats," *Confederate Veteran* 34 (June 1926): 211. A chain was also stretched across the Yazoo River in Mississippi during the Vicksburg Campaign but was soon broken by the strong current.

33. *OR A*, LII, pt. 2, 214–15, 216, 277; *OR N*, XXII, 799, 806, 807; Polk to wife, January 6, 1862, Polk Papers, US; "Torpedoes Used by the Confederate Government," in Ben LeBree, ed., *The Confederate Soldier in the Civil War* (Paterson, N.J.: Pageant Books, Inc., 1959), 438–39; *Daily Missouri Republican*, January 7, 8, 24, 1862; *Chicago Tribune*, January 6, 1862. It was December 12, 1862, before a torpedo in the West claimed its first prize—the ironclad *Cairo*.

34. *OR N*, XXII, 793–94, 806, 809, 811, 812–13, 821; Reed, *Combined Operations*, 76; William N. Still, Jr., *Iron Afloat: The Story of Confederate Armorclads* (Nashville: Vanderbilt University Press, 1971), 62; George W. Gift, "Exploits of the Ram Arkansas," in Ben LeBree, ed., *The Confederate Soldier in the Civil War* (Paterson, N.J.: Pageant Books, Inc., 1959), 404–08; *Memphis Appeal*, July 28, 1861, March 30, 1862.

35. Dufour, *Night the War Was Lost*, 323–26; Reed, *Combined Operations*, 77; Robert V. Bogle, "Defeat Through Default: Confederate Naval Strategy for the Upper Mississippi and Its Tributaries, 1861–1862," *West Tennessee Historical Society Papers* 17 (1963): 70–71.

36. *OR N*, XXII, 805; George N. Hollins, "Autobiography of Commodore George Nicholas Hollins," *Maryland Historical Magazine* 34 (1939): 228–38.

37. Paul H. Silverstone, *Warships of the Civil War Navies* (Annapolis: United States Naval Institute, 1989), 230, 244, 245; C. W. Read, "Reminiscences of the Confederate States Navy," *Southern Historical Society Papers* 1 (May 1876): 227–28; James M. Morgan, *Recollections of a*

Rebel Reefer (Boston: Houghton Mifflin Company, 1917), 61–62; *OR A*, VIII, 184; *Cincinnati Commercial*, March 14, 1862.

38. J. Thomas Scharf, *History of the Confederate States Navy* (New York: J. McDonough, 1887), 245; Dufour, *Night the War Was Lost*, 62; *Daily Missouri Republican*, April 11, 1862.

39. Still, *Iron Afloat*, 47–48; *Memphis Avalanche*, December 15, 1861. For Northern reaction, see *Daily Missouri Democrat*, December 1, 1861; *Chicago Tribune*, November 21, 1861; *New York Tribune*, April 5, 1862.

40. Morgan, *Recollections*, 62.

2. Too Much Haste Will Ruin Everything

1. John D. Milligan, "From Application to Theory; the Emergence of the American Ironclad War Vessel," *Military Affairs* (July 1984): 126; William N. Still, Jr., "Technology Afloat," *Civil War Times Illustrated* 14 (November 1975): 8–9; Paul H. Silverstone, *Warships of the Civil War Navies* (Annapolis: United States Naval Institute, 1989), 151; Howard P. Nash, *A Naval History of the Civil War* (New York: A. S. Barnes and Company, 1972), 26–27; Beringer et al., *Why the South Lost*, 119.

2. James M. Merrill, "Union Shipbuilding on Western Waters During the Civil War," *Smithsonian Journal of History* 3 (Winter 1968–69): 19; Florence Dorsey, *Road to the Sea: The Story of James B. Eads and the Mississippi* (New York, n. p., 1947), 2–25; Edwin C. Bearss, *Hardluck Ironclad: The Sinking and Salvage of Cairo* (Baton Rouge: Louisiana State University, 1980), 17.

3. Merrill, "Union Shipbuilding," 20; *Daily Missouri Democrat*, September 18, 1861; *Daily Missouri Republican*, September 21, 1861; William H. Fowler, Jr., *Under Two Flags: The American Navy in the Civil War* (New York: Norton, 1990), 139.

4. Robert E. Johnson, *Rear Admiral John Rogers 1812–1882* (Annapolis: United States Naval Institute, 1967), 166; Merrill, "Union Shipbuilding," 23.

5. *Daily Missouri Democrat*, February 3, 18, 1861; Benjamin J. Lossing, *The Pictorial Field Book of the Civil War in the United States of America*, 5 vols. (Hartford: Geo. Sinester, 1878), 2: 241–42; John D. Milligan, *Gunboats Down the Mississippi* (Annapolis: United States Naval Institute, 1965), 17, 23–24; James H. Merrill, *Battle Flags South* (Cranbury, N.J.: Fairleigh Dickinson University Press, 1970), 50; *OR N*, XXII, 314, 483, 494, 523, 527.

6. Reuben E. Stivers, *Privateers and Volunteers: The Men and Women of Our Reserve Naval Forces: 1776–1866* (Annapolis: United States Naval Institute, 1975), 250–58; *OR N*, XXII, 385, 459, 465, 494; Milligan, *Gunboats*, 53; Henry Walke, "Gunboats at Belmont and Fort Henry," in Robert C. Johnson and Clarence C. Buel, eds., *Battles and Leaders of the Civil War*, 4 vols. New York: Thomas Yoseloff, 1956), 1: 358–59; *Chicago Tribune*, November 30, 1861; *Daily Missouri Democrat*, February 26, 1862.

7. *OR N*, XXII, 495; *Daily Missouri Democrat*, February 3, 1862; *Chicago Tribune*, November 11, 1861.

8. *Daily Missouri Democrat*, November 23, 30, December 5, 14, 24, 1861; *Chicago Tribune*, December 5, 10, 26, 1861; Cooling, *Forts Henry and Donelson*, 26–27.

9. Reed, *Combined Operations*, 85; James McPherson, *Battle Cry of Freedom* (New York: Oxford University Press, 1988), 393.

10. Allan Nevins, *Ordeal of the Union*, 4 vols. (New York: Collier Books, 1992), 3: 12–13; Kenneth P. Williams, *Lincoln Finds A General*, 5 vols. (New York: The Macmillan Company, 1952), 3: 104–05; Page Smith, *Trial by Fire: A People's History of the Civil War and Reconstruction*, 5 vols. (New York: McGraw Hill, 1982), 5: 156; Hattaway and Jones, *How the North Won*, 54–55, 64.

11. *OR A,,* VII, 389–90, 402; McPherson, *Battle Cry of Freedom,* 350.

12. Williams, *Lincoln Finds a General,* 3: 124–25, 179; *OR A,* VII, 510, 525; *Daily Missouri Democrat,* January 7, 1862; *Chicago Tribune,* February 20, 1862.

13. Beringer et al., *How the South Lost,* 121; Williams, *Lincoln Finds a General,* 3: 66, 72, 78–80; *Daily Missouri Democrat,* February 3, 1862.

14. McPherson, *Battle Cry of Freedom,* 392; Beringer et al., *How the South Lost,* 120; Woodworth, *Davis,* 77–78; Milligan, "Emergence of the Ironclad," 129; *OR N,* XXII, 829–30.

15. Cooling, *Forts Henry and Donelson,* 129; *OR N,* XXII, 829–30.

16. Thomas L. Connelly, *Army of the Heartland: The Army of Tennessee, 1861–1862* (Baton Rouge: Louisiana State University Press, 1967), 113.

17. Beringer et al., *Why the South Lost,* 122–24, 130, 134; Edward Hagerman, *The American Civil War and the Origins of Modern Warfare* (Bloomington: Indiana University Press, 1988), 165–66; Archer Jones, *Confederate Strategy from Shiloh to Vicksburg* (Baton Rouge: Louisiana State University Press, 1961), 54.

3. Defense to the Last Extremity

1. McMurry, *Two Great Rebel Armies,* 122; T. Harry Williams, *P. G. T. Beauregard: Napoleon in Gray* (Baton Rouge: Louisiana State University Press, 1954), 120; Charles P. Roland, *Albert Sidney Johnston, Soldier of Three Republics* (Austin: University of Texas Press, 1964), 309; *OR A,* VII, 900.

2. Alfred Roman, *The Military Operations of General Beauregard in the War Between the States 1861 to 1865: Including a Brief Personal Sketch and a Narrative of His Services in the War with Mexico, 1846–48,* 2 vols. (New York: Harper & Bro., 1883), 1: 233–34; *OR A,* VII, 897; Joseph Parks, *General Leonidas Polk, CSA, the Fighting Bishop* (Baton Rouge: Louisiana State University Press, 1962), 213.

3. William N. Polk, *Leonidas Polk: Bishop and General,* 2 vols. (New York: Longmans, Green, and Co., 1915), 2: 75–80; Parks, *Polk,* 213–15; *OR A,* X, pt. 2, 311.

4. *OR N,* XXII, 826; *OR A,* VIII, 754.

5. Roman, *Beauregard,* 1: 236–37, 247, 361; *OR A,* X, pt. 2, 352.

6. Roman, *Beauregard,* 1: 236; Polk, *Polk,* 2: 82.

7. Roman, *Beauregard,* 1: 247, 352–53; 256, *OR A,* VII, 897; VIII, 757; *OR N,* XXII, 825, 826. Fletcher Pratt concluded that the true left of the Confederate line was intended to be Fort Pillow and that Island No. 10 was merely "a projection of the left." *Civil War on Western Waters* (New York: Holt, 1956), 61.

8. *OR A,* VII, 438, 853; VIII, 754; X, pt. 2, 377; *New Orleans Picayune,* February 16, 27, 28, 1862.

9. Jones, *From Shiloh to Vicksburg,* 16–17, 19–21, 25.

10. Connelly, *Army of the Heartland,* 21, 39, 129, 148.

11. Edward Younger, ed., *Inside the Confederate Government: The Diary of Robert Garlick Hill Kean* (New York: Oxford University Press, 1957), 25; Thomas Bragg Diary, March 6, 1862, SHC; Earl S. Miers, ed., *A Rebel War Clerk's Diary by John B. Jones* (New York: A. S. Barnes & Company, 1961), 69.

12. William C. Davis, *Jefferson Davis: The Man and His Hour* (New York: HarperCollins, 1991), 487; Scarborough, ed., *Ruffin,* 2, 249; William K. Scarbrough, ed., *The Diary of Edmund Ruffin* (Baton Rouge: Louisiana State University Press, 1976), 2: 249.

13. Archer Jones, *Civil War Command and Strategy: The Process of Victory and Defeat* (New York: The Free Press, 1992), 122–23, 162–63.

14. *OR A,* VIII, 754–55, 758, 761, 762.

15. Ezra T. Warner, *Generals in Gray: Lives of Confederate Commanders* (Baton Rouge: Louisiana State University Press, 1959), 14; Baker Diary, February 26, 1862, ADAH.

16. Woodworth, *Davis,* 264.

17. *ORA,* VIII, 125–27, 172, 754, 759; Benjamin D. Dean, *Reflections of the Twenty-Sixth Missouri Infantry in the War for the Union* (Lamar, Mo.: Southwest Missourian, 1892), 220–21; Baker Diary, February 28, March 4, 1862, ADAH; George V. Driggs, *Opening of the Mississippi or Two Years Campaigning in the South-West* (Madison, Wisc.: William J. Park and Company, 1864), 80; *Cincinnati Commercial,* March 19, 1862; *New York Tribune,* April 14, 1862.

18. Beauregard to Harris, March 14, 1862, Harris Papers, DU.

19. Jennings to brother, February 5, 16, 1862, Jennings Letters, UALR.

20. *ORA,* VIII, 149, 178; Gray to Gantt, February 16, 1862, quoted in *New York Times,* March 16, 1862.

21. *ORA,* VIII, 178, 754–55, 770.

22. Connelly, *Autumn of Glory,* 81; Hughes, *Belmont,* 37, 201.

23. *ORA,* VIII, 760, 762.

24. Stanley S. Arthur, *Old Families of Louisiana* (Baton Rouge: Louisiana State University Press, 1971), 95–96.

25. *ORA,* VIII, 149–51, 179, 186, 760; Joe Barbiere, *Scraps from the Prison Table, at Camp Chase and Johnson's Island* (Doylestown, Pa.: W. W. H. Davis, 1868), 64.

26. *ORA,* VIII, 186, 726; John B. Lindsley, ed., *The Military Annals of Tennessee, Confederate* (Nashville: J. M. Lindsley & Co., 1886), 790; L. B. Claiborne File, Civil War Times Collection, USMHI; *New Orleans Crescent,* March 15, 1862; *Cleveland Plain Dealer,* March 6, 1862.

27. *ORA,* VIII, 151, 762.

28. Ibid., 767.

29. McCown to Polk, March 5, 1862, Polk Papers, US; *ORA,* VIII, 149, 805; *ORN,* XXII, 824.

30. *ORN,* XXII, 824; *ORA,* VIII, 805.

31. *ORN,* XXII, 747–48, 832; *New York Herald,* April 15, 1862; *Chicago Tribune,* April 11, 1862; *New York Times,* April 14, 1862; *ORA,* VIII, 144, 151; McCown to Polk, March 5, 1862, Polk Papers, US.

32. McCown to Polk, March 5, 1862, Polk Papers, US; Harris to Jordon, March 9, 1862, Harris Papers, DU.

33. *ORA,* VIII, 148–49; Beauregard to Johnston, March 22, 1862, Letter Book of the Headquarters of the Western Department of the Confederate Army, Kuntz Collection, TU.

34. *ORA,* VIII, 150, 152, 153.

35. Ibid., 152, 774–75.

36. Edward W. McMorries, *History of the First Alabama Volunteer Infantry, C. S. A.* (Montgomery: The Brown Printing Company, 1904), 82–83; Daniel P. Smith, *Company K, First Alabama Regiment, or Three in the Confederate Service* (Gaithersburg, Md.: Butternut Press, 1984), 6–9; *ORA,* VIII, 778, 780; I. G. W. Steadman to son, June 1, 1891, Civil War Times Collection, USMHI; Brian M. Green, "Confederate Postal Use from Island Number Ten," *The Confederate Philatelist* 34 (November–December 1989): 187.

37. *ORA,* VIII, 152.

38. Beauregard to Johnston, March 2, 1862, Beauregard Memorandum, March 4, 1862 in Beauregard-Johnston Correspondence, Letter Book of the Western Department, Kuntz Collection, TU. Beauregard's troops were dispersed as follows: Island No. 10—7,000; Fort Pillow—2,500; Humboldt and Union City—7,000; Grand Junction—5,000; Corinth— 13,000; Iuka—2,500.

4. We Have Received Marching Orders

1. Bruce Catton, *Grant Moves South* (Boston: Little, Brown & Company, 1960), 188; *ORA*, X, pt. 2, 10; James Chumney, "Don Carlos Buell, Gentleman General," Ph.D. diss. Rice University, 1964, 65.

2. Hattaway and Jones, *How the North Won*, 147; *ORA*, VIII, 509–10.

3. Wallace J. Schutz and Walter N. Trenerry, *Abandoned by Lincoln: A Military Biography of General John Pope* (Urbana: University of Illinois Press, 1990), 4–5, 58–59, 60–61, 62, 64–66, 68, 71; *Philadelphia Inquirer*, April 9, 1862.

4. *ORA*, VIII, 452, 528, 820–23; *Chicago Tribune*, December 21, 24, 1861.

5. Force, *From Fort Henry to Corinth*, 66–67; William T. Sherman, *Memoirs of General William Sherman* (New York: Da Capo Press, Inc., 1984), 233; Hughes, *Belmont*, 45–46; *Cincinnati Commercial*, March 17, 1862.

6. *ORA*, VIII, 564; *Daily Missouri Democrat*, February 26, March 19, 1862; *Report of Major General John Pope* (Washington, D.C.: n.p., n.d.), 25; Dan Smith Diary, February 25, 1862, ILSHL; Arnold Miller Diary, February 27, 28, 1862, MSU.

7. *Daily Missouri Democrat*, February 22, 1862; *Cincinnati Commercial*, March 17, 1862.

8. Shelby County Historical Society, *Gold Rush and Civil War Letters to Ann from Michael Freyburger* (Shelbyville, Ind.: The Shelby County Historical Genealogical Society, 1986), 24; Martin V. Smith to "Dear Friends," February 17, 1862, Martin V. Smith Letters, IOSHS; *ORA*, VIII, 565; William Smith to wife, February 24, 1862, William S. Smith Letters, ILSHL; John Palmer to wife, February 24, 1862, John Palmer Letters, ILSHL; C. W. Reilly to Miss Ross, March 16, 1862, C. W. Reilly Letters, INHS.

9. Ezra T. Warner, *Generals in Blue: Lives of the Union Commanders* (Baton Rouge: Louisiana State University Press, 1964), 199–200, 358–59; John M. Palmer, *Personal Recollections of John M. Palmer: The Story of an Earnest Life* (Cincinnati: Robert Clark Co., 1901), 71–83; George T. Palmer, *Conscientious Turncoat: The Story of John M. Palmer 1817–1900* (New Haven: Yale University Press, 1941), 72, 76.

10. Marshall P. Thatcher, *A Hundred Battles in the West* (Detroit: L. F. Kilroy, 1884), 30, 32; Warner, *Generals in Blue*, 181.

11. J. W. Bissell, "Sawing Out the Channel Above Island Number Ten," in Robert C. Johnson and Clarence C. Buel, eds., *Battles and Leaders of the Civil War*, 4 vols. (New York: Thomas Yoseloff, 1956), 1: 460.

12. David S. Stanley, *Personal Memoirs of Major General David S. Stanley* (Cambridge: Harvard University Press, 1917), 84; Palmer to wife, March 9, 1862, Palmer Letters, ILSHL.

13. *ORA*, VIII, 559, 566, 570, 573; *Daily Missouri Democrat*, February 28, 1862.

14. *ORA*, VIII, 564–65; Smith to "Dear Friends," February 26, 1862, Smith Letters, ILSHL; Aden G. Cavins, *The War Letters of Aden G. Cavins Written to His Wife* (Evansville: Rosenthal-Kuebler Company, 1918), 4; Thomas H. Bringhurst and Frank Swigart, *History of the Forty-Sixth Indiana Volunteer Infantry* (Logansport, Ind.: Wilson, Humphreys and Co., 1888), 20.

15. *ORA*, VIII, 571; Oscar L. Jackson, *The Colonel's Diary, Journals Kept Before and During the Civil War* (Sharon, Pa., 1922), 44.

16. *Report of Major General John Pope*, 24–25; Force, *From Fort Henry to Corinth*, 71; Mullen, "Pope's New Madrid," 331; Hughes, *Belmont*, 5; *Philadelphia Inquirer*, March 31, 1862; Henry Walke, "The Western Flotilla at Fort Donelson, Island Number Ten, Fort Pillow, and Memphis," in Robert C. Johnson and Clarence C. Buel, eds., *Battles and Leaders of the Civil War*, 4 vols. (New York: Thomas Yoseloff, 1956), 1: 439.

17. *Cincinnati Commercial*, March 17, 1862; Bryon C. Bryner, *Bugle Echoes, The Story of*

the *Illinois Forty-Seventh* (Springfield: Phillips Bros., 1905), 36; Bringhurst and Swigart, *Forty-Sixth Regiment,* 21; Smith to wife, March 3, 1862, Smith Letters, ILSHL.

18. Thompson, *Reminiscences,* 142; *Memphis Appeal,* October 10, 1861.

19. *ORA,* VIII, 102, 110, 173, 573; Society, *Letters to Ann,* 25; Thompson, *Reminiscences,* 142–43; Bringhurst and Swigart, *Forty-Sixth Regiment,* 64; Benjamin F. Sweet, "Civil War Experiences," *Missouri Historical Quarterly* 43 (April 1949): 242; D. McCall, *Three Years in the Service: A Record of the Doings of the Eleventh Regiment Missouri Volunteers* (Springfield, Mo.: Baker and Phillips, 1864), 6; Smith to wife, March 3, 1862, Smith Letters, ILSHL; *Daily Missouri Democrat,* March 4, 1862; *Cincinnati Commercial,* March 4, 1862.

20. Cavin, *War Letters,* 4; Slack to wife, March 4, 1862, Slack Letters, INSL; Benson J. Lossing, *The Pictorial Field Book of the Civil War in the United States,* 5 vols. (New Haven: Geo. S. Lester, 1878), 2: 239; *Cincinnati Commercial,* March 10, 17, 1862; *New York Times,* March 17, 1862; Dean, *Recollections,* 277; Jackson, *Colonel's Diary,* 44–45.

21. *ORA,* VIII, 572, 580, 581.

22. Ibid., 587; *Cincinnati Commercial,* March 11, 1862; *Daily Missouri Democrat,* March 13, 1862; Driggs, *Opening of the Mississippi,* 79.

5. I Consider New Madrid of Great Importance

1. *ORA,* VIII, 758, 759, 761, 762, 763; *New Orleans Picayune,* March 2, 1862.

2. Baker Diary, March 1, 1862, ADAH.

3. Ibid., March 3, 1862; *ORA,* VIII, 162.

4. *New Orleans Delta,* March 8, 1862.

5. Thompson, *Reminiscences,* 65; Jennings to brother, March 18, 1862, Jennings Letters, UALR; Baker Diary, March 2, 1862, ADAH.

6. *ORA,* VIII, 102; Baker Diary, March 2, 1862, ADAH; Smith C. Twitty to wife, March 6, 1862, Smith C. Twitty Letters, Clements Collection; Charles W. Wills, *Army Life of an Illinois Soldier* (Washington, D.C.: Globe Printing Company, 1906), 64.

7. Baker Diary, March 2, 1862, ADAH; *Memphis Avalanche,* March 9, 1862.

8. Baker Diary, March 3, 1862, ADAH; Thompson, *Reminiscences,* 65; *ORA,* VIII, 675.

9. *ORA,* VIII, 81, 102; Smith to wife, March 3, 1862, Smith Letters, ILSHL; Baker Diary, March 3, 1862, ADAH; *Memphis Avalanche,* March 9, 1862; *Cincinnati Commercial,* March 10, 1862; C. W. Read, "Reminiscences of the Confederate States Navy," *Southern Historical Society Papers* 1 (May 1876): 337.

10. Lin Burtot to L. and R. Green, March 14, 1862, Lin Burtot Letters, NMHM; Bringhurst and Swigart, *Forty-Sixth Regiment,* 21; Slack to wife, March 4, 1862, Slack Letters, INSL; Cavins, *War Letters,* 6; Jackson, *Colonel's Diary,* 45; Palmer to wife, March 2, 1862, Palmer Letters, ILSHL; *Daily Missouri Democrat,* March 19, 1862; *Cincinnati Commercial,* March 10, 1862. The St. Louis journalist claimed that the Federals lost one killed and four wounded.

11. *ORA,* VIII, 81.

12. *Memphis Avalanche,* March 9, 1862. See also *Memphis Appeal,* March 5, 1862.

13. William S. Dillon Diary, March 4, 1862, UM; *ORA,* VIII, 765.

14. Morgan, *Recollections,* 67–68.

15. Baker Diary, March 5, 1862, ADAH; Dillon Diary, March 7, 1862, UM; Jennings to brother, March 10, 1862, Jennings Letters, UALR; Twitty to wife, March 6, 1862, Twitty Letter, Clements Collection.

16. Smith to wife, March 5, 1862, Smith Letters, ILSHL; Wills, *Army Life,* 65; Jackson, *Colonel's Diary,* 45.

17. *OR A,* VIII, 103, 105–06; Cavins, *War Letters,* 6–7; Daniel Smith to father, March 16, 1862, Daniel Smith Letters, ILSHL; Dillon Diary, March 4, 1862, UM; Baker Diary, March 5, 1862, ADAH; *Memphis Appeal,* March 7, 1862.

18. *OR A,* VIII, 588.

19. Ibid., 587–88.

20. Ibid., 591, 595; Stephen E. Ambrose, *Halleck: Lincoln's Chief of Staff* (Baton Rouge: Louisiana State University Press, 1962), 37–38; Force, *From Fort Henry to Corinth,* 74; Williams, *Lincoln Finds a General,* 3: 299.

21. *OR A,* VIII, 81–82, 113–14, 587.

22. *Memphis Appeal,* March 9, 1862; *Mobile Advertiser & Register,* March 22, 1862; *OR A,* VIII, 127; *OR N,* XXII, 751; Bryner, *Bugle Echoes,* 36. An unconfirmed report stated that the Federals dressed as women to lure the *Pontchartrain.*

23. *OR A,* VIII, 114; Morgan, *Recollections,* 64–65; Baker Diary, March 7, 1862, ADAH.

24. The 4th Tennessee of Stewart's brigade was already committed to New Madrid and is not included in the twenty-six hundred estimate. Such a distribution would have maintained Kennedy's small brigade and the 46th Tennessee at Island No. 10 for an emergency.

25. *OR A,* VIII, 127, 591–92, 775.

26. *Memphis Appeal,* March 9, 1862; *Memphis Avalanche,* March 14, 1862; *New Orleans Crescent,* March 24, 1862; *OR A,* VIII, 775.

27. *OR A,* VIII, 765, 766.

28. Roman, *Beauregard,* 1: 356; *OR A,* X, pt. 2, 329.

29. *OR A,* VIII, 770, 771, 772.

30. Roman, *Beauregard,* 1: 357.

31. *OR A,* VIII, 766, 771.

32. March 4, 1862 Memorandum in the Letter Book of the Headquarters of the Western Department, Kuntz Collection, TU; *OR A,* VIII, 778–79; Beauregard to Harris, March 14, 1862, Harris Papers, DU. Bragg had suggested a reinforcement of ten thousand. *OR A,* X., pt. 2, 328–29.

33. *OR A,* VIII, 772, 775.

34. Ibid., 771–72; Roman, *Beauregard,* 1: 356.

35. *OR A,* VIII, 787, 790, 791.

36. *Memphis Appeal,* March 7, 11, 1862; D. A. Turren to Miss Pink Willie, March 12, 1862, D. A. Turren Letters, INSL; William F. Mack to Colonel Cobb, April 1, 1862, William F. Mack Letters, NMHM; Baker Diary, March 10, 1862, ADAH; Jennings to brother, February 26, 1862, Jennings Letters, UALR.

37. Gaughen, ed., *Letters,* 35.

38. Palmer to wife, March 9, 1862, Palmer Letters, ILSHL.

39. *OR A,* VIII, 94–95; William E. Smith and Ophia D. Smith, eds., Colonel A. W. Gilbert, Citizen Soldier of Cincinnati (Cincinnati: Historical and Philosophical Society of Ohio, 1934), 82, 86; Stephen Z. Starr, *The Union Cavalry of the Civil War,* 3 vols. (Baton Rouge: Louisiana State University Press, 1985), 3:33.

40. Baker Diary, March 6, 1862, ADAH.

41. *OR A,* VIII, 98, 103.

42. Ibid., 106; Jackson, *Colonel's Diary,* 46.

43. Morgan, *Recollections,* 65. See also *New Orleans Picayune,* March 18, 1862.

44. *OR A,* VIII, 106; *Cincinnati Commercial,* March 11, 1862; Palmer to wife, March 9, 1862, Palmer Letters, ILSHL.

45. Alfred Gilbert to wife, March 8, 1862, Alfred Gilbert Letters, MUO; Hagan to Dear Sir, March 23, 1862 in Miles Papers, SHC; Jennings to brother, March 5, 1862, Jennings Letters, UALR; Palmer to wife, March 9, 1862, Palmer Letters, ILSHL.

46. Ephrain A. Wilson, *Memoirs of the War* (Cleveland: W. M. Bayne Printing Company, 1893), 67, 69; *ORA*, VIII, 594, 603; 16th Illinois Record Book, ILSHL; Driggs, *Opening of the Mississippi*, 81; Dean, *Recollections*, 132; S. H. M. Byers, *Iowa in War Times* (Des Moines: W. D. Condit & Co., 1888), 500.

47. Patricia L. Faust, ed. *Historical Times Illustrated Encyclopedia of the Civil War* (New York: Harper & Row, 1986), 543; Smith to wife, March 11, 1862, Smith Letters, ILSHL.

48. *ORA*, VIII, 95, 603, 605.

49. Wills, *Army Life*, 65–66; Matthew H. Jamison, *Recollections of Pioneer and Army Life* (Kansas City: Hudson Press, 1922), 173. See also Smith and Smith, eds., *Gilbert*, 82; Jackson, *Colonel's Diary*, 46; Arnold Miller Diary, March 9, 1862, MSU.

50. *Memphis Appeal*, March 9, 1862; Baker Diary, March 11, 1862, ADAH; *New York Herald*, March 18, 1862.

6. The Cowardly Rebels Run Away

1. Lossing, *Pictorial History*, 2: 240; *ORA*, VIII, 82; Lyman B. Pierce, *History of the Second Iowa Cavalry* (Burlington: Hawkeye Steam Book and Job Printing Company, 1865), 14; *New York Times*, March 17, 1862.

2. Wilson, *Memoirs*, 70–74; *Chicago Tribune*, March 19, 1862.

3. *ORA*, VIII, 165–166.

4. Ibid., 82, 96–97, 103; James R. Slack to Ann, March 15, 1862, Slack Letters, INSL; Benjamin T. Smith Diary, March 7 [13], 1862, ILSHL; Thatcher, *Hundred Battles*, 30; William D. Love, *Wisconsin in the War of the Rebellion* (Chicago, 1886), 467; *New York Times*, March 17, 1862; *Chicago Tribune*, March 19, 1862; "Sketch Shewing [*sic*] the Relative Position of the Enemy's Works and Our Batteries During the Attack of the 13th of March 1862. By F. Tunica, Engs.," Record Group 77, NA; Record of Company A, 16th Illinois Infantry Regiment, 39, ILSHL.

5. *ORA*, VIII, 96–97, 163, 166, 778–79, 788; Gilbert to wife, March 14, 1862, Gilbert Letters, MUO; *Memphis Avalanche*, March 15, 1862; Baker Diary, March 13, 1862, ADAH; *Memphis Appeal*, March 16, 1862; Wilson, *Memoirs*, 75; William C. Davis to mother, March 15, 1862, William C. Davis Letters, Civil War Misc. Collection, USMHI.

6. *ORA*, VIII, 166.

7. Baker Diary, March 13, 1862, ADAH; *ORA*, VIII, 96, 167; Slack to wife, March 15, 1862, Slack Letters, INSL; Wills, *Army Life*, 69; Wilson, *Memoirs*, 76.

8. *ORA*, VIII, 82; George H. Woodruff, *Fifteen Years Ago* (Joliet, Ill.: James Goodspeed, 1876), 183; Luther Bradley to wife, March 31, 1862, Luther Bradley Letters, USMHI; Slack to Ann, March 15, 1862, Slack Letters, INSL.

9. Gilbert to wife, March 14, 1862, Gilbert Letters, UMO; Smith and Smith, eds., *Gilbert*, 89; Jackson, *Colonel's Diary*, 46; *ORA*, VIII, 101; *Chicago Tribune*, March 14, 19, 1862. See also William Woodward Diary, March 18, 1862, USMHI.

10. Wilson, *Memoirs*, 76–77.

11. *ORA*, VIII, 163.

12. Ibid., 127, 162, 163, 167, 779; *ORN*, XXII, 749–50; *Memphis Appeal*, March 16, 1862; *Washington Telegraph*, August 13, 1862.

13. *ORA*, VIII, 164; *ORN*, XXII, 750.

14. *ORA*, VIII, 164–65, 167–68; Mack to Colonel Cobb, April 1, 1862, Mack Letters, NMHM; Jennings to brother, March 26, 1862, Jennings Letters, UALR; Force, *From Fort Henry to Corinth*, 77.

15. William Polk to sister, March 29, 1862, Polk Letters, US; Baker Diary, March 13, 1862, ADAH; *New Orleans Delta,* March 18, 20, 1862.

16. Wilson, *Memoirs,* 81; Jackson, *Colonel's Diary,* 48; Davis to mother, March 15, 1862, Davis Letters, USMHI; Stanley, *Memoirs,* 88. Stanley's report does not appear in the *ORA.*

17. *ORA,* VIII, 103–04, 108, 613; Slack to wife, March 15, 1862, Slack Letters, INSL; Bringhurst and Swigart, *Forty-Sixth Regiment,* 22; Davis to mother, March 15, 1862, Davis Letters, USMHI; C. W. Reilly to Miss Ross, March 16, 1862, C. W. Reilly Letters, INSL; *Cincinnati Commercial,* March 19, 1862.

18. Wills, *Army Life,* 67–68; Palmer to wife, March 14, 1862, Palmer Letters, ILSHL; Wilson, *Memoirs,* 82; *Memphis Appeal,* March 16, 1862; *ORA,* VIII, 83, 613–14; *Daily Missouri Democrat,* March 19, 1862; Frank Moore, ed., *Rebellion Record: A Diary of American Events, with Documents, Narratives, Illustrative Incidents, Poetry, etc.,* 10 vols. (New York: n. p. 1861–63), 4: 305.

19. *ORA,* VIII, 92–93, 168, 786; Palmer to wife, March 14, 1862, Palmer Letters, ILSHL; *New York Herald,* March 16, 1862; *Cincinnati Commercial,* March 19, 20, 1862; *Daily Missouri Republican,* March 15, 1862. The Cincinnati paper listed the following casualties on the 13th: 27th Ohio—one killed, three wounded; 43d Ohio—four wounded; 11th Ohio—one killed; 1st U.S.—one killed, five wounded; three others killed not in Ohio regiments. The Appeal of March 9, 1862, mentions seventeen Confederates having been killed to that date. Various anecdotal information confirms six killed and eight wounded prior to March 13. Gantt lost two killed, one wounded, and thirteen missing in the evacuation.

20. *ORA,* VIII, 766, 771; X, pt. 2, 340; Merrill, *Battle Flags South,* 113.

21. Baker Diary, March 13, 1862, ADAH; *ORA,* VIII, 138, 780–81.

22. *ORA,* VIII, 781–82, 138; Roman, *Beauregard,* 1: 358.

23. Baker Diary, March 13, 1862, ADAH; *Memphis Appeal,* March 18, 1862; *ORA,* VIII, 138; *New Orleans Delta,* March 21, 1862.

24. *ORA,* VIII, 132–33, 780–81, 785–86.

25. Ibid., 781–82, 138; Roman, *Beauregard,* 1: 358.

26. *ORA,* VIII, 598–99; Williams, *Lincoln Finds a General,* III, 299; Smith and Smith, eds., *Gilbert,* 86.

27. Schutz and Trenerry, *Abandoned by Lincoln,* 78; *ORA,* VIII, 613.

7. Why Can't Foote Move?

1. Foote, *Civil War,* I, 184; Bern Anderson, *By Sea and by River: The Naval History of the Civil War* (New York: Alfred Knopf, 1962), 23, 46, 86; Henry Walke, "Gunboats at Belmont and Fort Henry," *Battles and Leaders of the Civil War,* 4 vols. (New York: Thomas Yoseloff, 1956), 1: 359–60; *National Intelligencer,* March 10, 1862; *Philadelphia Inquirer,* March 26, 1862.

2. Foote to wife, February 16, 17, 23, 25, March 9, 1862, "Loose Papers, Mississippi River," Record Group 45, NA; Hoppin, *Foote,* 260.

3. *ORA,* VIII, 588, 590–91; *ONR,* XXII, 565, 651, 652, 657, 658, 662; Hoppin, *Foote,* 264.

4. Hoppin, *Foote,* 265; *ORA,* VIII, 595.

5. *ORN,* XXII, 503, 505, 659–60; Merrill, *Battle Flags South,* 118–19; Hoppin, *Foote,* 262, 265; *Daily Missouri Democrat,* January 21, 1862; *Daily Missouri Republican,* March 4, 1862.

6. *ORN,* XXII, 660; Hoppin, *Foote,* 259–62; *Cincinnati Commercial,* March 25, 1862; *Philadelphia Inquirer,* March 28, 1862.

7. Foote, *Civil War,* I, 309.

8. *OR N*, XXII, 663–64; Hoppin, *Foote*, 265–66.

9. *OR N*, XXII, 665, 685–87.

10. *Daily Missouri Democrat*, February 21, 27, March 4, 1862; *New York Herald*, March 8, 1862; *Daily Missouri Democrat*, March 12, 1862; *New York Times*, March 12, 16, 1862; *National Intelligencer*, March 18, 1862; *Chicago Tribune*, March 19, 26, 1862; Walke, "Western Flotilla," 439.

11. *Philadelphia Inquirer*, March 20, 1862; *Cincinnati Commercial*, March 18, 1862; *Chicago Tribune*, March 17, 1862; *Daily Missouri Democrat*, March 14, 1862; *New York Herald*, March 24, 25, 1862; *New York Tribune*, March 22, 1862; William A. Schmitt, *History of the Twenty-Seventh Illinois* (Winchester: Standard Steam Printing House, 1892), 4; *New York Times*, March 16, 1862; *OR N*, XXII, 693.

12. *New York Times*, March 30, 1862.

13. *OR A*, VIII, 115, 153; *OR N*, XXII, 773; *Daily Missouri Democrat*, March 19, 1862; *Daily Missouri Republican*, March 17, 1862; *Cincinnati Commercial*, March 18, 1862; *New York Tribune*, March 22, 1862; Milligan, ed., *From the Fresh Water Navy*, III, 41.

14. *Cincinnati Commercial*, March 18, 1862; *New York Tribune*, March 24, 1862.

15. *Cleveland Plain Dealer*, March 17, 1862; *OR N*, XXII, 693; *Daily Missouri Democrat*, March 19, 1862; *Chicago Tribune*, March 21, 1862; Milligan, ed., *From the Fresh Water Navy*, III, 42.

16. *OR A*, VIII, 159; *New Orleans Crescent*, March 26, 1862.

17. Milligan, ed., *From the Fresh Water Navy*, III, 41; *New York Tribune*, March 24, 1862; *Philadelphia Inquirer*, March 20, 1862; *Chicago Tribune*, March 21, 1862; *National Intelligencer*, March 18, 1862.

18. *OR A*, VIII, 159; *New Orleans Crescent*, March 26, 1862.

19. *OR A*, VIII, 159; *New York Tribune*, March 24, 1862.

20. *New York Tribune*, March 24, 1862; *Daily Missouri Democrat*, March 19, 1862; *OR N*, XXII, 770.

21. *OR A*, VIII, 153.

22. Edmund H. Cummings, "The Signal Corps in the Confederate States Army," *Southern Historical Society Papers* 16 (1888): 95; *OR A*, VIII, 159.

23. *Philadelphia Inquirer*, March 20, 1862; *Cleveland Plain Dealer*, March 17, 1862; *Cincinnati Commercial*, March 20, 1862.

24. *New York Tribune*, March 24, 1862; *OR A*, VIII, 153–54; *Philadelphia Inquirer*, March 20, 1862; *Cincinnati Commercial*, March 20, 1862.

25. *Chicago Post* quoted in *New York Times*, March 23, 1862; *Chicago Tribune*, March 24, 1862; *Philadelphia Inquirer*, March 20, 1862; *New Orleans Crescent*, March 26, 1862.

26. *Chicago Post* quoted in *New York Times*, March 23, 1862; *New York Tribune*, March 23, 1862; *New York Tribune*, March 24, 1862; *Philadelphia Inquirer*, March 20, 1862; *New Orleans Crescent*, March 26, 1862.

27. *Philadelphia Inquirer*, March 20, 1862; *OR A*, VIII, 154; Edward Crippen, "Diary of Edward W. Crippen, Private, 27th Illinois Volunteers, War of the Rebellion, August 7, 1861 to September 19, 1863," *Transactions of the Illinois State Historical Society for the Year 1900* (Springfield, Ill.: Illinois State Historical Society, 1910), 238; Woodruff, *Fifteen Years Ago*, 423. Trudeau incorrectly placed the incident at 1 P.M.

28. *OR A*, VIII, 154; *OR N*, XXII, 770, 773–74; William J. Putney Journal, 12, UMI; Crippen, "Crippen Diary," 238; *Daily Missouri Democrat*, March 21, 1862; Thaddeus C. S. Brown, Samuel J. Murphey, and William G. Putney, *Behind the Guns: The History of Battery I 2nd Regiment, Illinois Light Artillery* (Carbondale: Southern Illinois University Press, 1965), 10.

29. *ORA*, VIII, 154; Dillon Diary, March 17, 1862, UM; Baker Diary, March 17, 1862, ADAH.

30. *New York Tribune*, March 24, 1862; Charles Boynton, *The History of the Navy During the War of the Rebellion* (New York: D. Appleton and Company, 1867), 537.

31. Milligan, ed., *From the Fresh Water Navy*, 43; *Chicago Post* quoted in *New York Times*, March 23, 1862; *New York Times*, March 28, 1862; Albert D. Richardson, *The Secret Service, the Field, the Dungeon, and the Escape* (Hartford: American Publishing Company, 1865), 226; Henry Walke, *Naval Scenes and Reminiscences of the Civil War* (New York: F. R. Reed & Company, 1877), 104.

32. *Daily Missouri Democrat*, March 21, 1862.

33. *Philadelphia Inquirer*, March 24, 1862; Richardson, *Secret Service*, 226.

34. *ORA*, VIII, 154–55, 175; J. J. Neely to wife, J. J. Neely Letters, SHC; *New Orleans Crescent*, March 16, 1862; *Memphis Appeal*, March 20, 1862.

35. *New York Times*, March 28, 1862.

36. Richardson, *Secret Service*, 226–28; *Daily Missouri Democrat*, March 21, 1862; *Chicago Tribune*, undated article in Eltinge-Lord Papers, DU; *Cincinnati Commercial*, March 21, 1862; *ORN*, XXII, 693, 694; Charles C. Coffin, *The Boys of '61 or Four Years of Fighting* (Boston: Arno and the New York Times, 1885), 90; *New York Times*, March 19, 1862. The Associated Press reporter placed the *Benton's* casualties at one killed and six wounded, but the figure is not confirmed in official reports. *Boston Transcript*, March 19, 1862.

37. Clarence E. N. Macartney, *Mr. Lincoln's Admirals* (New York: Funk & Wagnalls, 1956), 105; Hoppin, *Foote*, 105.

38. Walke, *Naval Scenes*, 101.

39. Ibid., 102–04.

40. *ORA*, VIII, 125, 156, 160–61, 174, 180–81, 739; *Memphis Appeal*, March 21, 1862; Samuel B. Moore letter of March 31, 1862, quoted in *Cincinnati Commercial*, April 19, 1862; Edward Y. McMorries, *History of the First Alabama Volunteer Infantry, C. S. A.* (Montgomery: The Brown Printing Company, 1904), 36; *New Orleans Delta*, March 25, 1862.

41. *New Orleans Delta*, March 25, 1862.

42. *ORN*, XXII, 693–94; *New York Tribune*, March 24, 1862; *Cincinnati Commercial*, March 21, 1862.

43. *ORA*, VIII, 125, 128, 155–56; *Memphis Appeal*, March 21, 1862; *New Orleans Crescent*, March 26, 1862; *New Orleans Delta*, March 25, 1862; *Southern Confederacy*, April 4, 1862.

44. *ORA*, VIII, 150, 181; H. Blair Bentley, "Morale as a Factor in the Confederate Failure at Island Number Ten," *West Tennessee Historical Society Papers* 31 (1977): 126.

45. *Cincinnati Commercial*, March 21, 1862; Walke, *Naval Scenes*, 103; *New York Times*, March 22, 28, 1862; *ORN*, XXII, 770, 774–75; *Chicago Tribune*, March 21, 1862; *New York Tribune*, March 25, 1862; *New Orleans Crescent*, March 26, 1862.

46. Hoppin, *Foote*, 269.

8. We Think Foote and His Gunboats a Good Deal of Humbug

1. *ORN*, XXII, 692; *Report of Major General John Pope*, 30; W. A. Neal, *An Illustrated History of the Missouri Engineers and the Twenty-Fifth Infantry Regiment* (Chicago: Donohue and Henneperry, 1889), 41.

2. *ORN*, XXII, 697; Neal, *Missouri Engineers*, 41; *New York Tribune*, March 28, 1862; *Chicago Tribune*, March 22, 1862.

3. Walke, *Naval Scenes*, 117.

4. *OR N,* XXII, 697, 734; Neal, *Missouri Engineers,* 41.

5. Neal, *Missouri Engineers,* 41.

6. *OR N,* XXII, 700–01, 734.

7. Ibid., 698–99.

8. *OR N,* XXII, 770–71, 775–76; *New York Times,* March 22, 1862; *Daily Missouri Democrat,* March 23, 1862; *Cincinnati Commercial,* April 1, 1862; *Chicago Tribune,* March 27, 1862.

9. *New York Times,* March 25, 1862; Hoppin, *Foote,* 269.

10. Walke, *Naval Scenes,* 105; *Cincinnati Commercial,* March 22, 25, April 1, 1862; *New York Times,* March 22, 25, 29, 1862; *Daily Missouri Republican,* March 23, 1862; *Philadelphia Inquirer,* March 28, 1862.

11. Milligan, ed., *From the Fresh Water Navy,* III, 52; *Daily Missouri Democrat,* March 26, 1862; Richardson, *Secret Service,* 230.

12. *OR N,* XXII, 770; *New York Times,* March 25, 1862; *Cincinnati Commercial,* March 22, 1862; Franc B. Wilkie, *Pen and Powder* (Boston: Ticknor and Company, 1888), 151–53.

13. Walke, *Naval Scenes,* 105–06; *New York Times,* March 29, 1862; Crippen, "Crippen Diary," 239.

14. *Chicago Tribune,* March 21, 1862; *Daily Missouri Democrat,* April 3, 1862; *New York Times,* March 23, 1862; *New York Tribune,* March 31, 1862.

15. *New York Times,* March 21, 1862; *Philadelphia Inquirer,* April 4, 1862; Emmet Crozier, *Yankee Reporters 1861–65* (New York: Oxford University Press, 1956), 195.

16. *Chicago Tribune,* March 19, 1862; *Daily Missouri Republican,* March 18, 1862; *Cleveland Plain Dealer,* March 18, 1862.

17. *New York Herald,* March 28, 1862.

18. *New York Tribune,* March 17, 1862; *New York Times,* March 29, April 5, 1862; *Daily Missouri Republican,* April 3, 1862; Milligan, ed., *From the Fresh Water Navy,* III, 49.

19. *Philadelphia Inquirer,* March 26, 1862; *National Intelligencer,* March 18, 1862; *New York Times,* March 22, 1862; *Chicago Tribune,* March 21, 1862.

20. *Chicago Tribune,* March 29, 1862.

21. F. Stansbury Haydon, *Aeronautics in the Union and Confederate Armies* (Baltimore: Johns Hopkins Press, 1941), 238, 262, 264, 387–89, 392, 394–97; *OR N,* XXII, 771; *New York Times,* March 29, April 1, 1862.

22. Merrill, *Battle Flags South,* 125; *Daily Missouri Democrat,* March 22, 1862; *Daily Missouri Republican* of March 22, 1862 defended Foote; *New York Times,* April 1, 1862.

23. Milligan, ed., *From the Fresh Water Navy,* 49; Gilbert to wife, March 23, 1862, Gilbert Letters, MUO; Walke, "Western Flotilla," 441.

24. Hughes, *Belmont,* 19–21; Warner, *Generals in Blue,* 53–54; *New York Herald,* April 3, 1862; Love, *Wisconsin,* 461; O. H. Nelson, ed., *History of the Scandinavians* (Minneapolis: n.p., 1900), 154; Leslie Anders, *The Eighteenth Missouri* (Indianapolis: The Bobbs-Merrill Co., 1968), 36–37; *Daily Missouri Democrat,* March 18, 1862; *Chicago Post* quoted in *New York Times,* March 23, 1862.

25. Anders, *Eighteenth Missouri,* 38–39.

26. Theodore C. Blegen, ed., *The Civil War Letters of Colonel Hans Christian Heg* (Northfield, Minn.: Norwegian-American Historical Association, 1931), 66; William Onstott to brother, March 28, 1862, William Onstott Letters, ILSHL; Putney Journal, UMI; Crippen, "Crippen Diary," 238.

27. *New York Herald,* March 28, 1862; *New York Times,* March 20, 28, 1862.

28. *OR A,* VIII, 116, 117–18; *New York Times,* March 30, April 4, 1862; *Philadelphia Inquirer,* April 5, 1862; *New York Tribune,* April 5, 8, 1862; Blegen, ed., *Heg,* 70–74.

29. *Memphis Appeal,* April 3, 1862; *Charleston Mercury,* April 7, 1862; *Richmond Inquirer,* April 12, 1862; Beauregard to Polk, April 1, 1862, Beauregard Papers, LC.

9. Be of Good Cheer and Hold Out

1. *OR N*, XXII, 822; *OR A*, VIII, 782; Roman, *Beauregard*, I, 359.
2. There were thirty-five heavy guns at Fort Pillow, including seven columbiads and six 32-pounder rifles. The latter were so poor, however, that they were kept in a reserve position for fear that overuse would result in an explosion, *OR A*, X, pt. 2, 395.
3. *OR A*, VIII, 769, 793, 797.
4. Ibid., 794.
5. Ibid., 782, 785–86.
6. Ibid., 128; Dillon Diary, March 17, 1862, UM; Roman, *Beauregard*, I, 359; *New Orleans Picayune*, March 25, 1862.
7. *OR A*, VIII, 129, 795, 807; Roman, *Beauregard*, I, 359–60.
8. *OR A*, VIII, 807; X, pt. 2, 396.
9. *New Orleans Crescent*, March 26, 1862.
10. *New York Times*, March 22, 23, 26, 1862; *Chicago Tribune*, March 22, 1862; *Philadelphia Inquirer*, March 22, 26, 1862.
11. *OR A*, VIII, 128–29.
12. Green, "Confederate Postal Use," 188; *New Orleans Crescent*, March 26, 1862; Moore letter quoted in *Cincinnati Commercial*, March 31, 1862; *Daily Missouri Democrat*, April 3, 1862.
13. Green, "Confederate Postal Use," 188; *New Orleans Crescent*, March 26, 1862; *Cincinnati Commercial*, March 22, 25, 1862; *Daily Missouri Republican*, March 23, 1862; *Chicago Tribune*, March 28, April 1, 1862; *Philadelphia Inquirer*, March 30, 1862; *New York Tribune*, March 28, 1862; *New York Times*, March 31, 1862.
14. *New York Tribune*, March 27, 1862; *Chicago Tribune*, March 25, 29, 1862; *OR A*, VIII, 139, 144–45, 801; *OR N*, XXII, 747–48.
15. *OR A*, VIII, 139–40.
16. *OR N*, XXII, 740, 742, 743, 775; *OR A*, VIII, 156; *Memphis Appeal*, March 26, 27, 1862.
17. *Memphis Appeal*, March 28, 1862.
18. *Chicago Tribune*, March 29, 1862; *New York Times*, March 30, April 1, 1862; *New Orleans Crescent*, March 26, 1862; *New York Tribune*, April 15, 1862. The *Appeal* of March 26, 1862 claimed that no one had been killed since the attack of March 17.
19. Read, "Reminiscences," 337; Swigart and Bringhurst, *Forty-Sixth Regiment*, 23; Palmer, *Memoirs*, 98.
20. Swigart and Bringhurst, *Forty-Sixth Regiment*, 22–24; Palmer, *Memoirs*, 97–98.
21. Read, "Reminiscences," 338; *Memphis Appeal*, March 20, 1862; *Chicago Tribune*, March 29, 1862; Palmer to wife, March 20, 1862, Palmer Letters, ILSHL; Swigart and Bringhurst, *Forty-Sixth Regiment*, 24; Josh to Dear Friend, March 22, 1862, Josh Letters, MOHS; *Indianapolis Journal*, March 28, April 2, 1862. Pope's report of this action, not written until May 6, 1862, contained several inaccuracies. *OR A*, VIII, 85.
22. *Memphis Appeal*, March 20, 1862. The *Polk* must have appeared severely damaged, for the Northern press and official Union reports claimed that one Southern gunboat was sunk. *New York Times*, March 21, 1862; *OR A*, VIII, 85.
23. Swigart and Bringhurst, *Forty-Sixth Regiment*, 24–25; Augustus Sinks Memoirs, INSL; Palmer, *Memoirs*, 99.
24. Jackson, *Colonel's Diary*, 50–51; Palmer, *Memoirs*, 99.
25. *Memphis Appeal*, March 20, 1862; Read, "Reminiscences," 338; *OR N*, XXII, 740–41.
26. *New Orleans Crescent*, March 26, 1862.
27. *New Orleans Picayune*, March 25, 1862; *OR N*, XXII, 742.

28. Hollins, "Autobiography," 240; James H. Tomb, "Incidents of Naval Service," *Confederate Service* 34 (April 1926): 129.

29. *OR N*, XXII, 738; Read, "Reminiscences," 338.

30. *OR N*, XXII, 741, 756–57.

10. Someone Said Something about a Canal

1. Bissell, "Sawing Out the Channel," 460; *Philadelphia Inquirer*, March 28, 1862; *Chicago Tribune*, March 31, 1862; *New York Times*, March 25, 1862; *New York Tribune*, March 28, 1862.

2. *New York Tribune*, March 28, 1862; *Chicago Tribune*, March 31, 1862; Bissell, "Sawing Out the Channel," 460.

3. Neal, *Missouri Engineers*, 37, 42–43. Schuyler Hamilton later pointed to an article in the April 13, 1862 *New York Herald* titled: "The Schuyler Hamilton Canal," as proof that he originated the idea. "Comment by General Schuyler Hamilton," vol. 1 of *Battles and Leaders of the Civil War* (New York: Thomas Yoseloff, 1956), 462. It seems probable that both men independently originated the idea.

4. Neal, *Missouri Engineers*, 29, 37; Bissell, "Sawing Out the Channel," 461.

5. Bissell, "Sawing Out the Channel," 461; *New York Herald*, April 15, 1862; *Frank Leslie's Illustrated*, April 26, 1862.

6. Bissell, "Sawing Out the Channel," 461; *Frank Leslie's Illustrated*, April 26, 1862; Willis J. Abbot, *The Blue Jackets of '61* (New York: Dodd, Mead, and Company, 1886), 170.

7. Bissell, "Sawing Out the Channel," 461; Neal, *Missouri Engineers*, 38; *Philadelphia Inquirer*, April 2, 1862.

8. Bissell, "Sawing Out the Channel," 461; Neal, *Missouri Engineers*, 45–45; *OR A*, VIII, 656.

9. *OR A*, VIII, 650.

10. *New York Tribune*, March 28, 1862.

11. *Daily Missouri Democrat*, April 3, 21, 1862; *Daily Missouri Republican*, April 6, 1862; *New York Times*, May 10, 1862; *New York Tribune*, March 25, April 9, 1862; Gilbert to wife, March 23, 1862, Gilbert Letters, MUO; J. Cutler Andrews, *The North Reports the Civil War* (Pittsburgh: University of Pittsburgh Press, 1955), 171.

12. Wills, *Army Life*, 70; Driggs, *Opening of the Mississippi*, 82; David McLean to sister, April 5, 1862, David McLean Letters, UW; William Smith to wife, March 24, 1862, Smith Letters, ILSHL.

13. *Chicago Tribune*, March 28, 1862; *Philadelphia Inquirer*, April 7, 1862; Driggs, *Opening of the Mississippi*, 83; William S. Smith to wife, April 7, 1862, Smith Letters, ILSHL.

14. Confederate reports locate this battery at Dr. Martin's house. *OR N*, XXII, 749. The *Memphis Appeal* of April 9, 1862 makes reference to a Federal battery at Martin Toney's house, a mile south of the Dr. Martin house. (Toney's first name was, indeed, Martin, so there was no confusion by the journalist in mixing names. See *1860 Census for New Madrid County, Missouri*, 10.) The authors are convinced that these two references are to the same battery that was at the Toney house, directly opposite Dan Watson's.

15. William H. Ball to parents, March 21, 1862, William H. Ball Letters, USMHI.

16. *New York Times*, April 6, 1862; Swigart and Bringhurst, *Forty-Sixth Regiment*, 25; Palmer to wife, March 22, 1862, Palmer Letters, ILSHL; Justus Moore to "Dear Miss," March 28, 1862, Justus Moore Letters, INHS; Smith and Smith, eds., *Gilbert*, 87.

17. Palmer to wife, March 22, 28, 30, 1862, Palmer Letters, ILSHL; Swigart and Bringhurst, *Forty-Sixth Regiment*, 25.

18. Gilbert to wife, March 18, 1862, Gilbert Letters, MUO; Pinny to wife, March 23, 1862, Pinny Letters, WRHS.

19. *New York Tribune*, April 4, 1862; Ball to wife, March 28, 1862, Ball Letters, USMHI; Augustus Mower to parents, April 1, 1862, Augustus Mower Letters, UW (River Falls); *New York Times*, April 7, 1862; John Williams Diary, various entries in late March and early April 1862, UW (Eau Claire); Dan Smith Diary, March 27, 1862, ILSHL; Bradley to wife, March 31, 1862, Bradley Letters, USMHI.

20. Ball to parents, April 3, 4, 1862, Ball Letters, USMHI; *New York Times*, April 1, 1862; Wills, *Army Life*, 76; Pinny to wife, March 28, 1862, Pinny Letters, WSHS.

21. Gaughen, *Confederate Surgeon*, 38; Bentley, "Morale as a Factor," 127; W. T. Avery to wife, March 18, 1862, W. T. Avery Letters, TSLA; Moore letter quoted in *Cincinnati Commercial*, April 19, 1862. See also William Y. Thompson, *E. M. Graham: North Louisianian* (Lafayette, La.: Center for Louisiana Studies, n.d.), 37.

22. Poe, *Raving Foe*, 29–31; Mack to Colonel Cobb, April 1, 1862, Mack Letters, NMHM.

23. *OR N*, XXII, 757–58; Ball to parents, March 21, 1862, Ball Letters, USMHI; Smith to wife, March 18, 1862, Smith Letters, ILSHL.

24. *OR N*, XXII, 741; *Memphis Appeal*, March 23, 1862; Thomas Bragg Diary, March 26, 1862, SHC.

25. *OR N*, XXII, 748; *OR A*, VIII, 804.

26. *OR A*, VIII, 132; *Memphis Appeal*, April 4, 1862; *Cincinnati Commercial*, April 11, 1862.

27. *OR N*, XXII, 748.

28. Ibid., 749.

29. William W. Mackall, *A Son's Recollections of His Father* (New York: E. P. Dutton & Company, Inc., 1930), 169–70.

30. Ibid., 171; Roman, *Beauregard*, I, 359; *OR A*, VIII, 134, 804; *Memphis Appeal*, April 12, 1885.

31. Roman, *Beauregard*, I, 362.

32. *OR A*, VIII, 132, 805.

33. Ibid., 132, 807; Baker Diary, April 5, 1862, ADAH; *New York Herald*, April 10, 1862.

34. *OR A*, VIII, 809, 811.

35. Ibid., 809, 811–12.

11. Success Hangs upon Your Decision

1. *OR N*, XXII, 701.

2. Hoppin, *Foote*, 276–77; Scott to Stanton, March 30, 1862, Stanton Papers, LC; *OR N*, XXII, 702. See also *New York Times*, April 5, 1862.

3. *OR A*, VIII, 645–46.

4. *OR N*, XXII, 703; Walke, *Naval Scenes*, 117 18.

5. *OR N*, XXII, 706–08, 776; *New York Tribune*, April 4, 9, 1862; *New York Times*, April 4, 1862; Walke, "Western Flotilla," 444; Frazier Kirkland, *The Pictorial Book of Anecdotes and Incidents of the War of the Rebellion* (Hartford, 1866), 358–59.

6. *New York Tribune*, April 4, 1862; David McLean to sister, April 5, 1862, David McLean Letters, UW; Henry H. Eby, *Observations of an Illinois Boy in Battle, Camp and Prison, 1861–1865* (Mendota: by author, 1910), 39; Driggs, *Opening of the Mississippi*, 83; Smith to wife, March 5, 1862, Smith Letters, ILSHL; *Cincinnati Commercial*, April 7, 1862; *Richmond Inquirer*, April 8, 1862, Baker Diary, April 5, 1862, ADAH.

7. *OR A*, VIII, 653; Hoppin, *Foote*, 280.

8. *New York Times*, April 5, 6, 1862; *New York Tribune*, April 9, 1862; *New York Herald*, April 5, 6, 1862; *Cincinnati Commercial*, April 5, 7, 10, 1862; *OR N*, XXII, 745, 746, 776; *OR A*, VIII, 659. It is not clear whether Foote had previously planned the attack.

9. *OR A*, VIII, 653, 656.

10. A Confederate map reveals that there were actually two roads down Madrid Bend beginning at the same point and nearly paralleling each other. Both intersected at the Tiptonville Road about a mile apart. Apparently, the Federals knew about only the northernmost road. (See Gray report in *OR N*, XXII, 747–49).

11. *OR A*, VIII, 656.

12. Ibid., 657; Phillip Melville, "The Carondelet Runs the Gauntlet," *American Heritage* 10 (October 1959): 69.

13. Walke, "Western Flotilla," 442; Hoppin, *Foote*, 283–284; Walke, *Naval Scenes*, 124; H. Allen Gosnell, ed., *Guns on the Western Waters: A Story of River Gunboats in the Civil War* (Baton Rouge: Louisiana State University Press, 1949), 74–75.

14. Walke, *Naval Scenes*, 124; Walke, "Western Flotilla," 443.

15. Gosnell, ed., *Guns on the Western Waters*, 75; *New York Herald*, March 24, 1862; Melville, "Carondelet," 70.

16. Walke, *Naval Scenes*, 130; Gosnell, ed., *Guns on the Western Waters*, 76–78; *New York Herald*, April 15, 1862.

17. *New York Tribune*, March 27, 1862; *Chicago Times* article quoted in *New York Tribune*, April 1, 1862; *Daily Missouri Republican*, March 23, 1862.

18. Walke, "Western Flotilla," 444–45; Walke, *Naval Scenes*, 131–33; Hoppin, *Foote*, 287.

19. *OR A*, VIII, 171; J. M. Grace to father, April 6, 1862, J. M. Grace Letters, Lee Collection. For an example of the poor performance of the Confederate gunners, see *New Orleans Delta*, April 9, 1862.

20. Hoppin, *Foote*, 287; Walke, *Naval Scenes*, 132–33; Walke, "Western Flotilla," 444–45; *Cincinnati Commercial*, April 10, 1862; *New York Herald*, April 15, 1862.

21. Walke, *Naval Scenes*, 131–32; *OR N*, XXII, 709–10; Melville, "Carondelet," 76–77.

22. Ball to Peeples, April 15, 1862, Ball Letters, USMHI.

23. *OR N*, XXII, 710–14.

24. Ibid., 714–15.

25. *OR N.*, 715–16; *OR A*, VIII, 666.

26. *OR A*, VIII, 88, 887; *OR N*, XXII, 716–17, 726–27; Walke, "Western Flotilla," 445; Augustus Mower to parents, April 7, 1862, Augustus Mower Letters, UW (River Falls); *New York Times*, April 7, 1862.

27. *New York Times*, April 7, 1862; *Memphis Appeal*, April 9, 11, 12, 1862; Walke, *Naval Scenes*, 144; *Daily Missouri Democrat*, April 8, 1862.

28. Walke, "Western Flotilla," 445; Walke, *Naval Scenes*, 145; Palmer to wife, April 7, 1862, Palmer Letters, ILSHL.

29. *OR A*, VIII, 727.

30. *Philadelphia Inquirer*, April 11, 1862; *Chicago Tribune*, April 10, 1862; *New York Tribune*, April 14, 1862. The *Chicago Tribune* incorrectly reported that the *Pittsburg* had three barges beside her—two of hay and one of coal.

31. *Chicago Tribune*, April 10, 1862.

32. *New York Tribune*, April 14, 1862; Hoppin, *Foote*, 288; Milligan, ed., *From the Fresh Water Navy*, 55.

33. *New York Tribune*, April 14, 1862; *OR N*, XXII, 719, 727, 777.

34. Walke, *Naval Scenes*, 148.

35. *OR N*, XXII, 718, 727; Dan Smith to father, April 10, 1862, Dan Smith Letters,

ILSHL; Driggs, *Opening of the Mississippi*, 87; 16th Illinois Record Book, Civil War Misc. Collection, USMHI; Walke, *Naval Scenes*, 148.

36. Walke, *Naval Scenes*, 148, 150–51; *Chicago Tribune*, April 8, 1862; *OR N*, XXII, 718, 727.

37. Ball to wife, April 7, 1862, Ball Letters, USMHI.

38. *Daily Missouri Democrat*, April 8, 1862; William D. Hynes to father, April 7, 1862, William D. Hynes Letters, INSL; *Chicago Tribune*, April 12, 1862; Ball to parents, April 3, 1862, Ball Letters, USMHI; Wilson, *Memoirs*, 86.

39. *OR A*, VIII, 78, 89, 109, 670; *New York Times*, April 8, 1862; 16th Illinois Record Book, Civil War Misc. Collection, USMHI; Cavins, *War Letters*, 13.

40. *Chicago Tribune*, April 12, 1862; *OR A*, VIII, 109; Coffin, *Boys of '61*, 91–92.

41. *OR A*, VIII, 98; Jackson, *Colonel's Diary*, 51.

42. Stanley, *Memoirs*, 90.

43. *OR N*, XXII, 727; *OR A*, VIII, 645; Cavins, *War Letters*, 12; Dean, *Recollections*, 220.

12. The Only Point of Exit

1. Baker, "Island No. 10," 59–61; *OR A*, VIII, 133.

2. Baker, "Island No. 10," 61; *New Orleans Delta*, April 9, 1862; *OR A*, VIII, 133, 157–58, 175–76; Daniel P. Smith, *Company K First Alabama Regiment or Three Years in the Confederate Service* (Reprint, Gaithersburg, Md.: Butternut Press, 1984), 15.

3. N. B. Nesbitt, [untitled]. *Confederate Veteran* 4 (September 1896): 295; Edward Y. McMorries, *History of the First Regiment Alabama Volunteer Infantry, C. S. A.* (Montgomery: The Brown Printing Company, 1904), 37–38; Poe, *Raving Foe*, 31; *OR A*, VIII, 133.

4. Baker, "Island No. 10," 61.

5. Ibid., 62; White, "Federal Operations," 65; *OR A*, VIII, 133.

6. Baker, "Island No. 10," 62; Smith, *Company K*, 16; Poe, *Raving Foe*, 32; McMorries, *First Alabama*, 38; *OR A*, VIII, 109, 112; Wilson, *Memoirs*, 89.

7. *OR A*, VIII, 110, 112; *Chicago Tribune*, April 12, 1862; Jackson, *Colonel's Diary*, 52; 16th Illinois Record Book, Civil War Misc. Collection, USMHI; Wilson, *Memoirs*, 89–94.

8. *OR A*, VIII, 98–100, 669–700.

9. Ibid., 110; Smith, *Company K*, 17; Poe, *Raving Foe*, 32; McMorries, *First Alabama*, 38; Baker, "Island No. 10," 62.

10. *OR A*, VIII, 177; *Memphis Appeal*, April 12, 1862; *The Grayjackets: And How They Lived, Fought and Died for Dixie* (Richmond: Jones Brothers & Co., 1867), 209.

11. *OR A*, VIII, 158, 176.

12. *Philadelphia Inquirer*, April 16, 1862; *Cincinnati Commercial*, April 11, 1862; *New York Times*, April 10, 1862; *Chicago Tribune*, April 11, 1862; *OR N*, XXII, 721, 757; *Daily Missouri Republican*, April 11, 1862; *OR A*, VIII, 793.

13. *OR A*, VIII, 158, 177; *Memphis Appeal*, April 11, 12, 18, 1862; *Washington Telegraph*, April 13, 30, 1862; Edwin Rennolds, *A History of Henry County Commands Which Served in the Confederate States Army* (Reprint, Kennesaw, Ga.: Continental Book Company, 1961), 195–229. The *Appeal* placed the number of escapees at one thousand.

14. *OR A*, VIII, 136, 177, 772; Roman, *Beauregard*, I, 361; Edward A. Pollard, *The Lost Cause: A New Southern History of the War of the Confederates* (New York: E. B. Treat & Co., 1867), 236.

15. *OR A*, VIII, 177.

16. Ibid., 158–59, 177; *Grayjackets*, 209; Jennings to brother, April 12, 1862, Jennings Letters, UALR; *Mobile Advertiser & Register*, April 19, 1862. The *Appeal* of April 18, 1862

stated that only 132 men of the 1st Alabama made it to Memphis. Colonel Steadman had been previously removed to a private home to recuperate from illness and was subsequently captured.

17. Milligan, *From the Fresh Water Navy*, III, 56; *Daily Missouri Republican*, April 11, 1862; Junius Browne, *Four Years in Secessia* (New York: Arno & the New York Times, 1970), 128–29.

18. Browne, *Four Years in Secessia*, 130; *OR N*, XXII, 720, 771, 777.

19. *OR A*, VIII, 678; *OR N*, XXII, 720, 777; Blegen, ed., *Heg*, 77; James H. Wiswell to father, April 9, 1862 in Lyman Needham Letters, ILSHL; *New York Times*, April 14, 1862; Schmitt, *Twenty-Seventh Illinois*, 4; Browne, *Four Years in Secessia*, 133–34; *The Picket Line* (New York: n.p., n.d.), 89.

20. *Philadelphia Inquirer*, April 10, 1862; *Cincinnati Commercial*, April 11, 1862; *New York Times*, April 14, 1862; *Chicago Tribune*, April 11, 1862; *OR N*, XXII, 721.

21. *OR A*, VIII, 182–83; *Daily Missouri Republican*, April 11, 1862; Philadelphia Inquirer, April 15, 1862; Blegen, ed., *Heg*, 77.

22. *Chicago Tribune*, April 12, 1862; *Philadelphia Inquirer*, April 16, 1862; *Daily Missouri Republican*, April 11, 1862; Mower to parents, April 11, 1862, Mower Letters, UW.

23. *OR A*, VIII, 118–19.

24. *Chicago Tribune*, April 12, 1862; 16th Illinois Record Book, Civil War Misc. Collection, USMHI; *OR A*, VIII, 112; *Daily Missouri Republican*, April 11, 1862; Wilson, *Memoirs*, 95–96; Henry Strong Diary, April 9, 1862, INSL; *Cincinnati Commercial*, April 11, 1862.

25. *Daily Missouri Republican*, April 11, 1862; Gilbert to wife, April 9, 1862, Gilbert Letters, MUO.

26. *Daily Missouri Republican*, April 11, 1862; Wilson, *Memoirs*, 95–97; Ball to wife, April 11, 1862, Ball Letters, USMHI.

27. *Cincinnati Commercial*, April 11, 1862; Dwight to uncle, April 10, 1862, Dwight Letters, UW; McLean to sister, April 10, 1862, McLean Letters, UW; Dan Smith to father, April 10, 1862, Smith Letters, ILSHL; 16th Illinois Record Book, Civil War Misc. Collection, USMHI; Jamison, *Recollections*, 181.

28. Stanley, *Memoirs*, 91.

29. 16th Illinois Record Book, Civil War Misc. Collection, USMHI; *OR A*, VIII, 98; Frank Moore, ed., *Civil War in Song and Story 1860–1865*, 2 vols. (New York: n.p., 1980), 335.

13. Island Number Ten Is Ours!

1. *New York Times*, April 9, 1862; *Daily Missouri Democrat*, April 9, 1862; *Daily Missouri Republican*, April 9, 1862.

2. Mullen, "Pope's New Madrid," 342; *OR A*, VIII, 722, 724; Needham to Dear Friends, April 9, 1862, Needham Letters, ILSHL; Wiswell to father, April 9, 1862, Wiswell Letters, DU. See also H. Spaulding to uncle, April 16, 1862, Spaulding Letters, DU.

3. *National Intelligencer*, April 9, 1862.

4. *Report of Major General Pope*, 33, 58, 59; *Chicago Times*, April 14, 1862; *OR A*, VIII, 676; *Philadelphia Inquirer*, April 15, 1862; *Cincinnati Commercial*, April 11, 1862; John Y. Simon, ed., *The Personal Memoirs of Julia Dent Grant* (Carbondale: Southern Illinois University Press, 1975), 101.

5. Thomas L. Snead, "With Price East of the Mississippi," in Robert C. Johnson and Clarence C. Buel, eds., *Battles and Leaders of the Civil War*, 4 vols. (Reprint. New York: Thomas Yoseloff, 1956), 2: 721–22.

6. *OR A*, VIII, 90; *Cincinnati Commercial*, April 11, 1862; *Philadelphia Inquirer*, April

11, 1862; *Daily Missouri Republican,* April 11, 1862; A. T. Gay, "Correct History Wanted," *Confederate Veteran* 11 (November 1893), 337.

7. *Report of Major General Pope,* 33; "Map Showing Rebel Batteries at Island No. 10," April 7, 1862, LC; *Philadelphia Inquirer,* April 15, 1862; *Daily Missouri Republican,* April 11, 1862; *Chicago Tribune,* April 11, 1862.

8. *Memphis Appeal,* April 7, 1862; *Memphis Appeal,* April 11, 12, 1862.

9. *New Orleans Picayune,* April 10, 1862; *Richmond Enquirer,* April 11, 22, 25, 1862; Merrill, *Battle Flags South,* 141.

10. *Memphis Avalanche,* April 7, 1862; *Memphis Argus,* May 6, 1862; Merrill, *Battle Flags South,* 141.

11. Charles W. Dean, "New Madrid and Island Number Ten," *Military Order of the Loyal Union of the United States:* Illinois, 1 (1891): 91; Otto Eisenschiml and Ralph Newman, *The Civil War: The American Iliad* (New York: Mallard Press, 1991), 167.

12. Lossing, *Pictorial History,* II, 249; James D. Richardson, comp., *The Messages and Papers of Jefferson Davis and the Confederacy* (New York: Chelsea House-Robert Hector, 1966), II, 234–35.

13. Poe, *Raving Foe,* 35; Driggs, *Opening of the Mississippi,* 87, 89; *Daily Missouri Republican,* April 11, 1862; McMorries, *First Alabama,* 41; Gilbert, *Gilbert,* 89–90; Wilson, *Memoirs,* 97.

14. *Chicago Tribune,* April 11, 1862; Baker Diary, April 12–13, 1862, ADAH; *Cincinnati Commercial,* April 14, 1862; Rennolds, *Henry County Commands,* 183; McMorries, *First Alabama,* 41; *Chicago Times,* April 14, 1862.

15. Pope to William Butler, April 9, 1862, Pope Papers, CHS; Roy P. Basler, ed., *The Collected Works of Abraham Lincoln* (New Brunswick, N.J.: Rutgers University Press, 1953), V, 186–87; Schutz and Trenerry, *Abandoned by Lincoln,* 84–85; Maurice Melton, "The Struggle for Rebel Island No. 10," *Civil War Times Illustrated* 18 (April 1979): 46; Joseph E. Suppeger, "Lincoln and Pope," *Lincoln Herald* 77 (1975): 219.

16. Faust, ed., *Encyclopedia of the Civil War,* 266.

17. Ibid., 459.

18. Dean, "New Madrid and Island Number Ten," 91; Mackall, *A Son's Recollections,* 172–75.

19. *ORA,* VIII, 134; Mackall, *A Son's Recollections,* 171.

20. Melton, "Struggle for Rebel Island No. 10," 46; Hollins, "Autobiography," 243.

21. *Washington Telegraph,* April 2, August 13, November 5, 26, 1862, January 21, October 21, 1863; Fay Hempsteat, *A Pictorial History of Arkansas* (St. Louis: N. D. Thompson Publishing Co., 1890), n.p.

22. Fowler, *Under Two Flags,* 151, 171–72.

23. Edwin C. Bearss, *The Vicksburg Campaign* (Dayton: Morningside, 1986), II, 60, 262.

24. Alfred W. Ellet, "Ellet and His Steam-Rams at Memphis," in *Battles and Leaders of the Civil War* (New York: Thomas Yoseloff, 1956), I, 455–56. The Federals were preparing for a run past the Fort Pillow batteries when the fortifications were abandoned by the Confederates.

25. *Memphis Appeal,* April 17, 1862.

Bibliography

Manuscripts

"Account of John K. Craig Taking Food to Island Number Ten." New Madrid Historical Museum, New Madrid, Missouri.

Avery, W. T. Letters. Tennessee State Library and Archives, Nashville.

Baker, Alpheus. Diary. Alabama Department of Archives and History, Montgomery, Alabama.

Ball, William H. Letters. United States Military History Institute, Carlisle Barracks, Pennsylvania.

Beauregard, P. G. T. Papers. Perkins Library, Duke University, Durham, North Carolina.

Bradley, Luther. Letters. United States Military History Institute, Carlisle Barracks, Pennsylvania.

Burtot, Lin. Letter. New Madrid Historical Museum, New Madrid, Missouri.

Claiborne, L. B. File. Civil War Times Collection, United States Military History Institute, Carlisle Barracks, Pennsylvania.

Davis, William C. Letters. Civil War Misc. Collection, United States Military History Institute, Carlisle Barracks, Pennsylvania.

Dillon, William S. Diary. John Davis Williams Library, University of Mississippi, Oxford.

Ditto, George M. T. Letters in Hiram C. Crandall Papers. Illinois State Historical Library, Springfield.

Dwight, Edward C. Letters. State Historical Society of Wisconsin, University of Wisconsin, Eau Claire.

Eltinge-Lord. Papers. Perkins Library, Duke University, Durham, North Carolina.

Gilbert, Alfred. Letters. Miami University Library, Oxford, Ohio.

Grace, J. M. Letter. Richard Lee Collection, Perkinston, Mississippi.

Huger, T. B. Letter. Miles Papers, Southern Historical Collection, University of North Carolina, Chapel Hill.

Harper, Aaron C. Diary. United States Military History Institute, Carlisle Barracks, Pennsylvania.

Harris, David B. Papers. Perkins Library, Duke University, Durham, North Carolina.

Hynes, William D. Letters. Indiana State Library, Indianapolis.

Jennings, Roscoe A. Letters. University of Arkansas for Medical Sciences, Little Rock.

"Josh." Letter. Missouri Historical Society, St. Louis.

Letter Book of the Headquarters of the Western Department. Kuntz Collection, Tulane University, New Orleans.

"Loose Papers, Mississippi River." Record Group 45, National Archives, Washington, D.C.

McLean, David. Letters. State Historical Society of Wisconsin, University of Wisconsin, Eau Claire.

Mack, William S. Letter. New Madrid Historical Museum, New Madrid, Missouri.

Miller, Arnold. Diary. University Archives, Historical Collections, Michigan State University, East Lansing.

Morse, Justus. Letters. Indiana Historical Society, Indianapolis.

Mower, Augustus. Letters. University of Wisconsin Library, River Falls.

Needham, Lyman. Letters. Illinois State Historical Library, Springfield.

Neely, J. J. Letter. Southern Historical Collection, University of North Carolina, Chapel Hill.

Onstott, William. Letters. Illinois State Historical Library, Springfield.

Palmer, John. Letters. Illinois State Historical Library, Springfield.

Pinny, Oscar. Letters. State Historical Society of Wisconsin, Madison.

Polk, Leonidas. Papers. University of the South, Sewanee, Tennessee.

Pope, John. Papers. Chicago Historical Society, Chicago.

Putney, William J. Journal. Schoff Civil War Collection, William C. Clements Library, University of Michigan, Ann Arbor.

Records of Company A, 16th Illinois Infantry Regiment, Illinois State Historical Society, Springfield.

Reilly, C. W. Letters. Indiana Historical Society, Indianapolis.

Sinks, Augustus. Memoirs. Indiana State Library, Indianapolis.

Sixteenth Illinois Record Book. Civil War Misc. Collection, United States Military History Institute, Carlisle Barracks, Pennsylvania.

"Sketch shewing [*sic*] the relative positions of the enemy's works and our batteries during the attack on the 13th of March, 1862. By F. Tunica, Engs." Record Group 77, National Archives, Washington, D.C.

Slack, James. Letters. Indiana State Library, Indianapolis.

Smith, Benjamin T. Diary. Illinois State Historical Library, Springfield.

Smith, Dan. Diary. Illinois State Historical Library, Springfield.

Smith, Daniel. Letters. Illinois State Historical Library, Springfield.

Smith, Martin V. Letters. Iowa State Historical Society, Iowa City.

Smith, William. Letters. Illinois State Historical Library, Springfield.

Spaulding, H. Letters. Perkins Library, Duke University, Durham, North Carolina.

Twitty, Smith C. Letters. Mary Twitty Clements Collection, Bixby, Oklahoma.

Newspapers

Arkansas Gazette
Boston Transcript
Charleston Mercury
Chicago Times
Chicago Tribune
Cincinnati Commercial
Cleveland Plain Dealer
Daily Missouri Democrat
Daily Missouri Republican
Frank Leslie's Illustrated
Harper's Weekly
Indianapolis Journal
Memphis Appeal
Memphis Argos
Memphis Avalanche
Mobile Advertiser & Register
Nashville Daily Gazette
National Intelligencer
New Orleans Crescent
New Orleans Delta
New Orleans Picayune
New York Herald
New York Times
New York Tribune
Philadelphia Inquirer
Richmond Inquirer
Southern Confederacy
Washington Telegraph

Dissertation

Chumney, James. "Don Carlos Buell, Gentleman General." Ph.D. diss., Rice University, 1964.

Published Primary Sources

Abbot, Willis J. *The Blue Jackets of '61*. New York: Dodd, Mead, and Company, 1886.
Baker, Alpheus. "Island No. 10." *Southern Bivouac* (1882–1883): 54–62.
Barbiere, Joe. *Scraps from the Prison Table, at Camp Chase and Johnson's Island*. Doylestown, Pa.: W. W. H. Davis, 1868.
Baslor, Roy P., ed. *The Collected Works of Abraham Lincoln*. New Brunswick, N.J.: Rutgers University Press, 1953.
Bissell, J. W. "Sawing Out the Channel Above Island Number Ten." *Battles and Leaders of the Civil War*. Vol. 1. Ed. Robert C. Johnson and Clarence C. Buel, 1887–88. New York: Thomas Yoseloff, 1956.
Blegen, Theodore C., ed. *The Civil War Letters of Colonel Hans Christian Heg*. Northfield, Minn.: Norwegian-American Historical Association, 1931.
Boomer, George B. *Memoir of George Boardman Boomer*. Boston: Geo. C. Rand & Avery, 1864.
Bringhurst, Thomas H., and Frank Swigart. *History of the Forty-Sixth Indiana Volunteer Infantry*. Logansport, Ind.: Wilson, Humphreys and Co., 1888.
Brown, Isaac N. "The Confederate Gun-Boat 'Arkansas.' " *Battles and Leaders of the Civil War*. Vol. 3. Ed. Robert C. Johnson and Clarence C. Buel, 1887–88. New York: Thomas Yoseloff, 1956.
Brown, Thaddeus C. S., Samuel J. Murphey, William G. Putney. *Behind the Guns: The History of Battery I 2nd Regiment, Illinois Light Artillery*. Carbondale: Southern Illinois University Press, 1965.
Browne, Junius. *Four Years in Secessia*. New York: Arno & the *New York Times*, 1970.
Bryner, Bryon C. *Bugle Echoes, The Story of the Illinois Forty-Seventh*. Springfield, Ill.: Phillips Bros., 1905.
Burdette, Robert J. *The Drums of the Forty-Seventh*. Indianapolis: Bobbs-Merrill Company, 1914.
Cavins, Ader G. *The War Letters of Aden G. Cavins Written to His Wife*. Evansville: Rosenthal-Kuebler Printing Company, 1918.
Coffin, Charles C. *The Boys of '61 or Four Years of Fighting*. Boston: Arno & the New York Times, 1885.
Crippen, Edward W. "Diary of Edward W. Crippen, Private, 27th Illinois Volunteers, War of the Rebellion, August 7, 1861, to September 19, 1863." *Transactions of the Illinois State Historical Society for the Year 1900*. Springfield: Illinois Historical Society, 1910.
Cummings, Edmund H. "The Signal Corps in the Confederate States Army." *Southern Historical Society Papers* 16 (1888): 93–107.
Dean, Benjamin D. *Reflections of the Twenty-Sixth Missouri in the War for the Union*. Lamar, Mo.: Southwest Missourian, 1892.
Dean, Charles W. "New Madrid and Island Number Ten." *Military Order of the Loyal Union of the United States: Illinois* 1 (1891): 75–92.
Denslinger, C. W. *Civil War Diary of James Wesley Riley*. N. p., 1960.
Dorsey, Sarah A. *Reflections of Henry Watkins Allen*. New York: M. Doolady, 1866.

Driggs, George V. *Opening of the Mississippi or Two Years Campaigning in the South-West.* Madison, Wisc.: William J. Park and Company, 1864.

Eads, James B. "Recollections of Foote and the Gun-Boats." *Battles and Leaders of the Civil War.* Vol. 1. Ed. Robert C. Johnson and Clarence C. Buel, 1887–88. New York: Thomas Yoseloff, 1956.

Eby, Henry H. *Observations of an Illinois Boy in Battle, Camp and Prison, 1861–1865.* Mendota: By author, 1910.

Ellet, Alfred W. "Ellet and His Steam-Rams at Memphis." *Battles and Leaders of the Civil War.* Vol. 1. Ed. Robert C. Johnson and Clarence C. Buel, 1887–88. New York: Thomas Yoseloff, 1956.

Gaughen, I. J., ed. *Letters of a Confederate Surgeon.* Camden, Ark.: The Hurley Co., Inc., 1960.

Gay, A. T. "Correct History Wanted." *Confederate Veteran* 11 (November 1893): 337.

Gift, George W. "Exploits of the Ram Arkansas." *The Confederate Soldier in the Civil War.* Ed. Ben LaBree. Paterson, N.J.: Pageant Books, Inc., 1959.

Grant, Ulysses S. *Personal Memoirs of U.S. Grant.* 1885. Reprint, New York: Library of America, 1990.

The Grayjackets: And How They Lived, Fought, and Died for Dixie. Richmond: Jones Brothers & Co., 1867.

Hamilton, Schuyler. "Comment by General Schuyler Hamilton." *Battles and Leaders of the Civil War.* Vol. 1. Ed. Robert C. Johnson and Clarence C. Buel, 1887–88. New York: Thomas Yoseloff, 1956.

Hollins, George N. "Autobiography of Commodore George Nicholas Hollins." *Maryland Historical Magazine* 34 (1939): 228–43.

Jackson, Oscar L. *The Colonel's Diary, Journals Kept Before and During the Civil War.* Sharon, Pa.: n.p., 1922.

Jamison, Matthew H. *Recollections of Pioneer and Army Life.* Kansas City: Hudson Press, 1922.

Johnston, Joseph E. "Jefferson Davis and the Mississippi Campaign." *Battles and Leaders of the Civil War.* Vol. 3. Ed. Robert C. Johnson and Clarence C. Buel, 1887–88. New York: Thomas Yoseloff, 1956.

Knox, Thomas W. *Camp-Fire and Cotton-Field: Southern Adventure in Time of War.* New York: Da Capo Press, 1969.

McKall, D. Three Years in the Service: A Record of the Doings of the Eleventh Regiment Missouri Volunteers. Springfield, Mo.: Baker and Phillips, 1864.

McLean, William E. *Forty-Third Regiment of Indiana Volunteers.* Terre Haute: n.p., 1904.

McMorries, Edward Y. *History of the First Regiment Alabama Volunteer Infantry, C. S. A.* Montgomery: The Brown Printing Company, 1904.

Mahan, James C. *Memoirs of James Curtis Mahan.* Lincoln: The Franklin Press, 1919.

Miers, Earl S., ed. *A Rebel War Clerk's Diary by John B. Jones.* Reprint, New York: A. S. Barnes & Company, Inc., 1961.

Milligan, John D., ed. *From the Fresh Water Navy 1861–1864; The Letters of Acting Master's Mate Henry R. Browne and Acting Ensign Symmes E. Browne.* Annapolis: Naval Institute Press, 1970.

Morgan, James M. *Recollections of a Rebel Reefer.* Boston: Houghton Mifflin Company, 1917.

Neal, W. A. *An Illustrated History of the Missouri Engineers and the Twenty-Fifth Infantry Regiment.* Chicago: Donohue and Henneperry, 1889.

Nesbitt, N. B. [Untitled]. *Confederate Veteran* 4 (September 1896): 295.

"Obstructing Federal Gunboats." *Confederate Veteran* 34 (June 1926): 211.

Palmer, John M. *Personal Recollections of John M. Palmer: The Story of an Ernest Life.* Cincinnati: Robert Clark Co., 1901.

The Picket Line. New York: n.p., n.d.

Pierce, Lyman B. *History of the Second Iowa Cavalry.* Burlington: Hawkeye Steam Book and Job Printing Company, 1865.

Poe, James T. *The Raving Foe: A Civil War Diary and List of Prisoners.* Eastland, Tex.: Longhorn Press, 1967.

Pope, John. *Report of Major General John Pope to the Joint Committee on the Conduct of the War.* Washington, D.C.: n.p., n.d.

Porter, David D. *The Naval History of the Civil War.* Reprint, Secaucus, N.J.: Castle, 1984.

Read, C. W. "Reminiscences of the Confederate States Navy." *Southern Historical Society Papers* 1 (May 1876): 331–62.

Rennolds, Edwin. *A History of Henry County Commands Which Served in the Confederate States Army.* Kennesaw, Ga.: Continental Book Company, 1961.

Richardson, Albert D. *The Secret Service, the Field, the Dungeon, and the Escape.* Hartford: American Publishing Company, 1865.

Richardson, James D., comp. *The Messages and Papers of Jefferson Davis and the Confederacy.* 2 vols. New York: Chelsea House-Robert Hector, 1966.

Russell, William H. *My Diary North and South.* 1863. Reprint, New York: Harper, 1954.

Scarbrough, William K., ed. *The Diary of Edmund Ruffin.* Vol. 2. Baton Rouge: Louisiana State University Press, 1976.

Schmitt, William A. *History of the Twenty-Seventh Illinois.* Winchester: Standard Steam Printing House, 1892.

Shelby County Historical and Genealogical Association. *Gold Rush and Civil War Letters to Ann from Michael Freyburger.* Shelbyville, Ind.: The Shelby County Historical Genealogical Society, 1986.

Sherman, William T. *Personal Memoirs.* 1875. Reprint, New York: Da Capo Press, Inc., 1984.

Simon, John Y., ed. *The Personal Memoirs of Julia Dent Grant.* Carbondale: University of Southern Illinois Press, 1975.

Smith, Daniel P. *Company K First Alabama Regiment or Three Years in the Confederate Service.* Reprint, Gaithersburg, Md.: Butternut Press, 1984.

Smith, William E., and Ophia D. Smith, eds. *Colonel A. W. Gilbert, Citizen Soldier of Cincinnati.* Cincinnati: Historical and Philosophical Society of Ohio, 1834.

Snead, Thomas L. "With Price East of the Mississippi." *Battles and Leaders of the Civil War.* Vol. 2. Ed. Robert C. Johnson and Clarence C. Buel, 1887–88. New York: Thomas Yoseloff, 1956.

Stanley, David S. *Personal Memoirs of Major General David S. Stanley.* Cambridge: Harvard University Press, 1917.

Stevenson, William G. *Thirteen Months in the Rebel Army.* New York: Barnes, 1864.

Sweet, Benjamin F. "Civil War Experiences." *Missouri Historical Review* 43 (April 1949): 237–50.

Thatcher, Marshall P. *A Hundred Battles in the West.* Detroit: L. F. Kilroy, 1884.

Thompson, M. Jeff. *The Civil War Reminiscences of General M. Jeff Thompson.* Dayton: Morningside, 1988.

Tomb, James H. "Incidents of Naval Service." *Confederate Veteran* 34 (April 1926): 129–30.
"Torpedoes Used by the Confederate Government." *The Confederate Soldier in the Civil War.* Ed. Ben LeBree. Paterson, N.J.: Pageant Books, Inc., 1959.
Walke, Henry. "Gunboats at Belmont and Fort Henry." *Battles and Leaders of the Civil War.* Vol. 1. Ed. Robert C. Johnson and Clarence C. Buel, 1887–88. Reprint, New York: Thomas Yoseloff, 1956.
———. *Naval Scenes and Reminiscences of the Civil War.* New York: F. R. Reed & Company, 1877.
———. "The Western Flotilla at Fort Donelson, Island Number Ten, Fort Pillow, and Memphis." *Battles and Leaders of the Civil War.* Vol. 1. Ed. Robert C. Johnson and Clarence C. Buel, 1887–88. New York: Thomas Yoseloff, 1956.
Walton, Clyde C., ed. *Private Smith's Journal.* Chicago: R. R. Donnelley Company, 1963.
Wilkie, Franc B. *Pen and Powder.* Boston: Ticknor and Company, 1888.
Williams, John M. *The Eagle Regiment, Eighth Wisconsin Infantry Volunteers.* Belleville, Wisc., 1890.
Wills, Charles W. *Army Life of an Illinois Soldier.* Washington: Globe Printing Company, 1906.
Wilson, Ephraim A. *Memoirs of the War.* Cleveland: W. M. Bayne Printing Company, 1893.
Younger, Edward, ed. *Inside the Confederate Government: The Diary of Robert Garlick Hill Kean.* New York: Oxford University Press, 1957.

Secondary Sources

Books

Ambrose, Stephen E. *Halleck: Lincoln's Chief of Staff.* Baton Rouge: Louisiana State University Press, 1962.
Anders, Leslie. *The Eighteenth Missouri.* Indianapolis: The Bobbs-Merrill Co., 1968.
Anderson, Bern. *By Sea and by River: The Naval History of the Civil War.* New York: Alfred A. Knopf, 1962.
Andrews, J. Cutler. *The North Reports the Civil War.* Pittsburgh: University of Pittsburgh Press, 1955.
———. *The South Reports the Civil War.* Pittsburgh: University of Pittsburgh Press, 1970.
Arthur, Stanley S. *Old Families of Louisiana.* Baton Rouge: Louisiana State University Press, 1971.
Bearss, Edwin C. *Hardluck Ironclad: The Sinking and Salvage of Cairo.* Reprint, Baton Rouge: Louisiana State University Press, 1966.
———. *The Vicksburg Campaign.* Vol. 2. Dayton: Morningside Bookshop, 1986.
Beringer, Richard, Herman Hattaway, Archer Jones, and William N. Still, Jr. *Why the South Lost the Civil War.* Athens: University of Georgia Press, 1986.
Boynton, Charles. *The History of the Navy During the War of the Rebellion.* New York: D. Appleton and Company, 1867.
Byers, S. H. M. *Iowa in War Times.* Des Moines: W. D. Condit & Co., 1888.
Catton, Bruce. *Grant Moves South.* Boston: Little, Brown & Company, 1960.

Civil War Centennial Commission. *Tennesseans in the Civil War.* Vol. 1. Nashville: Civil War Centennial Commission, 1964.

Connelly, Thomas L. *Army of the Heartland: The Army of Tennessee, 1861–1862.* Baton Rouge: Louisiana State University Press, 1967.

———. *Autumn of Glory: The Army of Tennessee, 1862–1865.* Baton Rouge: Louisiana State University Press, 1971.

———. *Civil War Tennessee: Battles and Leaders.* Knoxville: University of Tennessee Press, 1979.

Cooling, Benjamin F. *Forts Henry and Donelson: The Key to the Confederate Heartland.* Knoxville: University of Tennessee Press, 1987.

Crozier, Emmet. *Yankee Reporters 1861–65.* New York: Oxford University Press, 1956.

Davis, William C. *Jefferson Davis: The Man and His Hour.* New York: HarperCollins, 1991.

Dew, Charles B. *Ironmaker to the Confederacy: Joseph B. Anderson and the Confederate Iron Works.* New Haven: Yale University Press, 1966.

Dorsey, Florence. *Road to the Sea: The Story of James B. Eads and the Mississippi River.* New York, 1947.

Dougan, Michael B. *Confederate Arkansas: The People and Politics of a Frontier State in Wartime.* Tuscaloosa: University of Alabama Press, 1976.

Dufour, Charles L. "The Conquest of the Mississippi." *The Image of War 1861–1865.* Vol. 2. Ed. William C. Davis. Garden City, N.Y.: Doubleday & Company, Inc., 1982.

———. *The Night the War Was Lost.* Garden City, N.Y.: Doubleday & Company, Inc., 1960.

Eisenschiml, Otto and Ralph Newman. *The Civil War: The American Iliad.* Reprint, New York: Mallard Press, 1991.

Faust, Patricia L., ed. *Historical Times Illustrated Encyclopedia of the Civil War.* New York: Harper & Row, 1986.

Foote, Shelby. *The Civil War: A Narrative,* Vol. 1. New York: Random House, 1956.

Force, M. F. *From Fort Henry to Corinth.* Reprint, Wilmington, N. C.: Broadfoot Publishing Company, 1989.

Fowler, William H. *Under Two Flags: The American Navy in the Civil War.* New York: Norton, 1990.

Gosnell, H. Allen, ed. *Guns on the Western Waters: A Story of River Gunboats in the Civil War.* Baton Rouge: Louisiana State University Press, 1949.

Hagerman, Edward. *The American Civil War and the Origins of Modern Warfare.* Bloomington: Indiana University Press, 1988.

Hattaway, Herman, and Archer Jones. *How the North Won.* Urbana: University of Illinois Press, 1983.

Haydon, F. Stansbury. *Aeronautics in the Union and Confederate Armies.* Baltimore: Johns Hopkins Press, 1941.

Hempsteat, Fay. *A Pictorial History of Arkansas.* St. Louis: N. D. Thompson Publishing Co., 1890.

Hoppin, James M. *Life of Andrew Hull Foote.* New York: Harper & Brother, 1874.

Horn, Stanley F. *The Army of Tennessee.* Indianapolis: The Bobbs-Merrill Company, 1941.

Hughes, Nathaniel C., Jr. *The Battle of Belmont: Grant Strikes South.* Chapel Hill: University of North Carolina Press, 1991.

Johnson, Robert E. *Rear Admiral John Rogers 1812–1882*. Annapolis: Naval Institute Press, 1967.
Jones, Archer. *Civil War Command & Strategy: The Process of Victory and Defeat*. New York: The Free Press, 1992.
Kirkland, Frazier. *The Pictorial Book of Anecdotes and Incidents of the War of the Rebellion*. Hartford, Conn.: Hartford Publishing Co., 1866.
Lindsley, John B., ed. *The Military Annals of Tennessee, Confederate*. Nashville: J. M. Lindsley & Co., 1886.
Lossing, Benson J. *The Pictorial Field Book of the Civil War in the United States of America*. Vol. 5. New Haven: Geo. S. Lester, 1878.
Love, William D. *Wisconsin in the War of the Rebellion*. Chicago: Church and Goodman, 1886.
Macartney, Clarence E. N. *Mr. Lincoln's Admirals*. New York: Funk & Wagnalls, 1956.
Mackall, William W. *A Son's Recollections of His Father*. New York: E. P. Dutton & Company, Inc., 1930.
McMurry, Richard M. *Two Great Rebel Armies: An Essay in Confederate Military History*. Chapel Hill: University of North Carolina Press, 1989.
McPherson, James M. *Battle Cry of Freedom: The Civil War Era*. New York: Oxford University Press, 1988.
Merrill, James H. *Battle Flags South*. Cranbury, N.J.: Fairleigh Dickinson University Press, 1970.
Milligan, John D. *Gunboats Down the Mississippi*. Annapolis: Naval Institute Press, 1965.
Monaghan, Jay. *Swamp Fox of the Confederacy: The Life and Military Service of M. Jeff Thompson*. Tuscaloosa: University of Alabama Press, 1956.
Moore, Frank, ed. *The Civil War in Song and Story*. Reprint, New York, 1970.
———. *Rebellion Record: A Diary of American Events, With Documents, Narratives, Illustrative Incidents, Poetry, etc.* 10 vols. New York: D. Van Nostrand, 1863–1867.
Nash, Howard P. *A Naval History of the Civil War*. New York: A. S. Barnes and Company, 1972.
Nelson, O. H., ed. *History of the Scandinavians*. Minneapolis: O. H. Nelson & Co., 1900.
Nevins, Allen. *Ordeal of the Union*. 4 vols. Reprint, New York: Collier Books, 1992.
Palmer, George T. *A Conscientious Turncoat: The Story of John M. Palmer 1817–1900*. New Haven: Yale University Press, 1941.
Parks, Joseph. *General Leonidas Polk, CSA, The Fighting Bishop*. Baton Rouge: Louisiana State University Press, 1962.
Penick, James Lal, Jr. *The New Madrid Earthquakes*. Columbia: University of Missouri Press 1981.
Polk, William N. *Leonidas Polk: Bishop and General*. 2 vols. New York: Longmans, Green, and Co., 1915.
Pollard, Edward A. *The First Year of the War*. London: George Phillip & Son, 1863.
———. *The Lost Cause; A New Southern History of the War of the Confederates*. New York: E. B. Treat & Co., 1867.
Pratt, Fletcher. *Civil War on Western Waters*. New York: Holt, 1956.
Reed, Rowenna. *Combined Operations in the Civil War*. Annapolis: Naval Institute Press, 1978.
Roland, Charles P. *Albert Sidney Johnston, Soldier of Three Republics*. Austin: University of Texas Press, 1964.

Roman, Alfred. *The Military Operations of General Beauregard in the War Between the States, 1861 to 1865: Including a Brief Personal Sketch and a Narrative of His Service in the War With Mexico, 1846–48.* 2 vols. New York: Harper & Bros., 1883.

Scharf, J. Thomas. *History of the Confederate States Navy.* New York: J. McDonough, 1887.

Schutz, Wallace J., and Walter N. Trenerry. *Abandoned by Lincoln: A Military Biography of General John Pope.* Urbana: University of Illinois Press, 1990.

Silverstone, Paul H. *Warships of the Civil War Navies.* Annapolis: Naval Institute Press, 1989.

Smith, Charles H. *The History of Fuller's Ohio Brigade 1861–1865: Its Great March, with Roster, Portraits, Battle Maps and Biographies.* Cleveland: A. J. Watt, 1909.

Starr, Stephen Z. *The Union Cavalry in the Civil War.* 3 vols. Baton Rouge: Louisiana State University Press, 1979–1985.

Still, William N., Jr. *Iron Afloat: The Story of the Confederate Armorclads.* Nashville: Vanderbilt University Press, 1971.

Stivers, Reuben E. *Privateers and Volunteers: The Men and Women of Our Reserve Naval Forces: 1776–1866.* Annapolis: Naval Institute Press, 1975.

Thompson, William Y. *E. M. Graham: North Louisianian.* Lafayette, La.: Center for Louisiana Studies, n.d.

Time Life Books. *The Civil War.* 10 vols. Alexandria, Va.: Time-Life Books, Inc.

Vandiver, Frank E. *Ploughshares Into Swords: Josiah Gorgas and Confederate Ordnance.* Austin: University of Texas Press, 1952.

Warner, Ezra T. *Generals in Blue: Lives of the Union Commanders.* Baton Rouge: Louisiana State University Press, 1964.

———. *Generals in Gray: Lives of the Confederate Commanders.* Baton Rouge: Louisiana State University Press, 1959.

Wideman, John C. *The Sinking of the USS Cairo.* Jackson: University of Mississippi Press, 1993.

Williams, Kenneth P. *Lincoln Finds a General.* 5 vols. New York: The Macmillan Company, 1949–1958.

Williams, T. Harry. *P. G. T. Beauregard: Napoleon in Gray.* Baton Rouge: Louisiana State University Press, 1954.

Woodworth, Steven E. *Jefferson Davis and His Generals: The Failure of Confederate Command.* Lawrence: University of Kansas Press, 1990.

Articles

Bentley, H. Blair. "Morale as a Factor in the Confederate Failure at Island Number Ten." *West Tennessee Historical Society Papers* 31 (1977): 117–31.

Bogle, Robert V. "Defeat Through Default: Confederate Naval Strategy for the Upper Mississippi and Its Tributaries, 1861–1862." *Tennessee Historical Quarterly* 27 (1968): 62–71.

Buttgenbach, Walter J. "Coast Defense in the Civil War: Island Number Ten." *Journal U.S. Artillery* 39 (May–June 1913): 331–38.

Cooling, Benjamin F. "Forts Henry and Donelson." *Blue and Gray Magazine* 9 (February 1992): 11–20, 45–53.

Green, Brian M. "Confederate Postal Use from Island Number Ten." *The Confederate Philatelist* 34 (November–December 1989): 183–93.

Melton, Maurice. "The Struggle for Rebel Island No. 10." *Civil War Times Illustrated* 18 (April 1979): 4–11, 43–46.

Melville, Phillip. "The *Carondelet* Runs the Gauntlet." *American Heritage* 10 (October 1959): 67–77.

Merrill, James M. "Union Shipbuilding on Western Waters During the Civil War." *Smithsonian Journal of History* 3 (Winter 1968–69): 17–44.

Milligan, John D. "From Theory to Application: The Emergence of the American Ironclad War Vessel." *Military Affairs* (July 1984): 126–32.

Mullen, Jay C. "Pope's New Madrid and Island Number 10 Campaigns." *Missouri Historical Review* 59 (April 1965): 325–43.

Roth, David E. "The Civil War at the Confluence." *Blue and Gray Magazine* 2 (July 1985): 6–20.

Still, William N., Jr. "Technology Afloat." *Civil War Times Illustrated* 14 (November 1975): 4–9, 40–47.

Suppeger, Joseph E. "Lincoln and Pope." *Lincoln Herald* 77 (1975): 218–22.

White, Lonnie J. "Federal Operations at New Madrid and Island Number Ten." *West Tennessee Historical Society Papers* 17 (1963): 47–67.

Index

Index

Larry J. Daniel received his bachelor of arts degree from Lambuth University in Jackson, Tennessee, and his master of divinity degree from Emory University in Atlanta. He has received the Fletcher Pratt Award of the New York Civil War Round Table and the Mrs. Simon Baruch University Press Award of the United Daughters of the Confederacy. Mr. Daniel has written two other books on the Civil War, *Cannoneers in Gray* (University of Alabama Press, 1984) and *Soldiering in the Army of Tennessee* (University of North Carolina Press, 1991).

Lynn N. Bock received his bachelor of arts degree from Westminster College in Fulton, Missouri, and was graduated cum laude from the Univesity of Missouri School of Law in Columbia. He is a member of the State Historical Society of Missouri, a trustee of the New Madrid Historical Museum, and past Missouri Society president of the Military Order of the Stars and Bars.